LAUER SERIES IN RHETORIC AND COMPOSITION

Series Editors: Catherine Hobbs, Patricia Sullivan, Thomas Rickert, and Jennifer Bay

LAUER SERIES IN RHETORIC AND COMPOSITION
Series Editors: Catherine Hobbs, Patricia Sullivan, Thomas Rickert, and
  Jennifer Bay

The Lauer Series in Rhetoric and Composition honors the contributions Janice Lauer Hutton has made to the emergence of Rhetoric and
Composition as a disciplinary study. It publishes scholarship that carries
on Professor Lauer's varied work in the history of written rhetoric, disciplinarity in composition studies, contemporary pedagogical theory, and
written literacy theory and research.

Other Books in the Series

Ancient Non-Greek Rhetorics, edited by Carol S. Lipson and Roberta A. Binkley

Roman Rhetoric: Revolution and the Greek Influence, Revised and Expanded
  Edition, Richard Leo Enos (2008)

Stories of Mentoring, Theory and Praxis, edited by Michelle F. Eble and Lynée
  Lewis Gaillet

Writers Without Borders: Writing and Teaching Writing in Troubled Times,
  Lynn Z. Bloom (2008)

1977: A Cultural Moment in Composition, by Brent Henze, Jack Selzer, and
  Wendy Sharer (2008)

The Promise and Perils of Writing Program Administration, edited by Theresa
  Enos and Shane Borrowman (2008)

*Untenured Faculty as Writing Program Administrators: Institutional Practices
  and Politics*, edited by Debra Frank Dew and Alice Horning (2007)

Networked Process: Dissolving Boundaries of Process and Post-Process, by Helen
  Foster (2007)

Composing a Community: A History of Writing Across the Curriculum, edited by
  Susan H. McLeod and Margot Iris Soven (2006)

*Historical Studies of Writing Program Administration: Individuals,
  Communities, and the Formation of a Discipline*, edited by Barbara
  L'Eplattenier and Lisa Mastrangelo (2004). Winner of the WPA Best Book
  Award for 2004–2005.

Rhetorics, Poetics, and Cultures: Refiguring College English Studies (Expanded
  Edition) by James A. Berlin (2003)

Transforming English Studies

New Voices in an Emerging Genre

Edited by
Lori Ostergaard
Jeff Ludwig
Jim Nugent

Parlor Press
West Lafayette, Indiana
www.parlorpress.com

Parlor Press LLC, West Lafayette, Indiana 47906

SAN: 254-8879

Library of Congress Cataloging-in-Publication Data

Transforming English studies : new voices in an emerging genre / edited by
Lori Ostergaard, Jeff Ludwig, Jim Nugent.
    p. cm. -- (Lauer series in rhetoric and composition)
  Includes bibliographical references and index.
  ISBN 978-1-60235-097-7 (pbk. : alk. paper) -- ISBN 978-1-60235-098-4
(hardcover : alk. paper) -- ISBN 978-1-60235-099-1 (adobe ebook)
  1. English philology--Study and teaching (Higher)--United States.
2. English language--Study and teaching (Higher)--United States. 3.
Education, Higher--Economic aspects--United States. 4. Education,
Higher--Social aspects--United States. 5. Language and culture--United
States. I. Ostergaard, Lori. II. Ludwig, Jeff. III. Nugent, Jim.
PE68.U5T73 2009
428.0071'173--dc22
                              2009006229

Cover image: "Grunge Scroll Background" © 2008 by Sam Alfano. Used by
    permission.
Cover design by David Blakesley.
Printed on acid-free paper.

Parlor Press, LLC is an independent publisher of scholarly and trade titles
in print and multimedia formats. This book is available in paper, cloth
and Adobe eBook formats from Parlor Press on the World Wide Web
at http://www.parlorpress.com or through online and brick-and-mortar
bookstores. For submission information or to find out about Parlor Press
publications, write to Parlor Press, 816 Robinson St., West Lafayette,
Indiana, 47906, or e-mail editor@parlorpress.com.

Contents

Foreword

Transforming the Discourse of Crisis

Gary A. Olson

Many speak of the discipline of English studies as being in crisis—a kind of identity crisis wherein we as a field are desperately attempting to pin down exactly what constitutes the discipline. Stanley Fish even suggests—in his instantly controversial and even reviled *Professional Correctness*—that English studies is in danger of rendering itself irrelevant. Fish claims that the field is expanding its borders so widely, is becoming so capacious, that it is losing its distinctiveness—the attribute that enables people to recognize exactly what a discipline is, what kind of intellectual work it engages in. He takes what in effect is a Derridian stance in pointing out that any given thing is defined in contrast to all things that it is not. English studies is what it is because it is *not* anthropology or biology or sociology, and so on—although it may borrow from these and other disciplines. That is, we understand a discipline to be what it is because it can successfully present itself to its own members and to the world at large as performing some specific set of tasks that only it can accomplish or that other disciplines are not as qualified to perform. Fish worries that the rush in English studies to embrace cultural studies, new historicism, and a range of other mostly political discourses will so dilute the discipline's distinctiveness that it will no longer be recognizable as engaging in work unique to itself. If the discipline does in fact abandon its distinctiveness, if it seems to be all things to all people (and thus nothing at all), then it will lose its *raison d'être* and consequently may well suffer the fate of classics in the university curriculum: near extinction.

While the discourse of crisis that Fish, James Berlin, and others adopt is a relatively recent phenomenon—and, I must add, an interested one, in that such language always works to make the author's particular agenda appear especially urgent and thus especially worthy of consideration—the kind of disciplinary reflection that they engage in is not new at all. Even before Richard Ohmann's canonical *English in America,* scholars have examined English studies as a discipline, noted its flaws, and recommended adjustments. The discourse of crisis notwithstanding, such meta-level reflection is healthy; it is what helps us all keep sight of our collective values and pursuits—our disciplinary distinctiveness—even when we can't all agree on precisely what those values and pursuits are. *Transforming English Studies: New Voices in an Emerging Genre* is the latest contribution to what—as the subtitle suggests—is becoming a critical genre in and of itself: the self-conscious, meta-level examination of the discipline *qua* discipline. The authors and editors undertake an ambitious effort to examine the status of English studies as a discipline and to serve as a positive alternative to the more fraught apocalyptic works that only envision disciplinary self-immolation were we not to follow a given path immediately and without waver. The works in this collection attempt to engage positively with how the discipline can transform itself to be responsive to its varied constituents and intellectual discourses. While not all the authors contained herein agree with one another on all points, their honest and constructive treatments of the subject add up to an energetic and refreshing exploration of English studies.

Unlike Fish, who defines the discipline in the narrowest of terms, the authors in *Transforming English Studies* attempt to account for the heteroglossia in the field—the multiple voices and varied perspectives that have come to constitute (like it or not) the modern discipline of English studies. In fact, it is exactly this attention to what the editors term "polyvocality" that makes this text stand out as a special contribution to the ongoing scholarly conversations about the discipline. Readers will find much here to contemplate as the field continuously reinvents itself—as it always has.

WORKS CITED

Fish, Stanley. *Professional Correctness: Literary Studies and Political Change.* Cambridge: Harvard UP, 1999.

Ohmann, Richard. *English in America: A Radical View of the Profession.* Oxford: Oxford UP, 1976.

Acknowledgments

Perhaps taking too literally Stephen North's suggestion in *Refiguring the PhD in English Studies* that "doctoral students must write their way into English Studies" (xiv) we began the process of compiling and editing these essays while still completing our doctoral degrees. This collection was born of our profound interest in the state of the discipline we were joining, and out of a curiosity about what questions might shape our lives' work. What we discovered through this process was that ours was a discipline that welcomed and even encouraged new voices, new perspectives, and new questions, and that it was a self-reflective discipline that was evolving before our very eyes. We also found that we were hardly three graduate students working in isolation: along the way we encountered people who were deeply interested in and committed to this project. Indeed, we couldn't have completed this collection without the support and guidance of many people.

We acknowledge a considerable debt to the Illinois State University department of English for providing an intellectual space where disciplinary critique and self-reflective practice are commonplace. We would like to thank that department for showing us how rewarding (if sometimes difficult) interdisciplinary conversations can be. This project also received material support from the Oakland University department of writing and rhetoric, for which we are very grateful. We owe many thanks as well to Patricia Dunn, Jan Neuleib, Ron Strickland, and Gary Olson who offered suggestions, strategies, and support throughout the creative process. We remain deeply indebted to our colleagues Jessica Barnes-Pietruszynski, Chris Breu, Charles Harris, Erik Hayenga, Doug Hesse, Cynthia Huff, Tim Hunt, Melissa Ianetta, Robert R. Johnson, Laurence José, Hilary Justice, Marshall Kitchens, Ken Lindblom, Becky Nugent, Jeff Pietruszynski, and Susan Stewart for their invaluable intellectual and emotional support. Lori would particularly like to thank her mother, Helen. Jeff would particularly like to thank April for her love and devotion, and to express his appreciation for his ever-accepting family. Jim would particularly like to thank his parents for their love and support.

Transforming English Studies

1 Introduction

Preservation and Transformation

Jim Nugent and Lori Ostergaard

James Berlin introduces his last book *Rhetorics, Poetics, and Cultures: Refiguring College English Studies* with a familiar alarm:

> English studies is in crisis. Indeed, virtually no feature of the discipline can be considered beyond dispute. At issue are the very elements that constitute the categories of poetic and rhetoric, the activities involved in their production and interpretation, their relationship to each other, and their relative place in graduate and undergraduate work. (xi)

Similar calls to field-wide crises have been proffered so frequently in recent times that the "English studies crisis" is now a firmly established phenomenon in our scholarship, if not in reality (North 57; Readings; Nelson; Richard Miller; Bérubé, *Employment;* Yood 526; Nicholson 125; Cain 83; Levine 13). These calls are offered in dire language that often portents disciplinary apocalypse: unless we act quickly, they assert, English studies faces disciplinary extinction, erasure, or irrelevance in the new university.

As Karen Fitts and William B. Lalicker note, different constituencies identify different geneses for the crisis, ranging variously from the fallout from the Culture Wars to the "struggles between literary studies and recently ascendant fields: writing, rhetoric, and culture and language study" (427). But whatever its motive or cause, the crisis in English studies is, by most accounts, constructed around the following pathologies:

3

- the collapse of tenure-line employment for English PhDs;
- a decline in the number of English majors;
- the "corporatization" of the university and the humanities;
- a crisis in scholarly publishing in English;
- budget crunches at local, state, and federal levels;
- the increasing disparity between how we value our work and how the institution and society value it; and
- the gross inequities of English's labor practices.[1]

These invocations of crisis and accounts of our disciplinary pathologies are, as Jessica Yood notes, part of our field's recent turn toward itself as an object of study. She identifies this condition as having emerged largely in the last decade of the twentieth century within the pages of the *ADE Bulletin* and *Profession,* as well in books by authors such as Michael Bérubé, Stephen North, John Guillroy, Robert Scholes, and Cary Nelson (535). These forms of self-conscious disciplinary critique, she notes, represent a new genre of scholarship: "The rhetoric of 'crisis' about the 'fate of the field' is not some elusive idea; it is the material of a new genre of writing. And this genre, emerging as I write, is reshaping the culture of academia" (526).

Like Yood, we believe in the potential of this new genre to refigure the discipline of English studies, and we believe in its potential to redress our disciplinary pathologies. We are also heartened and humbled by the work of scholars who have contributed to it. Works such as James Berlin's *Rhetorics, Poetics, and Cultures*; Susan Miller's *Textual Carnivals;* Sharon Crowley's *Composition in the University;* Richard Miller's *As If Learning Mattered;* and David Downing, Claude Mark Hurlbert, and Paula Mathieu's *Beyond English, Inc.*—to name only a few—have led us to a critical and self-reflexive engagement with issues surrounding the construction and identity of our discipline.

However, even in its seeming infancy, we have noticed a disturbing trend in the emerging genre of disciplinary self-reflexivity. We are concerned by the ways that many works within it invoke "crisis" and press us toward immediate action, while leaving unquestioned the basic assumptions that lie at the heart of the crises they construct. We are also concerned that many of these works depict the discipline in narrow ways that obscure its epistemological diversity, and use the name "English studies" as a tool to elide our differences and impose an imaginary unity on the field. Most importantly, we are concerned with the ways that many works seek to preserve the disciplinary *status quo* and offer short-term fixes and feints in lieu of genuinely transformative changes to the ideological and material foundations of our work.

This volume seeks to work against these troubling aspects of the genre of disciplinary self-reflexivity, even as it recognizes its place within it. This volume, like other works of the genre, is a concerned response to the pathologies that threaten the viability of English studies. Like other works, it offers new perspectives and approaches to constructing a more responsive and responsible figuration for the field of English studies. However, rather than envisioning field-wide crisis, the authors here envision opportunity. Rather than constructing a deliberately partial conception of the discipline, here you will find the voices of scholars from a broad range of English studies' subdisciplines. And rather than offering narratives of preservation for the field of English studies, here you will find narratives of transformation.

Through the voices of scholars from composition, technical writing, rhetoric, literacy studies, creative writing, computers and writing, linguistics, English education, literature, and children's literature, this volume offers diverse visions for moving forward in our negotiations and renegotiations of what it means to practice English studies, and to work toward resolving the pathologies that threaten the sustainability of our discipline. We believe that this volume offers what the new genre of self-reflexivity both demands and is found wanting: polyvocality. Only by drawing our visions for our discipline's future from multiple perspectives, we argue, can we avoid an English studies that is partial, incomplete, or constructed around limited interests. Only by inviting polyvocality, we maintain, can we elicit responses that advocate genuine transformation over preservation for the field of English studies.

THE TERMS *PRESERVATION* AND *TRANSFORMATION*

These two terms—*preservation* and *transformation*—are central to this project. In their 1996 volume *Refiguring the PhD in English Studies: Writing, Doctoral Education, and the Fusion-Based Curriculum,* Stephen North, Barbara A. Chepaitis, David Coogan, Lâle Davidson, Ron MacLean, Cindy L. Parrish, Jonathan Post, and Beth Weatherby articulate a vision for the future of English studies and its doctoral education. Drawing from the 1989 MLA study, *The Future of Doctoral*

Studies in English, North identifies three potential fates for the field: dissolution, corporate compromise, and fusion. Dissolution, he notes, results in dividing the body of English studies along largely predictable lines (69). Corporate compromise—the approach currently in place in many programs—is the strategy of "holding the conflicted enterprise together, however loosely, and then—for curricular purposes—finding some way to present *and* preserve all of its competing interests" (71). Fusion, the approach North and his collaborators ultimately advocate, involves bringing English studies' subdisciplines together in a radically transformative way "to harness the energy generated by the conflicts in order to forge some new disciplinary enterprise altogether" (73).

As North and his collaborators note, the goal of fusion "is not *preservation* but *transformation,* the production of new versions of English studies that will make sense—gain coherence—not by reference to activities under way elsewhere, nor to any other externally imposed norm" (94, emphasis added). Although our use of the terms preservation and transformation follow from the defining impulses of corporate compromise and fusion respectively, we would like to appropriate these terms for use in a more general, descriptive sense. We see these terms as a way to meaningfully characterize the responses that have been offered so far in the emerging genre of disciplinary self-reflexivity, and as a way to suggest new possibilities for performing productive work in this genre.

Of the works in this genre, we term those that trouble us most deeply—and those that this volume is articulated against—as preservationist. Preservationist responses, we argue, aim to reinstate or make relevant (again) the "work" that has traditionally been done in English departments, while treating as inviolable and axiomatic one or more aspects of the current disciplinary figuration. Although many preservationist responses are ostensibly transformative (many do, in fact, propose radical change), they nonetheless remain trapped within traditional constructions of disciplinary identity. In contrast to these responses are those rooted in the assumption that no aspect of our discipline is preordained or immune from interrogation—responses we term transformative. Although transformative responses may call for the maintenance of some element of our traditional disciplinary figuration, they nonetheless recognize the need to reexamine, re-theorize, and resituate our work at all levels. Transformative responses, we believe, offer us the most productive paths toward a sustainable disciplinary figuration.

Although we recognize North et al.'s vision of fusion as a truly transformative model of disciplinary reform, we would like to remain conceptually distinct from their vision in some ways. Our first point of departure is rooted in the metaphors that the authors use to describe the transformative effects of fusion: metaphors such as "bringing disparate elements together under sufficient pressure and sufficient energy," "harnessing the energy generated by the conflicts," and putting members of the discipline into "locked rooms" for "do-or-die negotiations" (73). We worry that these violent metaphors, while they suggest revolutionary paths to reform, do not accurately reflect how change is—and can effectively be—brought about in conservative institutions. We find ourselves in agreement with James E. Porter et al.'s contention that "[t]hough institutions are certainly powerful, they are not monoliths; they are rhetorically constructed human designs (whose power is reinforced by buildings, laws, traditions, and knowledge-making practices) and so are changeable" (611). We also agree with Porter et al.'s contention that the only alternative to recognizing the mutability of institutions is "political despair" (611). The voices in this volume, therefore, acknowledge the pressing need for transformative refiguration as well as the inevitability of working toward that end within the constraints of local and material contexts.

Second, we believe that North et al. too hastily dismiss dissolution as a viable option. Although the authors cite some possible benefits of a dissolution strategy, they dismiss it for two reasons: "First, there is the distinct possibility that employers [i.e., universities] simply will not care if English Studies breaks up" (254), and second, that dissolution will "water down still further any institutional clout the English professoriate might have left by dispersing it over two or more rival departments" (255). Although we admire North et al.'s attention to the immediate political consequences of dissolution, we feel that the strategy still bears consideration in our discussions of the discipline's future. In fact, echoing the work of Bill Readings, we feel that persistently interrogating the "if and why" of our being together—and by extension, keeping the prospect of dissolution on the table—can lead us toward a more sustainable, self-critical, and dynamic disciplinary figuration. Although this volume is, in its design, polyvocal, it does not summarily reject dissolution as a strategy, nor does it assume disciplinary unity to be preordained. Instead, our hope is that *Transforming English Studies* will expand the possibilities for transformative works, rather than limit them.

Third, the work of North et al. comes as a response to what they perceive as "a crisis of identity in English as both a discipline and a profession" (57). In a move characteristic of many preservationist responses, the authors seem to elide a number of genuine material and ideological differences between the subdisciplines by uniting them under a supposedly common exigence of crisis. Perhaps taking the lead from the larger political realm—in which calls to crisis have been used to advance and defend a war with Iraq, to hasten the passing of the USA PATRIOT Act, and to subvert domestic social programs— we remain skeptical of the construction of crisis in the work of North et al., as well as in many other works of the genre. The voices in this volume recognize that not all of English studies' subdisciplines suffer equally in a crisis of self-definition and articulation, nor do they share equal complicity in the disciplinary pathologies cited above. However, even as the voices here remain wary of calls to crisis, they nonetheless recognize that such calls can act as a convenient point of entry into critiques of the field—provided "crisis" is constructed not as a threat to disciplinary stasis, but rather as an opportunity for substantive disciplinary reform.

Finally, North et al. locate their hopes for disciplinary reform exclusively in doctoral-granting institutions, and envision reform being enacted by doctoral students empowered to write the future of the discipline against the Magisterial tradition. Although we agree with the authors that doctoral students are a vital resource and a powerful motive force for field-wide reform, we disagree with their assumption that established faculty act only to impede such work. As three of North's former students remind us in the first chapter of this volume, North et al. imagine change as "a generational dynamic," maintaining that disciplinary reform is the charge of the "next generation" of faculty. We suggest that North's generational dynamic may be unduly agonistic, and may offer us an unproductive model for working within local contexts toward substantive reform. In addition, we diverge from North et al. in our concentration on effecting reform within a variety of settings, including those beyond the English doctorate. As the essays in this volume attest, transformative disciplinary reform occurs not only through large-scale curricular changes and departmental recastings but also through our individual courses, our committee work, and our hallway conversations with colleagues. Rather than depicting reform as "do-or-die negotiations" with entrenched and obdurate senior faculty, the essays here envision reform as a gradual collaboration between all disciplinary stakeholders at the sites of the material and everyday.

PRESERVATIONIST RESPONSES

The new genre of disciplinary self-reflexivity has produced a class of responses that we term preservationist. These responses advocate—however implicitly or explicitly—the maintenance of one or more aspects of the *status quo* in English studies. In doing so, these responses employ a number of recurring strategies. The first of these is to work rhetorically to depict the field of English studies as unified and homogeneous, and to obscure substantive differences between the subdisciplines. This is accomplished most frequently by conflating the work of one subdiscipline (typically literary studies) with that of the larger discipline, and by uniting the field under powerful encompassing terms such as "English" or invocations of the disciplinary "we."

For instance, many articles within the *ADE Bulletin* elevate the work of literary scholars and teachers, and assume a generic commitment to literary study on the part of all English studies professionals. In her 1994 *ADE Bulletin* article "Reimagining English Departments: What is our Future?," Suzanne Gossett depicts a discipline founded on exactly two goals. According to her, the first goal, "one that departments in all disciplines share, is the empowerment of students," and the second goal is "the clarification and interpretation of texts, [which] becomes the characteristic and defining activity of our departments" (35). Although few in English studies would take issue with the first goal, the supposed "characteristic and defining activity" of the second goal immediately fails to account for much of the productive, noninterpretive work already being done by composition, rhetoric, creative writing, technical communication, and other subdisciplines.

Similarly partial depictions of the discipline are found in accepted institutional histories such as Gerald Graff's *Professing Literature*. Conspicuously absent from Graff's history are any substantive accounts of the role English's "other" subdisciplines have played in shaping present-day English studies. Although Graff makes a brief mention of literature's codependent relationship with composition in his introduction, this passing reference serves merely to excuse the absence of any critical engagement with the political consequences of this relationship in the remainder of his work. Because his response does not acknowledge other subdisciplinary specializations—let alone their institutional and disciplinary status—it continues to reify the work of literature within departments of English.

In their article "Invisible Hands: A Manifesto to Resolve Institutional and Curricular Hierarchy in English Studies," Fitts and Lalicker take the journal *Profession* to task for the ways in which it "marginalizes composition by almost entirely ignoring the perspective of those who see rhetoric and composition as legitimate professional work" (432). The journal's partial perspective, the authors argue, depicts "literary studies as the 'real' business of English Departments" (432), a move that they see manifested in *Profession's* "convention of using the titles 'English department' and 'literature department' interchangeably" (443).

A lot is at stake materially and politically in these partial, yet unifying depictions of the field. In his review of Richard Miller's *As if Learning Mattered,* John Brereton observes that, when books in the new genre of disciplinary self-reflexivity offer up partial depictions of the field, the concerns of his subdiscipline become marginalized:

> From my perspective as a writing teacher, some of the most prominent of these books—Alvin Kernan's *The Death of Literature,* David Damrosch's *We Scholars,* Bill Readings's *The University in Ruins,* John Guillory's *Cultural Capital,* Cary Nelson's *Manifesto of a Tenured Radical,* and Michael Bérubé and Cary Nelson's *Higher Education Under Fire*—fail to depict the world of English studies I know. Reading these books—conservative and liberal alike—I find only a few isolated sentences or paragraphs about composition, the largest part of most English departments' work and the largest single course in higher education. (495)

Brereton regrets that Miller's book "has been mostly ignored" by the field, and he suggests that the silence surrounding Miller's work "says something about who gets to dominate the conversation about the direction of English studies" (495). Like Brereton, we recognize that how "English studies" is constructed and depicted in our scholarship shapes and constrains the possibilities for field-wide reform, and we recognize the need to remain critical of disciplinary depictions that are partial or incomplete.

A second common strategy of preservationist responses is to delicately avoid the need to construct a set of defining principles for the discipline, a strategy accomplished by several means. On one hand, there are responses that recognize an immediate administrative need for a plausible "cover story" to explain our work to outsiders. As David Laurence relates in a 2002 *ADE Bulletin* article, in his role as director of the ADE he hears many members of the profession requesting "an account of what English departments do that is institutionally persuasive in that it will convey to administrators [. . .] and to parents, students, and the public that we know what we are doing and why it is worth doing" (17). In this and similar calls to pay attention to the articulation of our public identity (see, for instance, Culler, Laurence, Pratt, Scholes "Learning," Nicholson, Davidson, and Peltason), we see calls for after-the-fact justifications of disciplinary work already underway, rather than serious investigations into the foundations of that disciplinary work and what initially makes it worthwhile.

On the other hand, there are preservationist responses that argue against defining the discipline axiomatically. For instance, in his book *What Is English?*, Peter Elbow argues for embracing permanent ambiguity about the nature of the discipline. In his introduction, he characterizes his work as "trying to paint a picture of a profession that cannot define what it is" (v). He goes on to note: "Yes, it might be more comfortable and convenient if we knew just what English studies is, but this very absence of comfort and convenience in the profession is probably a good thing. [. . .] On good days I even say, 'It's about time we finally don't know what we are'" (v). In his spring 2000 *ADE Bulletin* article, Mike Heller takes similar relish in the indefiniteness of the discipline, while simultaneously valorizing the difficulties of avoiding self-definition. Heller suggests that "describing our discipline is something like describing the Tao" (20). To Heller, this near-mystical inscrutability is the discipline's strength: "the difficulty in articulating what we are about is itself a sign that we are on the right track. Important things in life are difficult to say" (21). A troubling aspect of this, however, is that Heller implicitly suggests that those who work in rhetoric, technical writing, composition, English education, linguistics, and other areas—subdisciplines that have typically had little dif-

ficulty articulating what they do and why it is valuable—may not be
engaged in important work.

Both of these responses—those for and against self-definition—
hold a particular allure for those seeking to preserve the disciplinary
status quo and to evade potentially transformative discussions about
how our work may find relevance with students and the larger public.
Rather than interrogate existing conditions in our departments and
our discipline, both responses depict our disciplinary pathologies as
mere problems of articulation, thereby circumventing meaningful examinations of the very practices that engendered those pathologies.

A third common move that preservationist responses make is to
work to maintain the distinction between the ideal and the material
aspects of disciplinary work and to uphold the ideal as the reified site
of academic labor. For instance, in addition to his mystical invocation
of the Tao, Heller suggests that the study of literature helps readers to
transcend the material world by way of its "spiritual presence," and
that "literature is about how we yearn for ultimate meaning" (23).
Even when not offered in such explicitly transcendental terms, many
preservationist responses find it hard to withhold their disdain for the
everyday and material. In his 1996 *ADE Bulletin* article "What We
Talk about When We Talk about English," Charles Harris bemoans
changes in the discipline that have, "among other adversities, forced
chairs to spend endless hours composing strategic plans that, if read at
all beyond the dean's office (if even there) seldom result in the resource
allocations that would make implementation possible" (25). To Harris, this kind of bureaucratic work "turns chairs into the very entrepre-
neurs many entered the profession to escape becoming" (25). He goes
on to couch this tension more explicitly in terms of the material and
the ideal, even suggesting that the material is the (presumably lowly)
province of non-academics: "unlike arguments in the public sector,
where the stakes are usually material, the fiercest of academic arguments are almost always about ideas" (25).

Jonathan Culler echoes Harris's reification of the ideal over the material in a 2002 *ADE Bulletin* essay. Here, Culler notes that "English
departments have generally been averse to strategic plans, recognizing
these for what they often are: time-consuming exercises that distract
one from the intellectually more valuable exercises of teaching and research" (51). Culler seems to view such administrative work as tedium
that we must resign ourselves to, "something as inevitable as death and

taxes" (51). Although he ultimately contends that English departments should become better at arguing for material resources, strategic plans are, in his depiction, a distraction from—rather than instrumental to—the intellectual work of English departments.

We believe that these three major strategies—the obfuscation of our epistemological diversity, the emphasis on disciplinary articulation over substantive interrogation, and the desire to somehow transcend the material conditions of our work—sustain traditional disciplinary figurations and frustrate efforts to work against our disciplinary pathologies.

Transformative Responses

The second major class of responses that we identify within the genre of self-reflexivity is of transformation. The primary characteristic of transformative responses is their persistent interrogation of the most basic, foundational, and ordinarily transparent assumptions of the field. For example, David R. Shumway and Craig Dionne introduce their collection *Disciplining English: Alternative Histories, Critical Perspectives* by suggesting that their "volume should lead us to question whether the particular practices and objects that English entails are justifiable given that there could be other practices and objects" (1). They further argue that "the most entrenched hegemony is not that of a particular theory, but of mundane assumptions and routine practices that are seldom noticed let alone questioned" (9). Likewise, in "Days of Future Past," Michael Bérubé suggests that when he ponders the future, he concentrates less on the "Next Big Thing" and more "on the mundane bookkeeping matters of the profession, out of the conviction that if the profession offers its aspirants good material and intellectual working conditions, the shape and the range of the knowledges produced in the profession will eventually take care of themselves" (20). Bérubé adds that "perhaps those bookkeeping matters are not quite so simple or mundane as I thought" (20). Following this, we believe transformative responses are shaped by their writers' willingness to question every seemingly mundane aspect of our disciplinary enterprise. We also believe that transformative responses engage with the material conditions from which crises emerge, even holding those conditions as the very object of study for the discipline of English. The aim of a transformative response, then, is not a return to the "real" work of an idealized discipline but rather to present a persistent intellectual engagement with the material and ideological contexts from which disciplines are constructed.

While the writer of a transformative response is unlikely to abandon the humanistic goals that brought them into the profession, what characterizes transformative responses most essentially, we feel, is their pragmatism. Works within this genre, such as Richard Miller's *As If Learning Mattered*, remind us that "making hortatory declarations about what must be done and extended critiques about what has been done is not, by any stretch of the imagination, the same thing as engaging in the entirely unglamorous, often utterly anonymous work of figuring out what can be done within a given institutional context" (22). Here Miller celebrates the very same "entrepreneurial" work that Harris earlier eschewed. Lying similarly in contrast to Harris's preservationist response is an article by Dianne F. Sadoff that appeared in the *ADE Bulletin* five years after Harris's. In this work, Sadoff argues that department chairs must take advantage of conditions in their universities and their departments to ask "how, when, and in what venues, during a time of intellectual and programmatic diversity, can the chair successfully stage a departmental discussion about [. . .] the English curriculum?" (27). We believe Sadoff's work represents a pragmatic model for thinking through curricular changes by way of the "institutional and management issues" chairs encounter (27). She encourages chairs to evaluate not only the reasons for curricular change but also the possibilities for change, the obstacles to it, and the unforeseen consequences of curricular discussions in their departments. In contrast to Harris's disdain for the "adversities" of material, bureaucratic work, we get the impression that Sadoff might even be energized by the rhetorical and intellectual challenges presented by writing strategic plans for college deans.

Elaine Hanson argues in her 2002 *ADE Bulletin* article "Reflections on Being Together" that those engaged in field-wide reform need to adopt "a very pragmatic, opportunistic sense of what a given set of faculty members in a given set of circumstances can, with its characteristic ways of thinking and teaching, accomplish in its local situation" (44). This kind of attention to local contexts and materiality can be seen as an essential component of transformative responses—not because the material intrudes upon and limits the possibilities for the discipline, but because "sustainable educational ventures have always worked *within* local, material constraints" (R. Miller 9). As Porter et al. note, institutional critique itself "is an unabashedly rhetorical practice mediating the macro-level structures and micro-level actions rooted in a particular space and time" (612). Transformative responses recognize, then, that disciplinary reforms are not just enacted *within* local and material constraints, they are born of them.

A third characteristic of transformative responses is their polyvocality. Such works, which include North et al.'s *Refiguring the PhD in English Studies* and Downing, Hurlbert, and Mathieu's *Beyond English, Inc.,* are coauthored or co-edited, and draw on scholars from different corners of English studies. By enacting the very forms of interdisciplinary engagement and negotiation they themselves advocate, these collaborative responses negate moves to preserve a traditional or partial disciplinary figuration, including the traditional reification of single-authored texts. We believe that the interdisciplinary nature of these coauthored responses compels their writers to foreground their assumptions about what English studies is and should be. As Donald Hall notes in his 2001 *ADE Bulletin* article, "[W]e can never detach ourselves wholly from ourselves or achieve anything like clarity in our perspective on ourselves. Thus as part of our ethical commitment we must energetically solicit the perspectives of others, who can add immeasurably to our partial views, even if the result will never be complete." (32). Collaboration across the hallway with our "other" English colleagues moves us beyond presumption and forces us to recognize the constructedness of our own practices. Interdisciplinary work renders visible our tacit assumptions, leads us to question our entrenched disciplinary processes and practices, and compels us to pay attention to all potential stakeholders in our conversations about the future of the discipline.

We believe that these characteristics—a prolonged interrogation of the discipline's seemingly mundane assumptions, a respect for how local contexts shape reform, and an acknowledgment of the diversity of our (inter)discipline—are necessary components of any transformative response within the new genre of disciplinary self-reflexivity. We also believe that these are the defining characteristics of the works that follow, works with the potential, to use Jessica Yood's words, for "reshaping the culture of academia" (526).

PART I: NEGOTIATION AND COLLABORATION

The chapters in this section explore models of negotiation and collaboration within the everyday material contexts of our departments, committees, and courses. In the first chapter, Chris Gallagher, Peter Gray, and Shari Stenberg reexamine their attempts to work toward the goal of Northian "fusion" at their respective institutions. Here they chronicle how they learned to negotiate change, and came to "re-see" fusion as *con/fusion:* an acknowledgment of the complexity of institutional reform. In the second chapter of this section, Susan Burt uses language and sociolinguistics as a metaphorical lens for examining the discipline of English studies. She analogizes our disciplinary alliances to ethnolinguistic identities, and she illustrates how linguistic and epistemological alliances may be forged between subdisciplines. And in the third chapter, Caren Town tells the story of the collaborative design of a methods course for English education majors at her university, a process complicated by the fact that the primary instruction for these future language arts teachers occurs across three separate departments: the Department of Literature and Philosophy, the Department of Writing and Linguistics, and the College of Education.

PART II: DISCIPLINARY ENACTMENT

The chapters in this section examine what our practices reveal about our values as a discipline. In the first chapter of this section, David Downing analyzes the valuing of different types of work within the discipline, illustrating how English studies can "actively transform the disciplinary economy of value" rather than "passively wait for the economy to turn some magical corner." He argues that moves to divide English studies into separate departmental units "plays easily into the hands" of administrators and permits "the 'outsourcing' and 'downsizing' of our limited resources." In the second chapter, William Banks interrogates moves to separate rhetoric and writing programs from English departments. Banks argues in this chapter that "avoiding conflict is the last place *rhetoric* needs to go—in practice or in theory," and he notes that the moves to divide English departments may stem more from our "exhaustion" over departmental infighting than from "our discipline's primary commitments to transformation and change." And in the last chapter of this section, Matthew Abraham examines rhetoric and composition's move toward theory as an attempt to legitimatize the work of administration as "intellectual work" rather than "mere" service. Abraham defines theory as the ability "to imagine what our environments might be like if we weren't so alienated, oppressed, and—most importantly—so obedient."

PART III: CURRICULAR DESIGN

The chapters in this section examine new curricular models that promise to refigure the diverse work of English studies in meaningful and sustainable ways. In the first chapter of this section, Marcia McDonald engages with civic rhetoric and "education for democracy" to construct an integrated English curriculum. McDonald ponders if "a dialogue between the university and English studies" might produce new directions for our work in the discipline. She examines four proposed curricula (those of Bérubé, Heath, Spellmeyer, and Culler), and she proposes her own model for an integrated English studies curriculum. In the second chapter, Lynée Lewis Gaillet suggests that we look to historical models to integrate the work of composition, technical writing, English education, rhetoric, cultural studies, and literature. Gaillet proposes that the integrated curriculum designed by eighteenth-century moral philosopher George Jardine may provide students with tools for advancement and civic engagement. And in the third chapter, Matthew Pifer responds to Ed Folsom's call to implement graduate programs in "small-college teaching" and his parallel call to develop a generalist theory to shape such programs. Pifer's chapter locates the generalist as not only a viable professional designation but also as an epistemology that will help English faculty reevaluate undergraduate curricular offerings.

PART IV: KAIROTIC APPROACHES

The essays in this final section respond to complaints about disciplinary crisis with proposals for new directions for the field. In doing so, they replace the rhetoric of fear with a rhetoric of opportunity, and they model a characteristic strategy of transformative works: adopting a stance that is *kairotic* and proactive, rather than neurotic and reactive. In the first chapter, Michael Pennell argues that English studies "is nearing, or traversing, a tipping point" but that the changing nature of writing in English studies has been largely ignored in our scholarship. Pennell offers two key concepts in English studies as it reaches this critical moment of transformation: corruption and non-place. In the second chapter, Christopher Schroeder argues that "while we can continue to declare literacy crisis after literacy crisis, we do so [. . .] at our own (disciplinary and personal) expense." In an essay that blends traditional scholarship with personal narrative, Schroeder offers a model of literacy that can provide the field of English with social legitimacy. In the final chapter, Michael Knievel critiques discourses about technology in English studies that focus on how technology may be transformed and "humanized" by its association with the discipline of English. Using pragmatist philosophy and three twentieth-century iterations of the *Humanist Manifesto,* Knievel argues for an English studies that is technology-inclusive.

NOTE

1. See Bérubé "Future Past"; Bousquet; Davidson; Gilbert et al.; Heller; Hutcheon et al.; Lauer; Laurence; Nelson; Nerad and Cerny; Nicholson; Peltason; Pratt; Scholes, "Learning"; Scholes, "Situation"; Yancey; among others.

WORKS CITED

Bérubé, Michael. "Days of Future Past." *ADE Bulletin* 131 (2002): 20–26.
—. *The Employment of English: Theory, Jobs, and the Future of Literary Studies.* New York: New York UP, 1998.
Berlin, James A. *Rhetorics, Poetics, and Cultures: Refiguring College English Studies.* 1996. West Lafayette, IN: Parlor Press, 2003.
Bousquet, Marc. "The Rhetoric of 'Job Market' and the Reality of the Academic Labor System." *College English* 66.2 (2003): 207–28.
Brereton, John C. Rev. of *As if Learning Mattered: Reforming Higher Education.* By Richard E. Miller. *College Composition and Communication* 51.3 (2000): 494–97.
Cain, Jeffrey. "On the Crisis of Self-Definition in English Studies." *Rocky Mountain Review* 55.1 (2001): 83–92.
Crowley, Sharon. *Composition in the University: Historical and Polemical Essays.* Pittsburgh: U of Pittsburgh P, 1998.
Culler, Jonathan. "Coping with Excellence." *ADE Bulletin* 131 (2002): 50–52.
Davidson, Cathy N. "Them Versus Us (and Which One of 'Them' is Me?)." *ADE Bulletin* 125 (2000): 3–8.

Downing, David, Claude Mark Hurlbert, and Paula Mathieu. *Beyond English, Inc.: Curricular Reform in a Global Economy*. Portsmouth, NH: Boynton/Cook, 2002.

Elbow, Peter. *What Is English?* New York: MLA, 1990.

Fitts, Karen, and William B. Lalicker. "Invisible Hands: A Manifesto to Resolve Institutional and Curricular Hierarchy in English Studies." *College English* 66.4 (2004): 427–51.

Gilbert, Sandra M., et al. "Final Report of the MLA Committee on Professional Employment." *ADE Bulletin* 119 (1998): 27–45.

Gossett, Suzanne. "Reimagining English Departments: What Is Our Future?." *ADE Bulletin* 108 (1994): 27–45.

Hall, Donald E. "Professional Self-Reflexivity." *ADE Bulletin* 129 (2001): 31–34.

Hanson, Elaine. "Reflections on Being Together." *ADE Bulletin* 131 (2002): 41–45.

Harris, Charles B. "What We Talk about When We Talk about English." *ADE Bulletin* 113 (1996): 21–29.

Heller, Mike. "What is Essential about the Teaching of Literature." *ADE Bulletin* 125 (2002): 20–23.

Hutcheon, Linda, et al. "Professionalization in Perspective." MLA Ad Hoc Committee on the Professsionalization of PhDs. *ADFL Bulletin* 34.3 (2003): 43–53.

Laurence, David. "The Latest Forecast." *ADE Bulletin* 131 (2002): 15–19.

Lauer, Janice. "Doctoral Program Reviews: Taking Charge." *ADE Bulletin* 119 (1998): 9–13.

Levine, George. "Putting the 'Literature' Back into Literature Departments." *ADE Bulletin* 113 (1996): 13–20.

Miller, Richard E. *As If Learning Mattered: Reforming Higher Education*. Ithaca, NY: Cornell UP, 1998.

Miller, Susan. *Textual Carnivals: The Politics of Composition*. Carbondale, IL: Southern Illinois UP, 1991.

Nelson, Cary. *Manifesto of a Tenured Radical*. New York: New York UP, 1997.

Nerad, Maresi, and Joseph Cerny. "From Rumor to Facts: Career Outcomes of English PhDs" *ADE Bulletin* 124 (2000): 43–55.

Nicholson, Gregory. "The English Discipline in the 1990s and Beyond: Perspectives of a New Graduate Student." *The Journal of the Midwest Modern Language Association* 36.1 (2003): 125–38.

North, Stephen M., with Barbara A. Chepaitis, David Coogan, Lâle Davidson, Ron MacLean, Cindy L. Parrish, Jonathan Post, and Beth Weatherby. *Refiguring the PhD in English Studies: Writing, Doctoral Education, and the Fusion-Based Curriculum*. Urbana, IL: NCTE, 2000.

Peltason, Timothy. "Making the Case for Literary Education." *ADE Bulletin* 125 (2003): 14–19.

Porter, James E., Patricia Sullivan, Stuart Blythe, Jeffrey T. Grabill, and Libby Miles. "Institutional Critique: A Rhetorical Methodology for Change." *College Composition and Communication* 51.4 (2000): 610–42.

Pratt, Linda Ray. "In a Dark Wood: Finding a New Path to the Future of English." *ADE Bulletin* 131 (2002): 27–33.

Readings, Bill. *The University in Ruins.* Cambridge: Harvard UP, 1996.

Sadoff, Dianne E. "The Curriculum and the Chair in an Age of Programmatic Diversity." *ADE Bulletin* 127 (2001): 27–31.

Scholes, Robert. "Learning and Teaching." *ADE Bulletin* 134–135 (2003): 20–26.

—. "The PhD Situation." *ADE Bulletin* 121 (1998): 9–15.

Shumway, David R., and Craig Dionne. *Disciplining English: Alternative Histories, Critical Perspectives.* Albany: SUNY P, 2002.

Yancey, Kathleen Blake. "Made Not Only in Words: Composition in a New Key." *College Composition and Communication* 56.2 (2004): 297–328.

Yood, Jessica. "Writing the Discipline: A Generic History of English Studies." *College English* 65.5 (2003): 526–40.

Part I

Negotiation and Collaboration

2 Making Trouble Elsewhere: Second-Generation Con/fusion

Chris W. Gallagher, Peter M. Gray, and Shari J. Stenberg

Think of it this way. If it turns out that we absolutely have to spend the rest of our working lives explaining that the experimental program that conferred our degrees is gone [. . .] we are determined to do all we can to ensure that it will have been an experiment that made a difference: had a lasting and positive impact on both how English Studies goes about preparing each new generation of doctoral candidates and—thereby—on the nature of the discipline itself.

—North et al., *Refiguring the PhD in English Studies*

North et al.'s messianic call speaks to us, inspires us, and—on darker days—haunts us. As three graduates of SUNY-Albany's "fusion-based curriculum," we have had very different experiences as faculty members at our respective institutions: a large, comprehensive state university (Chris), a small, Jesuit university (Shari), and an urban community college (Peter). But we all feel ourselves to be, as we joke, the seeds put to the wind by this experiment aimed at refiguring "the nature of the discipline itself" (232).

In more sober moments, we ask ourselves and each other: just how *does* disciplinary change occur? In particular, how *might* we ensure that experiments such as SUNY-Albany's have "a lasting and positive impact"? Perhaps this essay, aimed at addressing the former question, will go some way toward (re)figuring out the latter as well.

In what follows, we examine the reform model offered by North et al. in the context of our own efforts to enact change in the institutions where we took faculty positions. Doing so allows us to reflect on the institutional and political constraints and possibilities for "refiguring" English studies. While we remain committed to the idea of "fusion" as a touchstone for institutional and disciplinary change, we offer a Deweyan re-vision of that concept, which hinges on treating fusion as an "end-in-view" rather than a fixed end (Dewey 123). In so doing, we work away from the seeds-to-the-wind reform model and toward a reform model we term *con/fusion*.

The notion of *con/fusion* destabilizes but does not dismiss North et al.'s vision of change. It retains fusion as a goal, but does not insist on its full realization—even in the long run—as a condition for continued effort in its service. In fact, it insists on illuminating the complexity—the confusion—that accompanies change efforts in the academy, and more particularly, for our purposes, in English studies. Although *confusion* is typically understood as a negative condition from which one seeks escape, our experience as teachers and scholars of writing reminds us that revision (whether textual or institutional) should not, as Nancy Welch puts it, consist of "manag[ing] unruly voices and rein[ing] in excessive texts" (25). Revision, whether of texts or institutions or disciplines, requires "groping and stuttering," some "clumsy attempts and much improvisation," and venturing toward goals whose "very existence is not guaranteed in advance" (Le Doeuff qtd. in Welch 28).

We argue, then, that con/fusion—the coexistence of fusion as an end-in-view and confusion—is a *positive* condition that we should embrace. It is a necessary component of institutional change, and it values what Richard Miller calls the "entirely unglamorous, often utterly anonymous work" of mundane struggle over the hope of a one-time, transformational change (22). But in order to clear some conceptual space for this work, we turn first to North et al.'s notion of *fusion* and its implicit model of change.

SUNY-Albany's Fusion-Based Curriculum and the Possibility of Change

We note at the outset that North et al.'s challenge to the field—which essays in this collection, in part, seek to answer—is *not* to replicate SUNY-Albany's program elsewhere. Passing on the simple attraction of the replication reform model, North et al. insist that disciplinary change must be enacted locally, multiply, in concrete sites of teaching,

[handwritten margin note: not universal, rhetorically + institutionally situated...]

learning, and knowledge-making. Indeed, one of the core principles of the "fusion-based curriculum" is that each new program would gain "its coherence from the integrated interests of the *particular set of faculty and students who participate in it,* who taught and took its classes" (258, emphasis added). Thus, Albany is but one attempt—one enactment—of basic principles that foreground the need to integrate the interests of the various stakeholders who constitute graduate programs.

The central concept of SUNY-Albany's doctoral program is *fusion,* defined by North et al. as "bringing disparate elements together under sufficient pressure and with sufficient energy to transform them in a single new entity, one quite distinct from any of the original components" (73). This model challenges the current academic norm, *corporate compromise,* which sustains the illusion of unity for the sake of institutional federation, but ultimately allows each "component" (or individual professor or graduate student) to remain unchanged (73). In other words, corporate compromise is a kind of academic "I'm-OK-you're-OK," a marriage of convenience in which we agree not to interfere with one another for the sake of holding together our existing arrangement—loosely, and with as little friction as possible. In this way, it is decidedly "impure": it remains corrupted by selfish motives and is acquiescent to a *status quo* that supports unjust labor practices, lack of professional and disciplinary coherence, limited educational opportunities, and so on.

[handwritten margin note: shared purpose]

[handwritten margin note: yes packets]

To work against corporate compromise, fusion requires three commitments (North et al.). First, fusion demands that faculty from all constituent fields agree to be "sequestered in the disciplinary and professional equivalent of a locked room for what amount to do-or-die negotiations" (73). Fusion, after all, brings about a "new entity," one substantively different from any of the original component parts. Second, doctoral students must become *participants,* rather than spectators, in the design and operation of the program. It is their (new, intradisciplinary) expertise that will constitute change. In the graduate program that existed during our tenure at SUNY-Albany, this meant that student-driven, intradisciplinary inquiry occupied the center of its fusion-based doctoral program in "Writing, Teaching, and Criticism." The curriculum was designed to integrate the subfields of the discipline *within individual courses,* thereby encouraging doctoral students—whether rhetoricians, creative writers, literary scholars, literacy workers, and so on—to examine, from these various perspectives, the core elements of the program: writing, teaching, and criticism. In this way, the curriculum was not designed to transmit knowledge from master to apprentice, or to recreate students in the professors' image. Instead, it represented "a coordinated series of occasions for negotiating claims about who knows what, how, why, and to what ends" (North et al. 92).[1]

Third (and by extension), fusion requires willingness on the part of faculty to "renegotiate their disciplinary and professional expertise vis-à-vis the doctoral students" (75). This renegotiation takes place largely through the privileging of students' *writing*, which, North et al. are careful to note, will necessarily exceed the expertise of any of the assembled faculty. The students thus play a crucial role: they are not only responsible for contributing to the curriculum but also for bringing their disciplinary knowledge and professional identities to bear on the subject of each classroom they enter (96).

MAKING TROUBLE ELSEWHERE

In this essay, we are concerned with the *process* by which disciplinary/professional reform might be achieved. Certainly part of that process—and the part that receives the lion's share of attention in *Refiguring the PhD*—involves changes in the *written artifacts* of the discipline: what "counts" as scholarship, the arguments made in that scholarship, the visions it holds out for the future. On this count, SUNY-Albany's graduates have indeed made a mark (Cain, Gallagher, Hurlbert and Blitz, Kalamaris, Kameen, Owens, Stenberg, and others). In fact, several books produced by SUNY-Albany graduates appear in NCTE's Refiguring English Studies series.

However, the reform process must involve another, perhaps more important site: the institutions in which fusion-based programs' graduates take faculty positions and work with their own students—that is, where they help shape, in direct fashion, "the next generation" of professors, and where they reshape the discipline with undergraduate students in undergraduate English curricula. North et al. have much less to say on this score, but in his 2001 Conference on College Composition and Communication presentation, North, speaking about the demise of a thriving undergraduate writing sequence at SUNY-Albany that fused rhetoric and poetics, described the importance—indeed, the necessity—for graduates of SUNY-Albany and similar programs to "make trouble elsewhere" for both undergraduate and graduate education. But what does "making trouble elsewhere" mean, and how might it be enacted with our own vastly different students and colleagues?

In North et al.'s vision of reform, doctoral students are key players not only in shaping the curriculum in which they learn but also in "refiguring" English studies more broadly by carrying on the work of fusion elsewhere—specifically, in the institutions where they find faculty positions and in the discipline/profession at large. That is, change is imagined here as a generational dynamic: it is the responsibility of "the next generation," North et al. insist, "to work their way toward the new order" (106).

North et al. argue persuasively that because the discipline has been content to ensure its perpetuation through minting new professors in the image of the old, doctoral students have long been overlooked as potential *catalysts* for change. If disciplinary reform is desirable—as we are assuming for the purposes of this collection, and as many recent publications in the field suggest (consider, for instance, NCTE's Refiguring English Studies series)—North et al. contend that "doctoral students in English Studies, present and future, constitute the largest, best motivated, and most talented group of people the professoriate has any realistic chance of recruiting to help reform the way it creates the field's future generations" (248–49).

As the three of us entered our new institutions, we carried with us what we now view as a romanticized vision of the troublemaker: "the dreamer who is fundamentally opposed to the senseless but indomitable forces" of academic institutions (Miller 201). Emboldened by our training in SUNY-Albany's "Teaching, Writing, and Criticism" doctoral program, we naively imagined that we could transport the principles and practices that informed that program to our new institutions. Fusion, as we knew and had experienced it, was our ultimate professional goal.

Recall that North et al. frame fusion as a chemical process: "bringing disparate elements together under sufficient pressure and with sufficient energy to transform them into a single new entity, one quite distinct from any of the original components" (73). How, we wondered, could we serve as catalysts that would ignite fusion? A catalyst—to borrow again from chemistry—*increases the rate of a reaction, without being consumed by it*. The catch, though, is that a catalyst sparks a reaction that, even in its absence, would have occurred anyway. The catalyst speeds, but does not initiate, the process. And here lay the problem for us: to serve as catalysts, the will toward fusion in our departments needed already to exist.

To be sure, we found in our respective institutions warm collegiality and thoughtful conversation about curriculum. What we did not find was the potential to spark *fusion* in our new professional homes. Shari was hired to direct the first-year writing (FYW) program at a four-year private university, a program that, like so many FYW programs, remained entirely separate from the English major. The possibility for composition to "fuse" with other areas of the department was severely restrained by its position outside of the disciplinary enterprise. Chris moved into a department that had just completed a revision of its undergraduate major, which now had no fewer than ten concentrations in its undergraduate major. This new—and hard-won—arrangement was a poster child for corporate compromise. Peter was invited to lead a college-wide interdisciplinary inquiry into, and a potential reform of, general education after having worked for several years with faculty in other disciplines to create writing intensive courses at his community college. At his college, corporate compromise is writ large: the ability to imagine a fusion-based general education program is severely circumscribed by legacies of agreements among departments, professional programs, college and university committees, administrators, a central university administration, as well as established discourse in transfer agreements with other colleges and in state law.

For each of us—new, untenured faculty members—the pressure to adapt to our institutions seemed far greater than any pressure we could bring to bear on them. Joy Ritchie and David Wilson locate a similar phenomenon in their study of new K–12 teachers, who faced "powerful initiation into the culture of schools" (70). Not only did this initiation require complex identity negotiations for these teachers, but it often resulted in teachers trading in their hard-won beliefs, values, and commitments for the comforts of belonging in a new community. And as Wilson reports in *Attempting Change,* individual K–12 teachers who were dramatically changed by the experience of a National Writing Project workshop—much as we were changed by our fusion-centered doctoral program—often faced not only the problem of "translation—making sense of new concepts in old contexts," but also of maintaining the "'necessary strength and enthusiasm' to carry out [their] new concepts" (38).

We certainly did not face the kind of "hazing" (70) that some of Ritchie and Wilson's teachers did. But we did face our share of recalcitrant and indifferent responses to even modest recommendations for change. We also faced established, taken-for-granted procedures and practices; unquestioned and often unacknowledged values and commitments; institutional inertia; intergenerational skepticism; and so on. We suspect no institution is free of these dynamics.

The problem was that the reform model we embraced—fusion as the end goal—did not address how to negotiate the obvious but often ignored reality that educational change is "inevitably constrained by the presence of those already in the system" (Miller 204). For Shari, the "system" was a department that operated out of a clear hierarchy: literature on top, then creative writing, and finally composition. Whether a student chose to emphasize literature (dubbed the "standard" track) or creative writing, the major consisted predominantly of literature courses. Literature students were not required to take any writing courses. Composition, as a field of inquiry, was absent entirely from the major. For Chris, the "system" was a loose confederation of curricular areas seemingly designed to keep faculty from having to talk with one another about their responsibility to undergraduate education. Peter's systemic troubles played out on the college level. Asking, "Who is responsible for General Education?" brought faculty together, but it also highlighted the complexity of college-level hierarchy. The possibility to "fuse" in the context of undergraduate general education was fraught, to say the least, with territorial claims on knowledge and with concern about academic freedom and governance issues.

However, it would be far too simple to suggest that we—those who "got it"—found ourselves in institutions filled with conservative folks who didn't "get it." Indeed, as we look back now (several years later) on our experiences as new faculty, it seems to us that because we operated out of a flawed vision of change, we often missed out on the changes that were *already underway* in our respective institutions. What we saw as institutions refusing to change were in fact institutions changing in ways we didn't value—or even recognize.

LISTENING FOR CONNECTIONS

Shari's experience of working toward curricular change helps demonstrate the necessity of locating change already in process, that is, of developing institutional literacy. To be institutionally literate, according to Gallagher, is to "be able to read institutional discourses (and their resultant arrangements and structures) so as to speak and write back to them, thereby participating in their revision" (79). The assumption here is that institutions are indeed revisable—but also that revision is dependent upon a careful understanding and assessment of local contexts (see also Porter et al.). Institutional literacy also requires a two-way dynamic, whereby one critically examines local contexts at the same time she questions and reconsiders her desired end in relation to those contexts. In this way the institution, and fusion itself, are always under revision.

Shari began to realize the need for institutional literacy when she faced the reality of a major that centered on a coverage model of British and American literature. To move from a traditional, highly exclusionary model to a fusion-based curriculum seemed a daunting, if not impossible, task. So she decided to start small, by talking informally with colleagues about possibilities for curriculum revision. How had institutional change come to fruition in the past? What had been the most effective ways to initiate reform?

Two colleagues shared that she might begin not by recommending curriculum reform, but by working to integrate her ideas into courses already "on the books." Shari was at first discouraged by what felt like accommodationist advice. After all, her goal was not simply to make a corporate compromise and add her own interests to an already established curriculum. Still, it was a start. So she began immediately drafting a senior seminar course on "Writers Working Within and Against Academic Discourse," which she hoped would allow literature and creative writing majors to examine academic discourse as a value-laden construct, as well as to examine how writers transgressed discursive boundaries in their respective fields. In other words, Shari invited students to bring their knowledge and experience to bear on the subject matter of the course. It was the fusion model encapsulated into one course.

In teaching the course, Shari found that students were hungry to engage in this kind of dialogue. They were interested in engaging texts that looked vastly different from the scholarship they read in other classes, and they felt empowered to discover that the writings they took to be "natural" were indeed constructions—constructions that clearly didn't serve all members of the field equally. (Indeed, many felt relieved to express that they felt hindered by the *status quo*). So Shari wasn't working alone; she was working in dialogue with students, who could then raise these ideas elsewhere.

But as Shari began to discuss her course with other faculty members, it became clear that fusion-based goals were not hers alone. Two of the creative writers, for instance, had also taught senior seminars in which literature and creative writing students were invited to bring their knowledge to the collective table and were allowed to engage in either creative or literary projects. Both were valued. This allowed the variously situated students to learn from one another and to discover what is gained by bringing students' knowledges into dialogue with one another. Shari and these two faculty members began to talk: why aren't there more such opportunities for students? Why aren't there more connections between creative writing and composition? Why is composition left out of the major altogether?

Perhaps what surprised Shari most is that even those who were privileged by the current disciplinary structure were not necessarily satisfied with it. Some felt constrained and began to work "within and against" by adding a subtitle to the original course title in order to create room for more perspectives and areas of inquiry. Change was already occurring, but it was not made public. Shari also began to ask about the department's history, about why the curriculum was structured this way, and about prior efforts to change it—which indeed existed.

So rather than coming to the department with a proposal for dismantling the current system—insisting on fusion or nothing—Shari learned it was more useful to begin by making connections; by asking questions and listening to stories; by discovering where there existed some restlessness, and thus, potential for change. Once her chair at the time, a scholar in British literature, began to examine the multiple ways in which the curriculum hindered the current faculty (which had drastically changed demographically and in area of study since the last curriculum was designed), she suggested a yearlong discussion—not yet revision process—of the curriculum, and of curricular issues in English studies more generally. The result of those discussions (which were fruitful, energizing, painful, and exhausting) led to a second year of curricular revision. While the driving goal of the new curriculum is faculty inhabitation (the possibility for the greatest number of faculty to move in and out of as many courses as possible) and not fusion, there certainly exists much greater opportunity for fusion to take place. Moreover, these discussions have required faculty to learn a good deal about each other's work, something they were able to avoid nearly altogether before.

FROM FIXED-END TO END-IN-VIEW

What Shari learned—what each of us has learned—is that institutional change is a slow, messy, often frustrating process. We confess that at times, participating in such processes only heightens our temptation to renounce the impurity of corporate compromise and push for our vision of "fusion or bust." Even today, we sometimes want to shake the very foundations of the programs we "inherited," to get our colleagues to start from scratch, and to find some way—any way—to capture some of what we experienced at Albany. And if it turns out to be impossible to instigate the kind of change we are looking for, we can at least find redemption in our defeat: we may lose, but we're fighting the good fight.

While almost addictive, this narrative is a dangerous one. First, the all-or-nothing model violates the very definition of fusion, which is dependent upon meeting student and faculty needs, interests, and expertise (North et al. 258). Further, to assume that there is a pure and fundamental form of fusion is to deny the importance of local contexts. It is to risk acting out of a will to truth, which establishes fusion as a fixed and utopian end, and those who promote it as heroes or saviors. As John Rajchman argues, when discourses abide by a will to truth, their advocates use this will to protect themselves from "re-thinking and change. It turns what was once 'critical' in their work into a kind of norm or law—a final truth, a final emancipation" (qtd. in Gore 11). While we are clearly advocates of fusion, we also want to maintain a self-reflexive stance. It seems to us that fusion requires ongoing questioning, rethinking, and revising.

We want to resist, then, a notion of fusion that is founded upon what John Dewey would call a "fixed end": an achievable goal, and thus a terminus of action. For Dewey, the alternative to "fixed ends" are "ends-in-view." An end-in-view, unlike a fixed end, is a resource for present activity, but its achievement is not the sole motivator and determinant of that activity. While a fixed end determines and measures present activity, an end-in-view informs it while also allowing us to experience the intrinsic value of the present moment. So, for instance, if employment is the fixed end of education, we will design a strictly

change attachment to this model [handwritten marginal note]

functional, vocational program driven entirely by the specifications of
future employment opportunities. By contrast, if employment is an
end-in-view, we will design educational programs with an eye toward
preparing students for employment, while also providing them experiences that hold immediate significance and that may prepare students
for a host of other experiences as well (democratic citizenship, for instance).

Similarly, if we operated as new faculty members with fusion as the
fixed end, all of our work would function in service of realizing that
model in our new institutions. By this yardstick, the work the three
of us have done must be judged an unqualified failure. We have not
brought "fusion" to our institutions. On the other hand, we know
that our commitment to the *idea* of fusion—our having "fusion in
our hearts," as we joke—*has* informed our work throughout the early
phases of our careers. We can act on the principles of fusion without
holding out hope that this model will actually be realized. (Much in
the way, for instance, we work variously from/for the principles of participatory democracy or democratic socialism, knowing that we will
not see these models in practice in our lifetimes in the U.S.) In this
way, fusion is not only a product but also a process—an end in itself.
And this process creates moments of con/fusion that are worthy of
reflection.

ILLUMINATING THE CON/FUSION

Peter's experience working with his college's general education program helps demonstrate the importance not only of holding onto fusion as an end-in-view rather than a fixed end but also of making productive use of the con/fusing process accompanying this work. That
is, rather than aiming to sever or suppress con/fusing moments for
their hindrance to fusion as a fixed end, Peter found it important to
use these moments as a way, as Welch puts it, to "ask us new questions,
reveal our unexamined assumptions, [and] disturb any sense of a stable
model we embody" (63).

Unlike Chris and Shari, Peter was working in an interdisciplinary
context as the chair of a faculty inquiry group charged with examining
the current state of general education at his college (a group analogous
to the yearlong curriculum study group in Shari's department). Peter
went into the work imagining that the intradisciplinary fusion within
English found at Albany was to be the model for a meaningful inter-

disciplinary fusion-based general education program that joined the liberal arts and professional degree curricula.

The faculty inquiry group was part of the university-wide inquiry into General Education that all eighteen colleges in the system were conducting. Peter found an intense distrust of the very enterprise of the inquiry groups: was this just one more attempt by the university's central administration to impose a blueprint upon each of the (very distinct) colleges? As well, there was concern about the motives behind such a broad inquiry in the wake of efforts over the past decade by the central administration of the university to further alter the open admissions legacy of the university, including removing basic writing programs from the four year colleges and relegating it to community colleges, and reducing the number of credits necessary to graduate— policies with which the community colleges in the system, including Peter's, continue to struggle.

The previous year, Peter's college assessment committee began a formal expansion of a college-wide assessment program that asked each department and each faculty member to name and begin assessing teaching and learning goals for various courses. Framing this general education inquiry as an extension of these efforts, Peter hoped to move the conversation from individual and idiosyncratic pedagogies to commonly shared goals for students' learning experiences and faculty teaching goals across disciplines and professional programs. Could a faculty group that included members who were educated in Europe, South America, and North America, at land-grant, Ivy League, and state universities arrive at common understandings of what general education ought to be? The group members began with narratives of their own educational experiences, and from those narratives they collected the keywords that resonated across the conceptions of general education that appeared in those narratives: "breadth"; "mind-expanding"; "difference, dialogue, and respect"; "solid grounding"; "a rich gateway to ideas"; "thinking outside the box." With such generalities, it was easy enough for the faculty to claim broad agreement and go back home to their departments. Who could argue with a colleague who wrote that an undergraduate general education ought to promote "intellectual ambidexterity"? Setting these terms and their stories next the actual general education curriculum of the college, however, highlighted (created?) tension.

It quickly became clear that the college's general education program, if it could be called a program, was the product of compromise after compromise, producing a staggering sedimentation of detailed exceptions and accommodations. To inquire into its nature was to make uninvited trouble for many departments and many disciplines. But it also enabled the inquiry group members to recognize the history of previous decisions, to make them available for scrutiny, and to imagine alternative decisions. This preliminary process led Peter to ask the faculty group to name and think with the tensions they were feeling as they moved back and forth between asking broader questions about the purposes of general education and asking how the specific context of the college, the degree programs, and the departments coincided with "general education."

Using a template he created, Peter re-presented the tensions that appeared in the group's discussions and online exchanges. For example, should "breadth of knowledge" be experienced as a "grab bag" of disciplines that students variously and individually collect on their way to their degree ("students should have the autonomy to choose what they want"), or should the idea of "breadth" be deliberately facilitated by faculty and created as part of the curriculum through a capstone course ("students should be offered guidance in making connections across different kinds of knowledge")? Some faculty members strongly advocated for an intentionally designed and administered general education curriculum that established the same analytic goals across each course, regardless of discipline, explicitly designed to examine issues of interdisciplinarity. Even as they proposed it, many recognized that such an idea was in tension with the current practice of maintaining distinct departmental courses that were designed and taught as though they were part of a discipline-based major.

Instead of asking the group to come quickly to a *resolution* of each tension, Peter asked that they examine what these tensions could teach them. To this end, he asked colleagues to choose two tensions (or to create new tensions not already identified) and do three things: name current practices at the college that fell closest to each "pole" in the tension; identify a course that person taught and place it on each continuum, explaining how and why they did so; and identify what might have to change individually, departmentally, college wide, and university wide, to move that course closer to either of the poles. The tensions were intended to be understood as opportunities to inquire into their own practice, their departmental/discipline offerings, and the shape of the college curriculum, ideally seeking connections across all three. As the task indicates, the poles that established each tension were to be understood as creating a continuum rather than as defining oppositions; and moreover each faculty member's connection to each tension was to be seen as dynamic rather than as staking out intellectual territory.

The inquiry group shared their writing about the tensions, pushing and challenging and supporting and extending each other. Surprisingly, consensus did emerge in several areas. For instance, they agreed that the best way to teach general education was through a variety of different and connected learning activities that promote both student and faculty involvement. Learning communities, writing intensive courses, courses connected by certain themes, and collaborative learning appeared to be steps in the right direction. Similarly, the group agreed on the importance of mentoring and advising, and of developing good "habits of mind" in students, and of not assuming that they come to college already having learned them.

Holding fusion as a fixed end in this context simply made no sense because the faculty members involved did not control *a* curriculum that represented a discipline. Rather the faculty all participated in multiple curricula and degree programs, and each was embedded in overlapping networks of power and control. However, recognizing fusion as an end-in-view helped shape a set of conversations and the public exchange of writing (an unusual and uncomfortable process for many) about the aims and goals of general education at an urban community college that became strategic steps toward further inquiry. This process has drawn faculty colleagues out of their intradisciplinary conversations and into an interdisciplinary debate around a collective enterprise that holds out the promise of countering isolation and corporate compromise—ideally both within disciplines and across disciplines.

So far, these small steps have brought faculty together to create new learning communities independent of the inquiry group and to create a pilot transfer project in collaboration with a four year college that many of the college's students transfer into. Some faculty have expressed a renewed sense of investment in their working on the college assessment committee; others have begun revising the college's general education objectives in the hope of taking their revisions before the college community and ultimately the college senate. As well, the use of ongoing student focus groups—both current students and those who have graduated—to assess student input and feedback on their general education experiences has been recognized and asserted as fundamentally necessary to any future collective work.

Relational Work Toward Con/Fusion

As Shari and Peter both learned, institutional change is not the result of *individual* efforts. But if we are attendant to changes already under-way in our new institutions and if we keep fusion as an end-in-view rather than a fixed end, we may well serve as catalysts, sparking a reac-tion by forming coalitions and engaging in *relational work* with other colleagues or students. Relational work, according to Welch, involves

> learning through relationships how [our] individual stories [and ideas, visions, and values] join, disrupt, change, and are changed by the words of others, learn-ing within potential spaces how to rename their re-lationships to institutions from one of compliance or alienation to one of collective, responsible, and creative participation. (120)

Often, in fact, it is these communities that sustain us and prevent us from being consumed by the sometimes disheartening process of institutional revision.

Chris's experience demonstrates the importance of relational work, especially with students. Early on in his tenure track position, he taught a required course for MA students entitled Introduction to Lit-erary Scholarship. Despite that narrow title, the course functioned (or, in recent years had come to function) more like an Introduction to Graduate Studies in English course, focusing largely on the methods and practices of the fields within the discipline (now including atten-tion to composition and rhetoric, film studies, and creative writing, in addition to literary scholarship). Still fresh from his own program at SUNY-Albany, Chris designed a course in which graduate students would have the opportunity to think and write across the traditional boundaries of the discipline—to examine, for instance, intersections between composition and creative writing pedagogy or between liter-ary and rhetorical theory.

While such an approach might seem not entirely out of place in a generalist MA program, students nonetheless found it very difficult to do the kind of boundary-crossing work the course invited them to do. In fact, many of them chafed at this work, asking instead for a class that would be truer to the title of the course by immersing them in the tools and methods of their scholarly specialization (most of these students saw themselves as specializing in a literary field, typically identified by time period and nation: nineteenth-century British, twentieth-century American, and so on). This insistence among first- and second-year MA students on forging and working from a stable, specialized professional identity came as a surprise to Chris—at first.

Meanwhile, a departmental committee on which Chris served was working on changing the title of the course from Introduction to Literary Scholarship to Introduction to English Studies. The latter, broader title seemed better suited to the work of the course in its recent incarnations. Along with a few colleagues, Chris drafted "Aims and Scopes" documents to account for this broader approach. The course would be a space where students—variously situated—would inquire into the shape and nature of the discipline/profession, asking questions such as "What is English studies?" "What values and practices hold it together?" "What is the relationship between and among its constituent parts?" and "What is its place in the academy and in culture?" Students would survey a range of "critical and intellectual stances" in the discipline, with one eye on a subfield that they found particularly interesting and one on the broader discipline.

When these documents were brought to the department, however, some faculty demurred, claiming that students were better served by the more traditional "training" in the methods of literary scholarship. Don't students need to know how to use databases? Don't they need to learn how to cite sources accurately? Don't they need to know how to structure a journal article?

What became clear in the course of this conversation was how Chris's students responses to his course were shaped by the messages students were getting from the faculty: learn to do what we do. Specialize. *Be like us.* That these messages were coming through so clearly for MA students in a generalist program demonstrates the power of "corporate compromise" in the department. (This is the same department, recall, that established a ten-concentration undergraduate major.) The department meeting ended with a compromise: the course would be called Introduction to Research and Scholarship in English.

Chris's first response to this discussion, frankly, was to write off those colleagues who chipped away at his version of the course: they were passé, out of touch, irretrievably "corporately compromised." But committed more than ever to thinking through curriculum and knowledge-making in English studies, he designed a seminar called Emerging Models of English Studies: Rhetorics and Poetics, which explored intradisciplinary scholarship (including North et al.), curricula, and pedagogy. The course drew a small but lively group of students (for an extended discussion of this course, see Crisco et al.). Moved by the innovative, integrative thinking of many scholars and teachers in the discipline, the class decided to intervene in the local curriculum by proposing a new course, called Approaches to English Studies, which would do the work Chris and his colleagues had originally imagined under the auspices of Introduction to English Studies:

> This [. . .] course takes English studies, itself, as a sub-ject of inquiry. It will provide graduate students an op-portunity to map the field of English studies as it is enacted institutionally (in professional organizations, curricula and curricular reform efforts, and scholar-ly journals across the field). The course may [do the following]: 1) survey the historical development of English studies; 2) critically examine some of the key terms currently at the center of debates concerning the defining goals and purposes of the work of English de-partments; 3) create a collaborative, explicitly intradis-ciplinary forum to explore the often competing com-mitments of our discipline and to articulate the stakes (individual, field-wide, institutional, cultural) of the various approaches to reforming English studies; and 4) provide students with opportunities to locate them-selves and their professional commitments in relation-ship to the field of English Studies.

This course was approved and is now "on the books." The addition of a single course may be a humble intervention indeed; it hardly moved the department or the curriculum toward fusion. But if we view this series of events from the perspective of con/fusion—as an example of working relationally—it becomes an object lesson in the anatomy of change. Key to the admittedly modest change Chris and these students brought about was the formation of what we think of as a "troublemaking collectivity." The purpose of such a collectivity is to disrupt corporate compromise—in this case by carving a space in which the primary commitments of the curriculum in which the course is housed are systematically put under scrutiny through "explicitly intradisciplinary" study.

We have found that like fusion, con/fusion is not possible without the participation of students. Recall that a central aim of fusion is not to transmit knowledge from professor to student, but to facilitate a "series of occasions for negotiating claims about who knows what, how, why and to what ends" (North et al. 96). At Albany it was necessary for all who took part in the program to understand the fusion enterprise, and to view themselves as crucial contributors to a "nexus of discourse" (154). We have found, however, that too often students—graduate and undergraduate—at our respective institutions regard the curricular structure as natural, inevitable, fixed. It is something they must "get through," not something to which they are invited to contribute. For this reason, inviting student contribution is crucial. As both Chris and Shari discovered, by helping students to examine the (political) structure of English studies in and beyond their local institutions, students began to serve as catalysts themselves.

Go (Re)Figure

For us, fusion has become much more than a curricular model; it has become a way to name a set of commitments and values that we bring to all of our work within and beyond English departments. As we moved from being graduate students to new professors, our attempts to enact change in our new institutions were considerably more modest and more complicated—more confusing—than we had imagined they would be. But our will to make trouble for the academic *status quo*—corporate compromise—did not, and has not, dwindled. Instead, we have learned

- to be attendant to change already underway in our institutions;
- to keep fusion as an end-in-view rather than a fixed end, making productive use of con/fusing moments; and

- to imagine and pursue change (institutional and disciplinary) as relational work.

In his typical pragmatic fashion, Richard Miller contends that academics need to "leave off critiquing the academy for having failed to make good on its promise to deliver a meaningful, morally sacrosanct life and to begin, instead, to work within the fiscal and bureaucratic constraints that both enable the academic enterprise and limit its scope" (210). Although we consider ourselves pragmatists, we worry about the accommodationist premise in Miller's declaration. We should *never* leave off critiquing the academy—or the other institutions in which we live and work. The ethic informing con/fusion is decidedly critical; it teaches us that corporate compromise is not good enough and we must work with fusion as an end-in-view. We work in the service of fusion without insisting on its achievement as a precondition for carrying on. And we work against corporate compromise without insisting on its abolition as a precondition for carrying on. This ethic can serve as the foundation for troublemaking collectivities: alliances in which we make trouble *with,* not just *for,* those already in, as well as those entering, the systems in which we live and work. Such collectivities, we believe, are our best hope for refiguring "the nature of the discipline itself."

Note

1. In the years since our departures from SUNY-Albany, the graduate program has shifted away from the model we describe here; instead of an integrated "Writing, Teaching, and Criticism" program, the PhD now includes a small set of concentrations.

Works Cited

Blitz, Michael, and C. Mark Hurlbert. *Letters for the Living.* Urbana, IL: NCTE, 1998.

Cain, Mary Ann. *Revisioning Writers' Talk.* New York: SUNY P, 1995.

Crisco, Virginia, Chris W. Gallagher, Deborah Minter, Katie Hupp Stahlnecker, and John Talbird. "Graduate Education as Education: The Pedagogical Arts of Institutional Critique." *Pedagogy* 3.3 (fall 2003): 359–76.

Dewey, John. *Democracy and Education.* 1916. New York: Free P, 1966.

Gallagher, Chris W. *Radical Departures: Composition and Progressive Pedagogy.* Urbana, IL: NCTE, 2002.

Gore, Jennifer M. *The Struggle for Pedagogies.* New York: Routledge, 1993.

Kameen, Paul. *Writing/Teaching*. Pittsburgh: U of Pittsburgh P, 2000.

Miller, Richard. *As If Learning Mattered*. Ithaca: Cornell UP, 1998.

North, Stephen M. "It Only Looks Like We Lost: The Rise, Fall, and Legacy of a Writing Sequence through the English Major." Conference on College Composition and Communication. Denver. 14–17 Mar. 2001.

North, Stephen M., with Barbara A. Chepaitis, David Coogan, Lâle Davidson, Ron MacLean, Cindy L. Parrish, Jonathan Post, and Beth Weatherby. *Refiguring the PhD in English Studies: Writing, Doctoral Education, and the Fusion-Based Curriculum*. Urbana, IL: NCTE, 2000.

Owens, Derek. *Composition and Sustainability*. Urbana, IL: NCTE, 2003.

Ritchie, Joy S., and David E. Wilson. *Teacher Narrative as Critical Inquiry*. New York: Teachers College Press, 2000.

Porter, James E., Patricia Sullivan, Stuart Blythe, Jeffrey T. Grabill, and Libby Miles. "Institutional Critique: A Rhetorical Methodology for Change." *College Composition and Communication* 51.4 (2000): 610–42.

Stenberg, Shari J. *Professing and Pedagogy: Learning the Teaching of English*. Urbana, IL: NCTE, 2005.

Welch, Nancy. "Resisting the Faith: Conversion, Resistance, and the Training of Teachers." *College English* 55 (1993): 387–401.

Wilson, David E. *Attempting Change*. Portsmouth, NH: Boynton/Cook, 1994.

3 Sociolinguistics as a Lens for Viewing English Studies, or Wearing My Ever-Lovin,' Ever-Changin' Heart on My Sleeve

Susan Meredith Burt

This short chapter is in three parts. In the first part, I attempt to define my view of English studies by focusing on the sociolinguistic, sociohistorical position of the English language with respect to other languages of the world and to derive from that position examples of questions that can be used to define our hybrid and emergent discipline (if I decide to speak of it in the singular). In the second part of the chapter, I try to play with, and end up struggling with, an extended metaphor that is probably ill-advised, but I nevertheless use it to describe several types of English departments that we can find in the American academic landscape. The third part of the paper is truly odd, for me; perhaps it is a piece of English studies science fiction.

1. The Sociolinguistic Position of English, and What That Should Mean for English Studies

In 1992 Michael Krauss published an article in *Language* on the impending devastation of the world's languages. Discussing the entire world, continent by continent, Krauss argued that, given current rates of population dislocation, war, genocide, but also somewhat less violent methods of displacement such as language shift and television (which he called "cultural nerve gas") children had ceased learning a significant number of the world's approximately 6,000 languages, and that many of these languages were now moribund. Another significant percentage of languages is suffering a decline in the rate at which children within the group learn the heritage language as opposed to a dominant language—and these languages are endangered. Only 600 of the world's languages, 10 percent of the total, have sufficient population, educational infrastructure, and economic and institutional support to count as "safe." Some of these safe languages, of course, threaten smaller languages; in the process of language shift, these stronger and more dominant languages absorb speaker populations as families and individuals decide to speak Spanish rather than Aymara; Dutch rather than Frisian; English rather than Menomini, Ojibwa, Navaho, or Mandan—up to 80 percent of North American indigenous languages that are still spoken today are moribund. Language shift in the home territory of an indigenous language can lead to language death.

What happens to a language as it dies—as it ceases to be spoken in a fully functioning, self-reproducing human society—is a growing subfield of linguistics, largely launched by one of my mentors, linguist Nancy Dorian of Bryn Mawr College. As I began my own career as a scholar, however, I did not study language death (Dorian), or the preliminary process, language shift (Fishman, Gal), but was drawn to pragmatics, with its focus on situated language use, and to the theoretical attempts to understand interactions of various types and to understand our understanding of them. Only in the past few years have I had the opportunity to attempt to combine the two strands of endeavor: what can we learn about the changes that take place in interactions—and in people's understanding of them—in societies that are shifting their language loyalty from one language to another?

Language shift and language death are some of the possible eventual linguistic outcomes of a process that began centuries before now, with cultural contact, territory conquest, and/or colonization. Other outcomes of language contact can include stable bilingual or multilingual polities, the emergence of mixed languages, pidgins and creoles, the expanding use of *lingua francas*, and on the level of speaker behavior and capabilities, code-switching of various types, "interference" of various types (Thomason; Myers-Scotton), pragmatic failure and misunderstandings of various types (Thomas) and occasionally, first language attrition (Kouritzen), the loss of the ability to speak one's first language.

Linguists are inclined to consider issues of language shift with a focus on the language that loses speakers (or on the speakers who lose languages). But we can also turn our attention to the linguistic and cultural effects of this contact-induced shift process on the language that speakers shift *to*—such as English, in a growing number of cases (Kachru *Alchemy;* Kachru, *Other Tongue;* Crystal). How the shift to English transforms English and English texts are issues that I hereby nominate as possible defining questions for the offspring discipline that we parent at my home university and elsewhere—English studies. These can be some of any number of discipline-defining questions. Other questions of pedagogical, ethical, linguistic, sociolinguistic, rhetorical, and literary nature all spring from this sociolinguistic positioning of English as an increasingly dominant language in the world.

One question arising from the global spread of English that has already engaged the area of TESOL, for example, is the definition of Native Speaker. Ferguson (1992), for example, points out that the nonnative learners and users of English now outnumber its native speakers. It is no longer sufficient to connect automatically assumptions of linguistic proficiency with ethnic identity in an era when individuals migrate far from their "ethnic homeland," and learn to thrive socially, linguistically, and expressively in a second language and its society. Can they *become* Native Speakers of their second language? Can they claim all the rights, privileges and responsibilities of Native Speaker linguistic authority? Results of the decoupling of ethnicity and language "ownership" lend themselves to study by means of the various approaches that English studies, as a synthesis of linguistics, composition studies, and literary studies, makes available.

For example, what are the features of a literary creative text in English, produced by writers from outside of Braj Kachru's "Inner Circle" nations ("Standards"), whether those writers are immigrants to an Anglophone territory or speakers of a variety of English that has taken root far from the language's "ethnic homelands"? Faculty and students in postcolonial and immigrant literatures clearly contribute to our understanding of the global position of our shared language. Should we teach English to a group of people who will use English to find work in an economic enterprise that we fear will turn out to be exploitative of them and of others because the economic enterprise is being run by the usual corporate suspects? Robert Phillipson and Tove Skutmabb-Kangas warn the TESOL community against unwitting complicity with "Macdonaldization" (439). Deborah Cameron discusses the dangers of corporate exploitation of certain speaker groups, particularly women, in an economy where proficiency in languages and styles suitable for linguistic service work (such as staffing telephone call centers) is becoming a commodity. But Selma K. Sonntag (2003) demonstrates that English in its role as globalizing language is used for a variety of political ends, including resistance. Consequently, we have to ask whether we have the right to deny English instruction to eager learners who seem to really want it. These are the sorts of questions that arise out of this sociolinguistic moment in the life of the English language, and while I naturally incline to linguistic questions, these are not questions that would typically be central to a linguistics department, but I do think they could engage multidisciplinary departments of English studies.

Indeed, some of these questions already have engaged some of our students at Illinois State University. What are the pragmatic and rhetorical features of quasi-diplomatic, quasi-journalistic texts in English, produced by the official news bureau of North Korea? One of the graduate students in my department is tackling this one. Another has taken on defining the pedagogical responsibilities of a technical writer (who uses English, of course) teaching in a multilingual, West African context. These are questions that a mix of native speakers and second language speakers are best positioned to engage; departments that embrace ethnolinguistic diversity within their ranks can tackle questions such as these. We can expect questions like these to continue to emerge from the sociolinguistic dynamic that English is now a part of. If we want our emergent discipline to be able to work on these emergent questions, we need departments of English studies that reflect and connect to the different ethnic and national contexts in which the dynamic will play out. As Kachru suggests in a 1985 article ("Standards"), English studies needs an academic structure that can address its object language's unprecedented sociolinguistic role within the world. As the English-speaking world becomes more ethnolinguistically diverse, so must the discipline that hopes to understand it.

2. A Descriptive-Prescriptive Metaphor to Play With

In this section, I would like to propose that we consider our disciplinary allegiances as ethnolinguistic identities. If you will indulge me with this metaphor, I will sketch for you types of English departments using the levels of theoretical description that have developed in twentieth-century sociolinguistics. It will be apparent that some departments, in particular graduate programs, probably require the most recent type of sociolinguistic theory for their description—rendering them, to me at least, far more intellectually attractive than the alternatives, at least one of which I have lived in.

Consider then, the ethnolinguistic landscape, or, if you prefer, the ethno-disciplinary landscape, as describable using the earliest methods of dialect geography. Here, variation is described in terms of geographic region, and divisions are mapped in two dimensions. Typically in dialect geography, by the way, the map is drawn by someone from outside the region.

Thus, an English department of this sort might look like this:

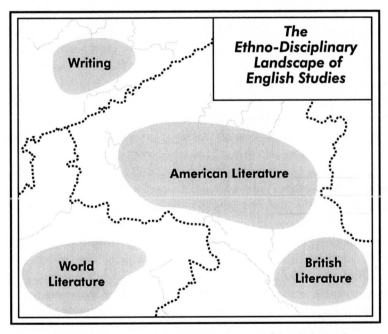

Figure 1: The Ethno-Disciplinary Landscape of English Studies.

We might describe such an intellectual region as the stereotypical English department ethnic homeland; British Literature was long ago the dominant ethnic group, but now American Literature seems to be ascendant. Nods are given in the direction of World Literatures, and more than a few sighs at the necessity for continued attention to writing instruction and its unattractive subordinate, Grammar. I have worked in at least one such department. What made it hard for me and all the inhabitants was a strict standardizing policy—we were all expected to assimilate and conform to a standard and universal dialect, as it were, in that we were all expected to be able to teach in any and all of the regions. There was, of course, some work that the native ethno-disciplinary groups found utterly distasteful—teaching that grammar course—and so, I was brought in as an ethno-disciplinarily different immigrant to take over that work. I too was expected to assimilate to the standard, but, like most adult immigrants, was too far past the critical learning period to be able to do so (as you can see, there is more than one meaning to an "English-only policy."). My attitude of personal ethno-disciplinary identity preservation must have offended the leadership, because, even as I attempted to expand the market for the work I performed, it became clear that an immigration quota would rule out the possibility that others from my ethno-disciplinary homeland would be allowed to enter, and indeed, after I left, there was scary talk of outsourcing my industry overseas to the Education college. Although most of the inhabitants of this region were friendly to me on an individual basis, only one showed any interest in learning more about my ethno-disciplinary heritage, predictably, the medievalist. I hope I have horrified you with this description, because, having lived in such an intellectual territory, I want never to do so again.

In the second half of the twentieth century, variationist sociolinguistics complicated dialect studies forever, as age, gender, ethnicity and identity began to crosscut the two-dimensional picture of the region. Now language variety—or intellectual identity, to pursue our metaphor—is understood not only in regional terms, but in regional plus demographic ones. Two-dimensional maps do not suffice—description must result in a three-dimensional model, but that model can be constructed either by someone from elsewhere or by someone from inside the region. My new department, like many, has been a community describable in these terms, as is any department that has complicated the traditional, two-dimensional picture of regional (or historical) divisions of English with other discipline-engendering categories such as race, gender, and age divisions cross-cutting ethno-disciplinary ones. In such departments, allegiances may be formed across ethno-disciplinary lines as "identity politics" complicates and enriches the academic political economy of curricula and the division of academic spoils.

In the last two or three decades, interactional sociolinguistics, discourse analysis, and pragmatics have complicated and continue to complicate the picture still further, bringing reflections of conversational dynamics, conflict, power relationships, social distance or closeness, speaker goals and intentions, and change into the theoretical machinery—where facets of our regional, gender and ethnic (or ethno-disciplinary) identities show through only from time to time, as their relevance rises and falls with our changing interactional goals. At least one school of thought that deals with interaction (conversation analysis) claims that accurate "mappings" of interactions should be drawn chiefly on the basis of reactions by the members, participants, insiders. Given that constraint, I don't know whether I can map departments at the level of complexity of interactional sociolinguistics or not, because I am still a disciplinary immigrant. However, I can bring in relevant questions that may help us construct the map: does our department (or our hybrid discipline) have an unspoken hierarchy of disciplinary importance, possibly derived or devolved from territory maps of earlier eras? If so, does that hierarchy get enacted or performed in our interactions, both political and interpersonal? Do such performances and interactions serve to reproduce the power hierarchies, as critical discourse analysts have claimed? (I am also not sure that the whole analogy doesn't completely fall apart here, but anyway, it was fun to try.) My point is that English studies now seems to be a discipline of immigrants, both ethnolinguistic and ethno-disciplinary, to the standard English department "homeland," and as the sociolinguistic position of the English language in the world continues to change, the intellectual richness and promise of the English studies enterprise will be greatest if we stay that way.

Should we remain the interesting intersection of layered ethno-disciplinary identities that I think English studies now is, or perhaps almost is, I envision a situation where interest in intercultural communication and its critiques take on new and crucial relevance. We will be able to assume less about each other than we now do, and will have to approach communication across the disciplinary boundaries within English studies with a cautious deference (as recommended for intercultural communication by Byrnes and Garcia, for example). While we should be deferential about recognizing the boundaries of other ethno-disciplinary groups, we should be prepared to have our own boundaries breached, because only in that way do we allow the immigration of ideas and approaches of the ethno-disciplinarily different to tweak, enrich or converge with our own. We should look for discipline-contact effects in our own talk and text. As one who has studied and experienced intercultural communication, I predict that we will find interdisciplinary communication to be frustrating and exhausting but also endlessly interesting.

3. THE ODD, THIRD PART

A native speaker of Linguistics (although her first language was Anthropology) encountered a native speaker of Creative Writing on the listserv, and later, again, in the hallway. As the Linguist does not speak Creative Writing—and the Creative Writing speaker knows some words of Linguistics, but feels shaky about the grammar part—they found it easiest to use the *lingua franca* of Pedagogy. Yet, as conversations across linguistic and cultural boundaries so often do, this one, too, went somewhat wrong, in a way that the Linguist, annoyed with herself, could not put her finger on. Perhaps she shouldn't have trotted out some of her most polysyllabic pieces of linguistic and cultural capital during the exchange. It was one of those E. M. Forster moments (the Linguist, like most first-language speakers of Anthropology, loves novels). Forster put it so well that famous linguist Deborah Tannen quoted him in her dissertation: "A pause in the wrong place, an intonation misunderstood, and a whole conversation went awry" (vii). An apology, a Speech Act in which the Speaker threatens her own Positive Face, was probably in order.

Sighing, our Linguist returns to the comfort of her home language, and talks with another Linguist about the encounter. He teases her, as he often does—nothing licenses a teasing relationship so well as that social closeness that comes from speaking the same minority language while surrounded by speakers of the culturally dominant tongue:

"Soooo, what have *you* been up to?"

"Talking with a Creative Writer."

"I can tell. It shows."

"What? Oh, come on. You know what those intercultural encounters are like."

"Well, it has affected you. You'd better scan all your texts for interdisciplinary interference."

"What? No way!"

The Linguist, now truly unsettled, checks her identity in the mirror—yes, she is still herself—and then checks on the language in her text. Yes, it's in Linguistics. It's clearly a Linguistics text. What else could it be? She is, after all, a Native Speaker. *So she gets to determine it...*

Thus, our disciplines, like our languages and our selves, are transformed through use, contact, and interaction. Whether the structures we build for our intellectual work can reflect those changes is a question that can shape the development of English studies.

Works Cited

Byrnes, Heidi. "Interactional Style in German and American Conversations." *Text* 6.2 (1986): 189–206.

Cameron, Deborah. "Language, Gender, and Globalization." *Sprak, Kön och Kultur.* Ed. Kerstin Nordenstam and Kerstin Norén. Göteborg: Institutionen för svenska spraket, 2001. 1–17.

Crystal, David. *English as a Global Language.* Cambridge: Cambridge UP, 1997.

Dorian, Nancy C. *Language Death: The Life Cycle of a Scottish Gaelic Dialect.* Philadelphia: U of Pennsylvania P, 1981.

Ferguson, Charles A. "Foreword to the First Edition. "*The Other Tongue.* 2nd ed. Ed. Braj Kachru. Urbana, IL: U of Illinois P, 1992. xiii–xvii.

Fishman, Joshua. *Reversing Language Shift.* Clevedon, UK: Multilingual Matters, 1991.

Gal, Susan. "Language Shift." *Kontaktlinguistik: Ein internationales Handbuch zeitgenössischer Forschung.* Ed. Hans Goebl, Peter H. Nelde, Zdenek Stary, and Wolfgang Wölck. Berlin: Walter de Gruyter, 1996. 586–93.

García, Carmen. "Apologizing in English: Politeness Strategies Used by Native and Non-Native Speakers." *Multilingua* 8.1 (1989): 3–20.

Kachru, Braj. "Standards, Codification and Sociolinguistic Realism: The English Language in the Outer Circle." *English in the World: Teaching and Learning the Language and Literatures.* Ed. Randolph Quirk and H. G. Widdowson. Cambridge: Cambridge UP, 1985. 11–30.

—. *The Alchemy of English.* Oxford: Pergamon, 1986.

—, ed. *The Other Tongue.* 2nd ed. Urbana, IL: U of Illinois P, 1992.

Kouritzin, Sandra G. *Face[t]s of First Language Loss.* Mahwah, NJ: Erlbaum, 1999.

Krauss, Michael. "The World's Languages in Crisis." *Language* 68.1 (1992): 4–10.

Myers-Scotton, Carol. *Contact Linguistics: Bilingual Encounters and Grammatical Outcomes.* Oxford: Oxford UP, 2002.

Phillipson, Robert, and Tove Skutnabb-Kangas. "English Only Worldwide or Language Ecology?" *TESOL Quarterly* 30.3 (1996): 429–52.

Sonntag, Selma K. *The Local Politics of Global English*. Lanham, MD: Lexington Books, 2003.

Tannen, Deborah. *Conversational Style: Analyzing Talk Among Friends*. Norwood, NJ: Ablex, 1984.

Thomas, Jenny. "Cross Cultural Pragmatic Failure." *Applied Linguistics* 4.2 (1983): 91–112.

Thomason, Sarah. G. *Language Contact: An Introduction*. Washington, DC: Georgetown UP, 2001.

4 We're *All* Teachers of English: The (Rocky) Road to Collaboration

Caren J. Town

Trying to create truly collaborative relationships between departments of English and secondary education can often seem like climbing switchbacks up a mountain: It looks like you're making no progress upward, the rocks hurt your feet, the goal is almost always out of sight, preliminary peaks masquerade as the real thing, and when you've finally reached the actual summit, the downhill trip is even *harder*. However, several of us at Georgia Southern University (GSU) have been trying over the years to make the climb, attempting to structure an interdisciplinary, cross-college program for training future language arts teachers.

MOTIVES FOR CHANGE

Prompted by concerns over high school students' SAT and other high-stakes test scores, pre-service teachers' certifying exam performances, university accrediting agency recommendations, and Georgia Board of Regents' policy changes, and facilitated by grants from the national Standards-based Teacher Education Program (STEP), faculty members from GSU's College of Education and the departments of Literature and Philosophy and Writing and Linguistics worked with language arts teachers from area high schools to begin discovering ways to better solve problems and meet expectations. We also hoped that such collaborative and interdisciplinary efforts would strengthen the somewhat tenuous connections between high school and university language arts programs.

In particular, we looked at ways to modify English, writing, and language arts methods courses in both the College of Education and the College of Liberal Arts and Social Sciences (CLASS) to help our shared students better meet the requirements of national and state organizations. These include the certifying exam (ours was until recently Educational Testing Service's PRAXIS II test), National Council of Teachers of English (NCTE) guidelines, National Council for Accreditation of Teacher Education (NCATE) Program Standards, the State of Georgia Board of Regents' Principles and Actions for the Preparation of Educators for the Schools, and Georgia's mandatory education standards (known at the time as the Quality Core Curriculum, or QCCs). Pulling these various (and sometimes contradictory) strands together was, of course, a monumental task.

To understand how complicated a job it was (and still remains), one must take a brief look at these conflicting expectations and their underlying assumptions about the teaching (and learning) of language arts. The PRAXIS II in English Language, Literature, and Composition, which was required in Georgia and many other states for teacher certification, is primarily a fact-based exam similar to the GRE, with emphasis on traditional content areas in language arts like literary/historical periods, literary genres and devices, critical reading, rhetorical terms, and grammar (*Study Guide*). (This test has recently been replaced by the instate Georgia Assessments for Certification of Educators—or GACE—a similar kind of exam.) NCATE's standards, which are based on NCTE guidelines, stress both content knowledge and skills, such as being able to "create various forms of oral, visual, and written literacy" and "demonstrate how to discover and create meaning from texts" ("NCATE Program Standards"). The QCCs, upon which Georgia's High School Graduation Test was based until very recently, asked students to "respond appropriately to questions about the author's purpose, character development, and plot structure," recognize cultural diversity, common elements of poetry, and literary elements, as well as respond creatively and choose literature according to personal interest ("Quality Core Curriculum"). (The QCCs has since been replaced by the Georgia Performance Standards, or GPS.)

These various requirements represent (at least) two conflicting models of language arts instruction and assessment: (1) a New Critical model of literary interpretation and instruction that expects students to absorb "objective" information about literature, and (2) a reader-response or cultural studies mode that stresses learning to be informed consumers of literature and emphasizes reading and critical thinking skills. Students wanting to become teachers (i.e., certified) had to absorb (and remember for four years) all the content information in their literature and composition classes, learn how to teach reading and writing skills in their methods classes, *and* reproduce both knowledge and skills on exams and in the classroom. It became clear during our STEP work that these areas of knowledge and *praxis* should not be separated; there needed to be both methodological discussions in the content courses and content discussions in the methods courses, or the students would never be able to come close to meeting the expectations placed on them for certification and on their students in high school classes.

We obviously had to find ways to collaborate across disciplines or fail at our task of training future teachers. As Annette Kolodny says in her fascinating description of her years as a dean of humanities, the curriculum of the next century must "evolve into permutations that are flexible, supportive of collaborative learning and research, genuinely interdisciplinary, and inventive of new disciplines when needed" (41). We were going to have to invent a new discipline for our pre-service teachers that combined theory and *praxis,* content knowledge and pedagogical skills. As Kolodny says, these new approaches will teach students "how to continue learning long after graduation and how to assess what they need to know in order to tackle any problem, however complex" (41). For future teachers, this means learning skills that will prepare them for the wide variety of challenges in today's classrooms. We also had to counter, especially in the content areas, what Vincent Leitch calls "the moribund modernist image of the university as ivory tower, peaceful, well-organized, and disengaged" (129). Ultimately, we needed to become committed to helping our students pass their qualifying exams, succeed in their classrooms, and eventually raise their students' scores on an ever-increasing number of high-stakes tests.

But first, we had to do our homework. To try to make sense of all these different expectations and see where we rose to the challenges and where we fell short, our STEP group met throughout the spring and summer of 2001 and made suggestions for curriculum and course revisions that more closely aligned these various requirements with teacher preparation. Perhaps more importantly, though, the meetings between English teachers from a variety of settings created a spirit of collaboration that we hope will benefit both university and high school language arts students and teachers in the future.

Why these meetings *needed* to take place should be explained in more detail (although it must be said that grants like STEP often create their own *de facto* justification). Over the past decade, state legislatures like Georgia's have begun more closely regulating the curriculum in public schools and colleges of education, in an attempt to control what they see—perhaps justifiably—as a crisis in American education. The scrutiny is especially intense if there is a perception that certain states are falling behind in SAT rankings, which is a particular problem in Georgia ("Mean SAT I"). This emphasis on standards and high-stakes testing is problematic in itself, but the special difficulty for content areas such as university literature and writing programs is that they have either not been made aware of these new requirements or they are deliberately resistant to them.

A Fraught History

The situation in the Georgia Southern Department of Literature and Philosophy is probably fairly representative of how these issues affect departments of English. As with many literature departments, we routinely teach both English majors and English education majors in our upper-level courses. English courses constitute the largest percentage of major courses in the English education program of study, so there has always been a certain amount of pressure from the College of Education to respond to the needs of "their" students in our classes. Many of our faculty members, however, have been unwilling and sometimes even hostile to what they perceive as interference in their curriculum and teaching practices. As Leitch puts it, "The disciplines are at once enabling and productive *and* restrictive and confining" (125). Literature faculty, especially, seemed reluctant to give up their disciplinary prerogatives. Clearly, much cross-disciplinary work needed to be done.

In our department, the collaboration story began in 1990, with the creation of an adolescent literature class, instigated by new state regulations that strongly suggested adding more content courses in the English education course of study. However, members of our department, from the chair down, felt that this course was imposed on the English department by outside forces, although we maintained control of the content and methodology (neither the adolescent nor children's literature classes at that time placed any emphasis on pedagogy). Still, we *were* collaborating, after a fashion, although, as Leitch warns, without actually changing existing disciplinary structures (126).

It is interesting to reflect on the fact that this first step toward collaboration (and site of contestation) took place around an adolescent literature course, a subject area that has been often undervalued by the academy (as has children's literature), and one which frequently uses non-canonical works to emphasize more contemporary, theoretically-informed ways of reading. Over the years, as future educators mix in these classes with English majors, strict formalist interpretive skills (traditionally the province of literary study) begin to overlap with reader-oriented approaches (more commonly used in language arts education). Also, because there is less likely to be an established canon in such courses, professors are freer to chose works that help students (and future teachers) approach reading more as a set of skills to be learned, rather than as pieces of knowledge to be swallowed and regurgitated. Content and pedagogy become much more intertwined; everyone begins to realize the ways in which we construct—rather than just absorb—knowledge.

This tentative first step in collaboration resulting from the creation of such a cross-disciplinary course, however, was undermined by the transfer in the middle of the 1990s of BS Ed. English majors from the English Department to the College of Education's advisement center. This caused many members of the English department to feel that their influence over English education students had been diminished and their hold on disciplinary boundaries loosened. The result of this was strengthened resistance to courses that straddled disciplinary lines, such as children's and adolescent literature. "As long as there are disciplines," Leitch says, "there will be interdisciplinary formations framed as minor offshoots and faced with precarious futures" (126). Increasingly, professors warned students that such courses were "minor offshoots," inappropriate for majors intent on graduate work in English.

This presented an opportunity, however, for "teaching the conflicts," as Gerald Graff would say (*Culture Wars* 12). By discussing these departmental squabbles in class, I could help students begin to distinguish between two radically different definitions of "English"— one reserved for the discipline-only canonized authors and time-honored critical approaches (usually formalist, teacher-centered) and another that stressed the need to challenge the canon and emphasized students' interpretive skills. Graff makes the point that "students learn not just by exposure to individual instructors, but by sensing how the teaching aggregate hangs together or divides, so that to obscure these relations robs students of one of the central means of making sense of education and the cultural world" (*Professing* 9). He later notes that "interdisciplinary conflicts go unperceived by students, who naturally see each discipline as a frozen body of knowledge to be absorbed rather than as social products with a history that they might have a personal and critical stake in" (258). The conflicts in our department and between colleges certainly helped make these divisions clear to our students and showed them that language arts instruction is "a social product with a history" (258).

In 1997, our "teaching aggregate" divided even further, when the English Department split into the Department of Literature and Philosophy and the Department of Writing and Linguistics, which meant, unfortunately for pre-service teachers, that instruction in composition, rhetoric, and linguistics was now being offered in a separate department from courses in literary history, interpretation, and criticism. For a future language arts teacher, who will be required to teach writing *and* literature, this further departmentalization meant, at the very least, that he or she would have to take courses in three separate departments with very different conceptualizations of the "language arts." For example, the emphasis on process-oriented writing and the move away from literature-based first-year composition courses meant that students coming into their literature courses in their sophomore year would have had little or no preparation (outside of high school) in the reading and interpretation of literature. In our department, literature professors have often not placed enough emphasis on the value of writing as a way of understanding.

However, Georgia Southern's conversion to the semester system in 1998 (with its accompanying mandate to revise programs during the change) led to the creation of new courses and improved relations with the College of Education. An Introduction to Literary Studies course emphasizing critical theory, current issues, and writing in the discipline was added to the requirements for the English major in the late 1990s, and a course called Teaching Literature to Middle and Secondary Students (taught in the Literature and Philosophy Department) was also created. Both of these courses are now part of the English education program of study, in part because of the STEP committee's advocacy.

The Department of Writing and Linguistics also added courses on teaching writing and grammar in the secondary schools, which have been added to the language arts education program of study.

However, the struggle wasn't over. Not surprisingly, members of the Literature and Philosophy Department objected to what they saw as the large number of Writing and Linguistics Department and College of Education courses required for the BS Ed. in English, and several professors argued that education majors should be required to take specific courses that were *not* required for English majors (like Shakespeare, for example) because education majors *clearly* weren't as prepared (or, perhaps by implication, as intellectually flexible) as English majors. Also, until fairly recently, the university catalog description for Teaching Literature read that "admission to the teacher education program" was required for admission to the course. Although this requirement could not be enforced for English majors who were interested in the course (and intrepid enough to question the prerequisite), the clearly intended effect was to limit the number of non-education majors who signed up for the course. Finally, the logistics of course scheduling has been intermittently problematic. For example, department chairs over the years have continued to schedule the teaching adolescent literature courses at times that are inconvenient for practicing and student teachers.

Some work has been done over the years to smooth relations between the various groups, however, through communication among department chairs, meetings with faculty in all three areas, work by the STEP committee mentioned earlier, participation by literature and writing faculty on College of Education committees, and the creation of a Secondary Education Committee in CLASS; however, more communication and discussion are needed. Clearly, what we thought was the summit was really just a minor mountain obscuring the real peak, and, regardless of how much hard climbing we have done, we are nowhere near the top.

A SAMPLE CLASS

Perhaps one advantage of the Georgia Southern teacher preparation program is that we offer a number of variously focused methods courses, in line with the argument advanced by Peter Smagorinsky and Melissa Whiting in their 1992 study of language arts methods course syllabi that "the potential for learning about teaching seems much greater when a course has a more specific focus and strives for fewer, more reachable goals" (11–12). Also, by requiring a *variety* of methods courses, taught in the College of Education and in content areas, students have the opportunity to learn to teach language arts in situational, transactional, process-oriented, reflective, and holistic ways. The bottom line is that "those who prepare teachers not try to satisfy all of [these goals] in a single course" (Smagorinsky and Whiting 105).

The focus of our department's segment of methods instruction has been refined over the years through theoretical discussions of teaching language arts with literature and education faculty, student comments, suggestions from high school teachers, and a developing sense of what will best serve the needs of future teachers and accommodate the ever-changing state and national requirements. My personal goal has been to keep the course relevant and useful, while maintaining high critical/theoretical standards. I am more interested in teaching critical frameworks than methodologies, and I hope that students will learn to articulate not just the *how* of teaching English but the *why*— both of the content and of their methods. My course follows the model advocated by Smagorinksy and Whiting that such courses should be "theoretically strong so that students emerge from the methods class with an understanding of how students learn rather than emerging with a bag of tricks to use" (23). I would much prefer that students be able to describe *why* they would teach a particular poem or short story in a certain way, rather than be able to list a variety of specific classroom activities.

Ideally, this model would extend to all English courses, so students who plan to be teachers could use effectively in their own classrooms what they learn in every content and methods course. As James Berlin says, "English courses must become self-consciously committed to the study of divergent reading and writing practices. Whatever literary and rhetorical texts are chosen, all must be considered in relation to their conditions of production, distribution, exchange, and reception" (114). I hope that, at least in my courses (both those explicitly for teachers and those designed for English majors), students will become aware of "divergent reading practices" and the wider psychological, social, political, and economic contexts in which they read literature (114). This is especially important for high school teachers, who will have to make the literature their students read relevant to their lives (if they want to engage their attention at all!).

The original motivation for the course came from a question by a student in my adolescent literature class, who asked me for suggestions for teaching *The Scarlet Letter,* which was her student teaching assignment. I offered some ideas, but I wondered aloud why she hadn't learned these things in her education methods courses. She said that they didn't have time for talking about teaching particular works, and that they concentrated on making lesson plans and teaching reading and writing, all of which is useful for the pre-service teaching but no help at all with Hawthorne. Fortuitously, the conversation coincided with our first STEP work, and this harmonic convergence led to the creation of the course. Of course, I had no real idea how to structure a course on teaching literature, other than anecdotal evidence from my twenty years of teaching in college classrooms. I also had (probably misplaced) confidence in what Pamela Grossman and others call an "apprenticeship of observation" (10), years of watching teachers and being a student, which, according to Grossman, "may not result in a clear vision of the different purposes for teaching a school subject" (11). Still, my lack of "pedagogical content knowledge," (Grossman 7), didn't deter me, although it probably should have. I thought that I knew, intuitively, how to teach students to teach literature.

The first semester a small group of seven students read *The Scarlet Letter* (of course), two Modern Language Association books on teaching Dickinson and Arthur Miller, and selections from *The Bedford Introduction to Literature* anthology. My first goals were modest: to expose students to a wide variety of literary types, from canonical to contemporary, and to start a discussion about how to teach those works. I would have to say that my successes were modest as well. Like several of the new teachers Grossman describes, my students still "had no framework around which to interpret and organize their insights" about either reading or teaching literature (109). I like to think they did come to understand *The Scarlet Letter* (and perhaps how to teach it) a bit better, though.

Undaunted, the next semester I discarded the MLA books (which I thought were too oriented toward college teaching) and added books on teaching multicultural works. Clearly, I was moving toward a more explicit focus on pedagogy, although I was becoming even more worried about my expertise in the field (which may have been a good thing). As a result of my increasing anxiety, I changed the focus the following semester to something I *do* know: critical theory. I devoted the first part of the term to discussing the use of critical theoretical frameworks, using Deborah Appleman's excellent *Critical Encounters in High School English*, which asks students to explore the ways in which critical theory can provide a series of "lenses" for the teaching and reading of literature. From this starting point, I asked students on their exams and final papers to articulate their own philosophies of teaching literature and to show the ways in which certain literary theories enhanced their philosophies and pedagogies.

Again, the emphasis was on *why* they chose a particular methodology, not *how* they would implement it. I also concentrated on having students reflect on their successes and failures in the student teaching experience and exposed them to perspectives of former students who had become teachers. What I was finally starting to work toward was helping students gain, in Grossman's words, "[k]nowledge that helps prospective teachers develop a sense of the overarching purposes for teaching subject matter and the strategies that are consistent with those larger purposes" (137). I wanted students to move from the *why* to the *how*—from the "overarching purposes" to "strategies consistent" with those purposes (137).

While Jane Agee points out that "[a]ttempting to bring conceptual change may not only be difficult but also a risky proposition for both teachers and students" (88), I have found that students, after some initial reluctance, are embracing critical theory and incorporating it into their practice. Many experienced teachers report that, while they have never really analyzed their own ideology, they discover that they have been using the various critical "lenses" without being aware of them. One pre-service teacher said that reading Appleman "has been very helpful for me when trying to pinpoint my own critical theories [. . .] Studying the theories in detail is helpful with understanding how I comprehend texts and furthermore how I will teach in the future." Another experienced teacher said that now that she is aware of the extent to which she uses literary theory, she is "more comfortable pursuing lines of questioning and letting go of the 'control' of my classroom discussion."

Of course, not everyone has been willing to embrace the more contemporary and perhaps controversial literary approaches; several students still favor using a formalist approach in their teaching, endorsing what Agee says, that "[e]ntering conceptions" students have "strongly shape" their responses to teaching and learning (87). However, while these students say that their familiarity with the formalist approach is "comforting," they appear willing to let teacher-centered formalism "spin off into a discussion of other approaches," and they hope that experimenting with different theories will help them "find a new way of teaching that [they] could find comfortable [. . .] but new and challenging for [their] students." One eighteen-year veteran says she was skeptical at first about teaching literary theory, but upon studying it further she recognizes that she already employs some of the reading approaches, and she says that "naming some of my teaching practices helped me to see why I teach the way that I do." This is in line with Robert Scholes's observation that: "The graduates of English programs should have found the method or methods that work best for them as readers and writers—and they should know the virtues and limitations of their preferred critical and interpretive methods" (141). The same thing holds true, it seems to me, for future secondary school teachers; they should be able to assess both the strengths and the weaknesses of the various methods they plan to employ in the classroom.

As a teacher, I, too, have moved from unreflective formalism to interactive poststructuralism. The course has shifted from one that was almost entirely text-based to one that depends more and more on a shared community of teachers and learners. At first I saw myself as the one with the content knowledge and the critical expertise that students were lacking. Now I find that I am reflecting more on my *own* practice as a teacher, and (I hope) conveying to my students that we are all engaged in the process of learning how to teach the literary works that we love and that continue to challenge us. To these ends, I evaluate each class (with the help of extensive student comments—both at midterm and the end of the course) in order to adapt to changing student needs and expectations.

As well as engaging in ongoing assessment of the course, I am also trying to encourage more of my literature department colleagues to join me in this enterprise, as I believe it would benefit our department and our future teachers if we share both the responsibility and the challenge of exploring various ways to train, be, and become more effective literature teachers. Most of my colleagues, not surprisingly, are not interested. In fact, as of this time, only one other faculty member (not in the Department of Literature and Philosophy, but an associate dean) has taught the course. This is a small step, however, toward a shared sense of ownership between content areas and the College of Education in the training of teachers.

Finally, the real key to the evolution of this course has been the movement from trying to fill gaps in teacher preparation (the nobody-was-teaching-them-how-to-teach-*The Scarlet Letter* problem) to learning how to articulate and share what it is that English departments do best: provide students with theoretical, historical, and cultural contexts for understanding and teaching literature. It is not our job, nor should it be, to replace colleges of education (although some of my colleagues may disagree). It is our responsibility to *help* train teachers of literature that we would be proud have in our state's classrooms, indeed that would we would be glad to have teaching our own children—teachers who are thoughtful, reflective, innovative and, most of all, able to justify and explain the reasons why they love to read and study literature. We may not have made it to the end of the switchbacks, and we cannot yet see over that highest ridge, but I know that I, for one, am starting to enjoy the trip.

The Uncertain Future

The most constant thing in education (either of K–12 students or student teachers) is change. In response (in part) to the national No Child Left Behind initiative, Georgia's high school curriculum is once again under review. As mentioned earlier, the Quality Core Curriculum has been changed from an extremely detailed list of elements to be learned, which the state Board of Education itself acknowledges "lacks depth and could not be covered in a reasonable amount of time," to "Georgia Performance Standards" that concentrate on "reading, writing, conventions, as well as listening, speaking, and viewing." The primary goal of these new standards is "media literacy" ("Georgia Performance Standards"). This change will align the standards more closely with NCTE/NCATE objectives and make it easier to decide what and how to teach the secondary education language arts classes. However, this does not eliminate the specter of high-stakes testing. In 2003, Georgia's students were ranked fiftieth in SAT scores ("Mean SAT I"), and students still face a high-school graduation test that measures their abilities in reading and responding to literature, critical thinking, and writing/usage/grammar.

Change is in the air for teacher training as well. Politicians at the state and national level, it seems, can't resist meddling in education

policy and changing the requirements for teacher certification nearly
every year. Any problem in the public schools, from low SAT scores,
to teenage pregnancy, to gun violence, they think, can be solved by
reconfiguring they way we educate and train our teachers. Ironically,
given all the brouhaha in the early 1990s at GSU about the movement
of BS Ed. majors to the College of Education, Georgia's Board of Regents has now mandated that Georgia's teachers have stronger content
preparation at all levels, which means that many Georgia schools, like
GSU, have moved to a Masters in Teaching (MAT) program, and all
secondary education students are now required first to get a degree in
a content area and then to take all their education courses and do their
student teaching at the graduate level. The BS Ed. no longer exists,
and English majors have come *back* to the department they left more
than a decade ago.

This change may not solve all—or even most—of our various problems with collaboration, however. Properly advising future teachers in
language arts, social studies, and the sciences, whose eventual teaching
responsibilities cross the university's disciplinary boundaries, remains
a challenge. It also isn't clear at this point whether moving to an MAT
program will encourage more or less collaboration among faculty from
different colleges in the years to come, although it may satisfy those
who (rightly or wrongly) think that teachers are currently not getting
enough content knowledge. It also appears that content areas will have
relatively little participation in the MAT, and currently the College of
Education is not seeking help with program development by faculty
outside the college. However, the Georgia Board of Regents continues
to insist that "teacher preparation programs will be the shared responsibility of education faculty, arts and sciences faculty, and classroom
teachers in the schools" ("Principles"). These groups should:

> 1) define and ensure the subject matter competence
> of all teacher candidates; 2) ensure that all teacher
> candidates can make the connections between subject
> matter knowledge and the learning needs of children;
> and 3) ensure that all teacher candidates can promote
> student learning within the realities of the classroom.
> ("Principles")

This means, at least in part, that faculty from outside the College of Education will remain involved—in some shape or form—in decisions about education curriculum.

After this ongoing struggle to create collaborative language arts instruction, the question arises: Are we moving toward a more coherent and collaborative way of teaching our future teachers, or are we merely solidifying our disciplinary boundaries and leaving our pre-service teachers out in the cold? To dust off that now rather tired metaphor of climbing the mountain, we are in for a long hike. The important thing, though, is that we are still making progress, even if the end is nowhere in sight.

Works Cited

Agee, Jane. "Negotiating Different Conceptions about Reading and Teaching Literature in a Preservice Literature Class." *Research in the Teaching of English* 33 (1998): 85–124.

Appleman, Deborah. *Critical Encounters in High School English: Teaching Literary Theory to Adolescents.* New York: Teachers College Press NCTE, 2000.

Berlin, James A. *Rhetorics, Poetics, and Cultures: Refiguring College English Studies.* 1996. West Lafayette, IN: Parlor Press, 2003.

"Georgia Performance Standards." 2005. 27 Jan. 2009. Georgia Department of Education. <http://www.georgiastandards.org>.

Graff, Gerald. *Beyond the Culture Wars: How Teaching the Conflicts Can Revitalize American Education.* New York: Norton, 1992.

—. *Professing Literature: An Institutional History.* Chicago: U of Chicago P, 1987.

Grossman, Pamela L. *The Making of a Teacher: Teacher Knowledge and Teacher Education.* New York: Teachers College Press, 1990.

Leitch, Vincent B. "Postmodern Interdisciplinarity." *Profession* (2000): 124–31.

Kolodny, Annette. *Failing the Future: A Dean Looks at Higher Education in the Twenty-First Century.* Durham, NC: Duke UP, 1998.

"Mean SAT I Verbal and Math Scores by State, with Changes for Selected Years." 2002. The College Board. 14 Dec. 2004 <http://www.college-board.com>.

"NCATE Program Standards: Program for Initial Preparation of Teachers of English Language Arts for Middle/Junior High and Senior High School Teaching.". National Council for Accreditation of Teacher Education. Oct. 1997. 17 Dec. 2004 <http://www.ncate.org/standard/ncte-97.pdf>.

"Principles for the Preparation of Educators for the Schools." Board of Regents of the University System of Georgia. 16 Dec. 2006. 12 Sept. 2008 <http://www.usg.edu/academics/initiatives/teachprep/principles.phtml>.

"Quality Core Curriculum—Ancillary Information—Language Arts." Georgia Department of Education. 1999. 22 Aug. 2000 <http://www. Glc.k12.ga.us/qstd-int/ancill/langart/mx-la13.htm>.

Scholes, Robert. *The Rise and Fall of English: Reconstructing English as a Discipline.* New Haven, CT: Yale, 1998.

Smagorinksy, Peter, and Melissa E. Whiting. *How English Teachers Get Taught: Methods of Teaching the Methods Class.* Urbana, IL: NCTE, 1995.

Study Guide: English Language, Literature, and Composition: Content Knowledge. Princeton, NJ: Educational Testing Service, 2001.

Part II

Disciplinary Enactment

5 Beside Disciplinary English: Working for Professional Solidarity by Reforming Academic Labor

David B. Downing

Even at the dawn of professional literary studies, educational consensus was already profoundly shaky.

> —Gerald Graff and Michael Warner,
> *The Origins of Literary Studies in America*

The difficulty with the separatist position [is] its promotion of "separate but equal" status may result in entrenchments of existing inequities for those inside—a "new ghetto," but a ghetto nonetheless.

> —Susan Miller, *Textual Carnivals*

The sustainable [. . .] scenario is radically different. Local cultures are emphasized within the curriculum. Intercultural student exchange is facilitated [. . .] and the curriculum is inherently interdisciplinary, flexible, and directed toward individual student needs.

> —Derek Owens, *Composition and Sustainability*

Disciplinary Dreams and Working Nightmares

English studies is the worst of academic sinners. The humanistic study of signifying practices has devolved into the most dehumanistic of higher education territories. No other field can shamefully claim, as we can, that in many departments over 75 percent of the courses are taught by "flex labor," part-time, temporary employees. These circumstances have a great deal to do with the systemic operations whereby the economic restructuring of higher education has taken an especially hard toll on workers in our field. As Stephen North suggests, College English Teaching, Inc. has some accounting to do for the ways it has arranged its workplace (233). In short, our own disciplinary practices have fueled the inequities in our labor force even as many practitioners clamor for the very principles of disciplinarity that were supposed to transcend those troubles.

David Harvey's description of the restructuring of the labor market provides a remarkably precise account of what has been happening over the past thirty years in English departments: a shrinking core of tenured faculty presides over an expanding array of part-time, temporary instructors and graduate students. As Ohmann puts it in his 1995 introduction to the re-issuing of *English in America*, "English has, it would almost seem, served as a small laboratory for innovative uses of flexible labor" (xxxix). We are now experiencing increasing internal professional class differences between the core and periphery of the academic labor market, at the same time that there are heightened "inter-familial" tensions between the competing subdisciplines of English studies, especially those between literature, composition, and creative writing (see especially Bousquet, Scott, and Parascondola; Nelson; Schell; Schell and Stock).

A common view of these employment problems in English studies is that we are at the mercy of a "market logic" whereby there's nothing much we can do but hold tight, cut down on the number of PhDs we produce, and wait out the cyclical spin-down of the economy. But Marc Bousquet's groundbreaking work on academic labor has forcefully demonstrated the limitations of this passive plan of inaction. Whereas the neoliberal discourse seems to be taking seriously the job crisis brought on by the relentless "market knowledge," Bousquet analyzes how the latter term can be seen as merely "a rhetoric of the labor system and not a description of it" ("Rhetoric" 209). Consequently, "the ideology of the market returns to frame the solution, blocking the transformative potential of analysis that otherwise demonstrates the necessity of non-market responses" (209). Once framed as a market problem, there is no need to transform the inevitable, rational system of disciplinarity whereby the university sustains its elite disciplinary archives on the backs of its transient, less-disciplinary graduate students, part-time, and temporary instructors. This essay focuses on how we might actively transform the disciplinary economy of value in English studies rather than passively wait for the economy to turn some magical corner. Of course, how we got ourselves into this situation is a longer story than any single chapter can narrate, but a view of the big picture can be a useful theoretical move as we try to locate possibilities for solidarity and action within our institutions.

In the next section I offer two forays into the founding moments of the disciplinary archive of English studies. My analysis is complementary to that of others who have told these stories more fully elsewhere although primarily as an ideological battle. I have turned my lens upon the systemic emergence of disciplinarity as exemplified in these cases through the injurious splitting between reading and writing done to our subject matter right from the beginning as it struggled for legitimacy in the modern university. The first case traces the contours of how Francis James Child moved from his gentlemanly position as Boylston Professor of Rhetoric to his "exemplary" status as the first English Professor at Harvard. This brief snapshot of Child's inventiveness models for us how he became a "sublime master" (Bové xiv) of the new field by creating one influential possibility for a paradigm of the literary side of English studies. The second traces less the fate of the exemplary figure, Adams Sherman Hill, than the institutional consequences of his founding English A as the prototype for university-wide writing courses that was imitated by virtually every institution of higher education in America. Writing and teaching suffered the same fates of being unable to meet the demands of the new disciplinary ecosystem except as reduced forms of social discipline that protected the bountiful gardens of disciplinary knowledge from contamination. Whether configured as a ghetto or a desert, many occupying the lowly terrains have seen their dreams of disciplinary fruition turned into a nightmare of cheap labor. But let's turn from the abstract registers to the case studies.

KICK-STARTING THE DISCIPLINARY GARDEN BY
ESCAPING THE "UNFLOWERING DESERT"

How far Francis James Child kicked the chair across the Harvard classroom one afternoon in the mid-1870s seems to be a matter of what you want the incident to reveal, or on what side of the lit-comp divide you take your stand. In a wonderfully revealing essay, Patricia Harkin examines the different stories that have entered the lore of English studies as legends about one of its founding figures ("Child's Ballads"). According to the account rendered by one of Child's admiring students, Francis Gummere, the chair only made it halfway across the floor, a measured sign of the dignified disdain Child registered for his years of grading themes. While lauding Child's wonders as a teacher, Gummere clearly sees Child's greatness embodied in his heroic crossing of the great divide between the old liberal arts colleges and the emerging research university. As pioneer of the new field, Child exemplified how the science of philology could be creatively adapted to bring a whole new kind of scholarly practice to literature. Rather than the wayward impressions of literary tastes characteristic of the belletristic tradition carried on by the likes of Longfellow and Lowell, Child's newly minted criteria for the gathering and compilation of hard evidence based on historical and comparative objectivity raised the disciplinary bar. Together with those fellow compatriots who had traveled to Germany for the same purpose, Child's scholarly standards set firmly on American soil the model for the disciplinary methods Child had learned in his three years' study of philology at the University of Gottingen.

The transition across the great divide separating the "drudgery" of grading themes from the spiritual rewards of literary research was more gradual than Child himself might have liked, at least according to some accounts, and that's where the legend of the chair comes into play. In Gummere's version, the idealized Child asks "solemnly" but portentously of his companion, "Do you know that I corrected themes in Harvard College for twenty-five years?" (qtd. in Harkin 27). Child had only placed "his foot on a light chair," and he "never lifted his voice unduly; but some sort of physical emphasis was imperative, and this was furnished by the chair. As he pronounced the 'twenty-five years' with most exact and labored utterance, his foot was released, and the chair found a new site half-way across the room" (27).

The dignified manner of the "physical [. . .] imperative" of the (presumably) gently sliding chair, metonymically registers the triumph of research over teaching, literature over composition, and career-calling over job drudgery as Harvard became a modern university. Gummere sees nothing but elation and triumph in that gesture, quietly graceful as it may be for the first real "Magister" of English studies whose eminence as an exemplary figure in the emerging paradigm could not be undone by any too violent image of his own behavior. Child was sliding, or kicking, the chair at about that very moment when Charles Eliot made him the first Professor of English at Harvard as he out-bid Hopkins's President Gilman in one of the first contractual alterations that signaled the coming of age of the new discipline of English studies. As Harkin explains, the "Hopkins offer changed the economic frameworks, and Eliot's new judgment was that Child's teaching literature would make Harvard competitive with Johns Hopkins" (31). But the founding gesture of leaving composition in its literary wake has been recast by others in a different light.

As recently as 1982, when Donald Stewart retells Child's incident with the chair, the shift in the tone and content of the anecdote registers what by then had become for many workers in English a longstanding anger at the very shift that Gummere celebrated many years earlier. In Stewart's words, "Child angrily kicked a chair across a room, complaining bitterly about the years he was wasting correcting student themes" (qtd. in Harkin 32). There was no "half-way" in this version of the narrative. Literature's triumph was composition's demise, and Child becomes refigured as a literary elitist who has no truck with the drudgery of student compositions.

All the fine histories we now have of the rise of literature at the expense of composition, reveal how in the course of the many years since the first Harvard English professor enjoyed his respite from grading themes, "composition" faced some pretty rough calls as it got cast into the ghetto (see especially Berlin, Connors, Crowley, Faigley, Graff, Harkin, Kitzhaber, Susan Miller, Thomas Miller, North, Scholes, and Winterowd). Henry James referred to it as a "loathsome chore" and a "burden;" Child's successor to the Boylston Chair, George Lyman Kitteridge repeatedly called it "drudgery," as did Charles Eliot, who also saw it as nothing but "routine work." By 1967, William Riley Parker called the grading of themes and teaching of composition "slave labor," unrewarding "service," a "dismal, unflowering desert" (see Harkin

23–29). No wonder Stewart and others whose professional identity is affiliated with writing might personally feel, and thus represent, the significance of Child's kick with more vehemence than practitioners of the more sanctified disciplinary gardens of literary criticism.

The ideological force of the kick originates when the aesthetic/ poetic version of cultural modernity triumphs over the reductively mechanical version of what writing came to be in most composition courses that for so many years modeled themselves after the 1885 for- mation of English A at Harvard. As Susan Miller explains, "the dual curriculum in English after its establishment at Harvard between 1873 and 1895 was quickly outlined and nationally delivered as an arche- typical negative for reproduction across the country" (52). But beside the ideological triumph of the "high" sensibility of literature over the "low" drudgery of composition, my brief foray into this historical ar- chive is to more fully emphasize the function of disciplinarity in these institutional battles. And the latter emphasizes the power of societal modernity with its rational bureaucracies and institutional mecha- nisms for reproducing specific sets of material social hierarchies.

In this respect, Child's career shift as he recreated himself as per- haps our first "sublime master" or exemplary figure of English is es- pecially revealing partly because he himself had to cross over from the older college's curriculum into the modern disciplinary univer- sity. Indeed, Child first began as a tutor of mathematics at Harvard. This was not at all unusual since mathematics, the classical languages (Greek and Latin), and a mix of classical (Quintilian and Cicero) and eighteenth-century British (George Campbell and Hugh Blair) ver- sions of rhetoric formed the fixed, non-elective undergraduate curricu- lum. And since there were no separate departments, professors were expected to perform multiple duties. Child's personal transformation into a literary scholar crosses through philological study in Germany, as it did for most professors trying to imitate the new disciplinary models of academic work. But it took twenty years or more after his return from Germany for his scholarly accomplishments to empower the institutional formation of a new department designating the dis- cipline of English.

What exactly is it that Child brought from Germany that played out so well for him and some others in America? What exactly is it that enabled him to produce new forms of knowledge under the emerging research emphasis so as to escape the drudgery of his proscribed position? The general answer, of course, is modern science with its impressive methods of invention. This modern, empirical discourse could demonstrate its control of nature with a reliability that every emerging division of knowledge could not help but admire and aspire to. But the question was: how could the discipline of science be carried over in practice to a field like literature that otherwise seemed inimical to the discourse and practices of the laboratory? Societal modernity's call for rational organization in the structure of educational institutions that could then be bureaucratically regulated faced some stiff challenges from the belletristic tradition. "Taste," after all, was not something that one could measure in the same way as, say, caloric intake. But preparations for such a reduction were well under way by the late-eighteenth century. As W. Ross Winterowd argues, the eighteenth century rhetoricians had paved the way for one kind of stability: George Campbell (*The Philosophy of Rhetoric*) and Hugh Blair (*Lectures on Rhetoric and Belles Lettres*), and others had purified classical rhetoric of the sublime, inventive, creative, so that "rhetoric left the agora, the public arena, and retreated to the drawing room" (66).

But philology was much better than rhetoric at this game, because language could be objectified in historical study that did not depend on idiosyncratic rhetorical performances nor on the waywardly subjective composings of any individual. In this sense, language could be seen as based on universal principles and laws, much like the Newtonian version of the physical world. However, whereas the laws of the internalized "human mind" might be difficult to objectify, as the eighteenth-century rhetoricians had tried to do, language could be seen to have an external, objectifiable referent in the various European languages with their philological roots grounded deeply in Greek and Latin grammar. And as Gerald Graff explains, "grammar for Hegel, as for later philologists like Friedrich Max Muller, was the alphabet of the Spirit itself" (*Professing* 29).

In Germany, Child was re-schooled not in rhetoric, but in philology, or what will later become a discipline and department of its own in linguistics. Despite this training, his love, his "calling," was for literature, and he invented the passage over: literature could be objectified, systematized along the lines that philology objectified language, through the study of detailed patterns, etymological roots, and syntactical forms pertinent to the history of those literary texts. In some pretty impressive new ways, the disciplinary side of literary research would adopt the new sets of objectifying practices since their objects had a kind of formal integrity and stability of form. Thus, in one of his first scholarly books, his 1855 edition of *The Poetical Works of Edmund Spenser,* Child's preface and annotations document with especial care the sources, allusions, and some of the errors in earlier editions in order to produce this standardized text.

In short, Child had created a bridge between cultural modernity with its valuing of the literary aesthetic and societal modernity with its needs for rational institutional organization. He did so mainly by not paying much heed to the belletristic concern for beauty, taste, and sensibility as a methodological principle but, rather, as a kind of bonus-value that added prestige to the calling (see Yood 528). Child was motivated by his great love for the beauty of the ballads as well as for the great authors of English literature, but he recognized that there was no way to turn love and sensibility into a method. From a disciplinary perspective, it was not the ballads themselves that mattered so much as the knowledge produced about the ballads that had been so skillfully converted into the exchange value of published research. Given Child's exemplary productions, university presidents could hire others to perform paradigmatic imitations of Child's model as part of the normal practice opened up for the fledgling discipline to create its own new territory of objective knowledge. And for the most part, that is exactly what happened as the new forms of academic disciplinarity began to shape the contours of emerging fields.

Child's synthetic performance joining the symbolic generalizations, models, and values established his own status as an exemplary figure for the emerging discipline. No one else had quite done things this way before. Prior to his labor, the ballads he studied might well have seemed casual, unimportant, or anomalous to the more rigorous philological standards of disciplinarity, just as they might have seemed less than literary to the belletristic tradition of fine art. Child's revolutionary performance was to demonstrate that they were not on both counts: philological complexity matched literary complexity by the shear weight of evidence he brought to bear upon the ballads. Indeed, Child's multi-volume study has been recently reprinted by Loomis House Press as a sign of its persistent influence. Of course, Child himself is neither the problem nor the solution: rather, it was the institutional consequences of his own exemplary performance that served to establish an influential form of normal practice for English, and those practices then became the source of institutional demands. To that extent, he did indeed change "the conditions of academic labor" (Harkin 34) as others found ways to ground their own expertise on Child's impressive accomplishments as a master of the new field.

As Graff and Warner put it, this rigidly disciplinary side of the emerging English studies competed with the belletristic tradition, formerly represented by writers like Longfellow and Lowell, whose chairs at Harvard were endowed as gentlemen of taste, not analyzers of technical matters pertaining to history, bibliography, and grammar. From this perspective, the history of the profession of English studies is "not the triumph of philology" but the conflict "between competing professional models" (6). That is, the disciplinarians could never completely colonize the terrain of professional tasks, especially where the spiritual as well as nationalistic values of the literary held such powerful sway. Cultural modernity would not so easily fit into Child's innovative adaptation of societal modernity in the form of a new academic discipline of English. Consequently, practitioners of the new field struggled to carve out spaces for their own work, sometimes by enacting a version of positivistic scholarship that could claim full disciplinary status, generally by following an historical or formalistic bent. Much of their work, however, continued to occupy professional academic spaces below, beside, or other than that rewarded by the emerging standards of disciplinarity. The contentious battles between competing forces seeking disciplinary unity for the entire profession subsided slightly only during the relatively brief sway of the New Critics which I will say more about in the next section. But in these founding moments, Child's invention of a new disciplinary space was accomplished in tandem with the "other" subordinated space allotted to the role of writing.

When Hill invented English A in 1885, he did so to try to defuse the rising clamor in American newspapers and magazines about "the growing illiteracy of American boys" (Kitzhaber 45). It was supposed to be a stopgap measure: "a temporary course in remedial writing instruction" which as Robert Connors explains, would be required "of all incoming freshman," but only "until the crisis had passed" (11). Charles Eliot had hired Hill to assist Child in transforming the new English department along the lines of the German university model, but the problem was that in the German model, writing was a presumption necessary for any disciplinary work. In America, students

were clearly unprepared to meet these minimum disciplinary standards, so English A was established as a kind of remedial course. Hill
was a "lawyer-turned-newspaperman" (Baron 146), whose basic assignment was to recast the traditional four-year program in rhetoric of
the classical curriculum into a one year course in composition. That
the course lasted on the Harvard catalog until 1951 suggests that the
crisis had a hard time passing. But it modeled the disciplinary hierarchy that would structure English departments throughout the land.
The discipline exercised in English A was not an exercise in emerging
forms of research as the lynchpin of disciplinarity, as we have seen in
the case of Child's work, but rather as an initial gatekeeper, protecting
the more advanced domains of "new" knowledge from contamination
from below.

In other words, English A was cast outside and below the more specialized ecosystem of academic disciplinarity, but directly in the line
of Michel Foucault's general description of the disciplinary society: a
place for the disciplining of the docile bodies of young men, but with
a ramped up force drawn by association with the new forms of disciplinarity as well as with the new corporate economy. The narrowly
conceived problem of getting your commas in the right place through
learning the rules of proper usage rose right out of the classical curriculum of the old colleges, hardly skipping a beat. Michel Foucault's
description of the disciplinary society had already established the conditions for this kind of surveillance, so there was very little new about
it. That is, English A could claim to be part of the discipline of English, but only as a kind of charade, the wearing of the feathers of prestige earned elsewhere under the new forms of academic disciplinarity
emerging from Child's exemplary research on ballads and literary heroes like Chaucer and Spenser.

Hill brought about some significant alterations in the rhetorical
preeminence of oratory and the performance of declamations in the
classical curriculum. As Reid explains, with "rhetoric's abandonment
of oratory," "the term 'rhetoric' fell out of fashion" as the new courses
tended to be called "'composition,' or simply 'English'" (253). Even
written exercises assigned in the old college meant that the teacher
determined the subject matter as well as the proper forms for argumentation. Hill's work as a journalist writing about the affairs of the
world might have contributed to his willingness to have students write
themes about their everyday life. But even with this focus on the indi-

vidual experience, the ideology of individuality and autonomy aided
the necessary qualification of those writings: they had to be objective examinations of those experiences. The only kind of imaginable
objectivity that he, and his successor, Wendell Barrett, could inscribe
within these parameters would have to be grammar and proper usage.
Under these constraints, the "daily theme" became a new instrument
of surveillance with which to implement the standards of correctness.

Indeed, English A was a place where students could be subjected
to Harvard's disciplinary demands by forcing "them to recognize the
power of the institution to insist on conformity with its standards"
(Crowley 74). The exams administered in this class and for admission to the college "were not intended to test students' ability to use
English; rather, they tested their knowledge about stuff taught in an
emerging academic discipline called 'English'" (75). But using "discipline" in this sense has nothing to do with producing new knowledge
for the emerging research university although it has much to do with
reproducing correctness. "Discipline" in this sense is simply a form of
social control. From this perspective, English A was more of a carry-
over from the old college idea of "mental" discipline that could now
be more efficiently and technically administered on the basis of standards, forms, and correctness of character as well as grammar that
simply had to be inculcated through imitation.

There was nothing "new" about any of this, in Arjun Appadurai's
sense of research as creating the new. Rather the institutional function of such disciplinary work reduced the epistemological dynamics
of disciplinarity to exchange value as a marker of easily coded differences. While waving the flags triumphing the rising standards of the
modern, disciplinary university, in English A disciplinarity had been
reduced to little more than social control masking itself as educational
value.

These systems of reduction had emerged earlier in the eighteenth
century through the power of the exam, the seminar, and the laboratory (Hoskins). English A elaborated on the disciplinary principles of
the exam which could so successfully objectify error. As Susan Miller
argues,

> the practice of attending to mechanical errors allowed
> written texts to become instruments for examining
> the "body" of a student, not just the student body.
> This attention allows a teacher (an "auditor" in both

> aural and accounting senses) to examine the student's
> language with the same attitude that controls a clini-
> cal medical examination. (57)

Thus in English A and the new Harvard entrance examinations, we find the perfect exemplification of how disciplinary forms of formal objectification under dominant scientific paradigms seek to objectify and falsify "errors" in the object through a method similar to the "clinical medical examination." Indeed "[w]riting, in fact, exposes errors and infelicities that speech might elide" (57). Control and command operate much more than investigation and inquiry, as always happens when disciplinarity gets reduced to its lowest common denominator.

The contrast between Hill's and Child's work highlights the shape of the new field. Whereas Child's love of literature fueled the transition to the modern university insofar as he was able to work out in practice societal modernity's version of technical analysis and diagnosis upon cultural modernity's literary objects, Hill had a different task. In contrast, all the efforts in the world to try to perform Child's set of objectifying operations on student writing could only yield propriety, grammar, or at best, the modes of discourse. But there was a payoff for this reduction, not to be lost on practitioners in the field. As David Russell explains, "English, unlike the other humanities, was able to construct itself through composition as a service to other disciplines within the university and indirectly to the emerging corporate economy—and thus gain credit and resources that, say, history and philosophy did not" (41). The split between reading (literature) and writing (composition) was deeply fueled by these economic forces which enabled the alibi where the "discipline" of English could be seen to comprise both ends, when only one really counted under the conditions of academic disciplinarity: "By constructing composition as a practical, remedial service, with no systematic training necessary to teach it and no research expected of those who did, large numbers of courses could be taught by low-paid, part-time staff, usually women" (51). Russell believes, therefore, that the injurious split occurred in "constructing literature and composition as two separate activities, one professional, the other not" (40). In such a formulation, Russell equivocates disciplinarity and professionalism, but I think there are good reasons to make a distinction. That is, the "low-paid, part-time staff" are professionals in that you don't hire just anybody to teach these subjects, so they have a degree of professional status, no matter how low it is, and they are indeed contractually obligated to fulfill their duties in the academy no matter how exploited the terms of those contracts. But their professional work does not count for much under the terms of academic disciplinarity.

Converting some of what they do into the establishment of the more strictly disciplinary parameters of research and training, as the field of composition has now quite successfully done since the 1960s, will no doubt be an important part of refiguring English studies. But the work of teaching, and engaging the dispersive, experiential, non-disciplinary, carnivalesque characteristics of many forms of both reading and writing, need professional recognition not just in the terms of disciplinary hierarchies of value. As Crowley puts it, "The invention of Freshman English enabled the creation of English studies" (59), but only, I would add, in tandem with Child's exemplification of the new possibilities for the literary discipline. The professional worth of writing teachers needs to be greatly enhanced because it is cruel and exploitive not to do so. And that kind of transformation is as much at the level of job action and collective bargaining as it is at the level of disciplinary purification and justification.

Consolidating the Split between the Garden and the Desert

From one perspective, what Child and Hill accomplished, together with their accomplices, was better than what a lot of their followers have been able to do ever since in the way of configuring the subdisciplinary desert and planting the disciplinary garden. Indeed, making English into a respectable academic discipline that could organize a coherent curriculum has generally been a contentious project. Ever since, English professors have struggled, at times with success but often with great difficulty, to adapt what they do to disciplinary practices, such as identifying stable bodies of knowledge and methodically verifying truth claims, practices better suited to the needs of scientists. Of course, while the strict processes of disciplining have become the quintessential measure of academic value, the institutionalized protocols for disciplinary practices often exclude or delimit a significant range of socially valuable intellectual labor. Messer-Davidow, Shumway, and Sylvan explain that "as inquiry came to assume a disciplinary form, alternative configurations of knowledge were excluded" (viii). This is especially the case for certain activities many English practitioners

perform: research or teaching that focuses on ameliorating the local
needs of specific groups of people, post-process tasks of invention and
composing that do not always narrowly define objects of investigation (see Kent), work that engages alternative discourses or rhetorical
modes other than expository argumentation (see Bernstein; Blitz and
Hurlbert; Owens, *Resisting Writings;* Schroeder, Fox, and Bizzell; Sirc),
or writing for broad audiences through publication in non-academic
magazines and books (a feather for academic celebrities, but a risk for
junior faculty seeking tenure credentials). In English departments,
disciplinarity perpetuates some of the basic conditions established by
Child's and Hill's models for both facilitating and justifying the subordination of writing to literature, even though, ironically, writing serves
a fundamental role in the practices of examining and grading across
all disciplines. The institutional principles of disciplinary knowledge
will always favor those domains where the objects of knowledge, such
as literary texts (or, as in the disciplining of cultural studies, cultural
texts), can be more successfully designated than the carnival of unruly
composings that students bring into the academy.

The guild nature of the disciplines means that the expository arguments suitable for scholarly publication produce knowledge if those
arguments can be measured or "refereed" by an audience of trained
professionals (who might be considerably divorced from the local contexts and issues). As Ohmann puts it, disciplinary practices can be
performed merely to re-enforce "loyalty to the guild rather than to the
college or university" (220), or to the students or the local community
or the public, for that matter. The disciplinary measure of success,
therefore, purposefully displaces any accountability to people immediately affected by a practical innovation, such as the development of
an interactive website linking local high school, community college,
and university English departments in a collaborative network. While
it is no doubt possible to give credit for such work, academic forms of
disciplinary pressure will inevitably tend to give greater significance to
the published article about the website than reward those who created
it and participated in its ongoing success.

From the opposite direction, efforts to speak beyond the disciplinary guild to nonacademic audiences also run the risk of being "un-
scholarly," and these risks persist despite an increasing concern within
the profession to gain what Bérubé calls "public access" (28). Such
instances register forms of disciplinary injustice, although in other

contexts such disciplinary distancing of local interests from broader knowledge claims has tremendous value for certain kinds of work. Argument is what the academy does best, and as John Michael contends, becoming "masters of our specific disciplinary technologies" (3) is part of what it means to be a critical intellectual in the contemporary world. Even though as Graff points out, some of the most influential academic works successfully negotiate the tension between the academic and the vernacular (*Clueless*), the press of disciplinarity can curtail such performances within a pretty narrow range, more accessible by tenured faculty than those trying to affiliate with a disciplinary specialty. When claims for knowledge are in dispute, disciplines can sometimes serve as critical arbiters for equality, even though race, class, and gender differences, as well as corporate interests often compromise claims of disciplinary autonomy. Non- or post-disciplinary activities will be in tension with disciplinary forms of argumentation, so the hard work will always depend on understanding when and for whom the discipline provides a measure of justice.

The picture is especially complicated in English because of the range of professional tasks we regularly perform. Knowledge production under the conditions of disciplinarity seeks to narrow that range by specifying the primary objects of study, such as literary or cultural texts, and the secondary critical methods for producing knowledge about those objects through expository prose. Any successful paradigm, as in the case of Francis Child, mediates the particular relations between objects and methods. Even so, textual objects themselves always exceed the mediations of any given paradigm's models and symbolic generalizations about those objects. And here lies the great irony: disciplinarity simultaneously devalues the rhetorical practices of poetic, aesthetic, and imaginative forms of discourse and artistic production, even as it claims to be producing knowledge about those forms. As James Berlin succinctly casts the story of our disciplinary history, poetics took precedence over rhetoric, but it did so not as the active creation *of* poetic texts but through the secondary activity of publishing expository arguments *about* poetic texts themselves (*Rhetorics*). Consequently, the domination within institutional evaluation practices of disciplinary discourse has often meant the crippling and devaluing of some of our most crucial concrete labor practices.

Working under the institutionalized version of managed disciplinarity, English departments grew dramatically in symbiosis with the tremendous growth of the university in the first half of the twentieth century. Despite the statistical successes in rising numbers of faculty and students, English professors competed for disciplinary justifications equal to those of the sciences, even while the intellectual tasks of English professors did not always measure up to disciplinary criteria. Graff details the battles for the literary terrain between the scholars and the critics, but the most painful disciplinary squeeze happened to writing practices which followed the social control model of discipline worked out in English A, even though they were the skills most highly in demand. In order to identify their objects and methods as well as literature professors, composition specialists had little choice but to adapt accordingly. Disciplinary pressure for such specification led to the predominance of what Berlin has called "current-traditional" rhetoric (*Rhetoric and Reality* 36), a kind of re-scripting of the principles Hill outlined in *Principles of Rhetoric* that were really principles of grammar, not dimensions of classical rhetoric. By reducing classical concerns for the social significance of universals to narrowly conceived grammatical objectifications suitable for scientific research, such formalist adaptations of rhetoric to disciplinary criteria followed the reductions of classical rhetoric to what Winterowd called the "managerial rhetoric" (66) of Campbell and Blair. Of course, a great deal of writing gets excised from the academy as it narrows the range of writing practices at all levels with, of course, dire consequences for the politics of writing specialists within English departments (Crowley, S. Miller, Ohmann, Scholes, Winterowd). As we have seen in the exemplary case of Child, because "literature" had become a privileged term in cultural discourse since the romantic period (1770–1830), it could better meet the requirements for disciplinary discourse. This was particularly the case when the corporate models of management were tied to the political mission of the nation-states, and literature could be seen to inculcate a form of nationalist identity and cultural pride (Readings, S. Miller).

The principles of scientific management had thereby adapted the disciplinary conditions for the production of knowledge insofar as they served as viable institutional mechanisms to measure and evaluate success in terms of the quantity and quality of publication. Teaching, which had always been associated with English A's instruction of writing, became simply superfluous in upper division literature courses because the latter were supposed to "teach themselves" (see

Graff, *Beyond*): all the valuable labor investment was in the emerging paradigms of literary and critical research. In short, both pedagogy and writing were "defined as extrinsic to the 'serious' work of the discipline, the systematic analysis of language and literature" (Graff and Warner 3). Consequently, under this disciplinary regime, teaching became so clearly subordinated to research that, for instance, the MLA abandoned teaching in 1916 by revising a clause in the constitution that originally described "the object of the Association as 'the advancement of the *study* of the Modern languages and their literatures'" to read "the advancement of *research* in the Modern languages and their literatures" (*Professing* 121). With its formation in 1911, NCTE became the home for teaching and writing in the profession, and the basic splits between composition and literature, teaching and research, became solidified as prestige accrued, naturally enough, to the more specifically academic forms of disciplinary research.

Historical studies such as Graff's, Shumway's, Applebee's, Leitch's and others document the intellectual content of the battles to make the unruly field of the literary into a respectable academic discipline so I will not rehearse them here. The point I draw from those ongoing battles is that although the category of the literary may be easier to objectify than even the broader subject of writing, that relative ease, of course, does not mean that consensus can be reached on this object with the same kind of disciplinary precision modeled by the sciences. So historical scholars, literary critics, linguists, and creative writers battled to win the war that would end when their paradigm could represent the field as a unified whole. Needless to say, it is an endless war because there can be no victors, only perpetual quarreling between paradigms, none of which can ever claim to objectify the field or subject matter in any final way.

But even so, a temporary plateau was reached with the rise of New Criticism during the period from 1930s to the 1960s. What is relevant here is that the basic principles of New Criticism gave rise to the greatest period of disciplinary stability for English departments. They authorized English departments to develop curricula that enabled them to define their objects and methods, the primary characteristics of disciplinary discourse, with almost as much confidence as the sciences (see Kamuf 77, 84). Ideological claims for the spiritual richness of the unmediated, un-paraphraseable "verbal icon" of the poetic experience justified study of the "intrinsic" properties of the text as an object of knowledge, but the ideological claims mattered far less than the powerfully consistent disciplinary practices that became institutionalized in everyday use. They no longer had to fall back on philology, or linguistics, to substantiate the scientific basis of their object and methods. Although the New Critics themselves evidenced a much wider range of ideological beliefs about the transcendent values of literary art than many of their critics have acknowledged, their curricular successes depended less on such literary values as upon their working practices with respect to the discipline. With literature as the object, close reading as the method, and expository critical writing about canonized texts as the verifiable procedures for producing knowledge, the program for an English major could now be succinctly mapped out by organizing a series of courses based on the coverage model of the periods and genres of English and American literature beginning with Chaucer and leading up to the Modernists. The period/genre curriculum provided a relatively objectified map of the disciplinary objects constituting the field of knowledge. Despite the considerable variation within the major English departments in America, all these curricula "have a common basis" (Ohmann, *English in America* 222), and it is that disciplinary basis that I am referring to here.

But, again, what tends to slip out of view are the categories of difference and the culture of diversity, and not just among the disciplinary objects but among the workers in the profession itself. No one particularly needed to pay attention to the fact that the profession of literary studies "was for all practical purposes a brotherhood based on race, citizenship, and class, bound together by what might be called, in a play on both its literal and figurative senses, the old school tie" (North 22). Even more, with the basic machinery of the transformations of English A into the university-wide composition courses set up as the gatekeeper, the field had successfully reduced the disciplinary procedures to techniques of social control, as many have now documented in the case of English A. Since English A converted to composition service courses hardly depended at all on the disciplinary procedures for producing new knowledge, and since anyone with sufficient talent to pursue graduate study in English must have already acquired such rudimentary discipline as grammar, graduate students became a ready labor force for occupying the unflowering desert.

With college enrollments nearly quadrupling between 1945 and 1970, the basic inequities of the disciplinary system of English could be tolerated, if not camouflaged, by the post-war economic boom in corporate America. Challenges to the system from new areas of investigation, such as women's studies and African American studies, could be addressed by adding to the existing curriculum without fundamentally changing the orthodox curriculum of literary periods and genres, because there were always enough students to fill whatever classes were offered. Moreover, the corporate structuring of disciplinary hierarchy consolidated itself during the period of New Critical hegemony. North describes how the general shape of undergraduate and graduate English education took the shape of what he calls "College English Teaching, Inc." (233). In this system, the main task of tenured senior professors was to replicate themselves through graduate education via the PhD and the apprenticeship program whereby graduate students could do the dirty work of servicing the industry by teaching the composition courses while the professors could develop their literary research specializations in graduate seminars. The ongoing corporate need for writing skills could thus be met in a system calling for increased numbers of PhDs even when graduate training itself had nothing to do with teaching or writing. As North explains, "What has always made the credit-generating factory possible was the understanding— often tacit, to be sure, but unmistakable—that such teaching could be turned over to the less-than-fully-compensated and/or less-than-fully-qualified since it was not itself directly tied to the discipline's core activities" (235). In short, the "discipline" set the criteria by which the "less-disciplined" could be exploited, and in times of relative bounty, few complained vociferously. By the 1970s, however, College English Teaching, Inc. began to experience deeper signs of crisis.

The Curriculum is the Message: Towards a Sustainable English Studies

William Riley Parker got it wrong: there *are* flowers in the desert, but you have to know where to look for them. The ecology of the desert has its own kind of sustainability, even if humans cannot inhabit such spaces for very long without help. Ecologists have now taught us a great deal about how such harsh environments have their own sustainable, if fragile, ecosystems which can be so easily disrupted by human intervention, waste, and exploitation. But to bring the metaphor home, the ecosystem of academic disciplinarity can be toxic to some forms of human survival, especially in the humanities quarters of the academic world, where it is now proving to be not very ecologically sustainable. The latter term, as Derek Owens explains, has become a kind of buzzword since it "started surfacing with growing regularity in the early 1980s" (*Composition* 21). But in the strong and good sense in which he defines it, "*sustainability* means meeting today's needs without jeopardizing the well-being of future generations" (1). The growing problem of the exploitation of "flexible" labor practices in English studies has been too well fueled by the disciplinary economy of value that continues to jeopardize the well being of many students and teachers. How we can sustain work in English studies so that the genuinely flexible contours of our labor in a multicultural, global context do not just operate according to the un-ecological, exploitative, and deceptive forces of the "faux local" (Gee et al.) powers of global capital may be the most crucial phase of our various strategies for professional solidarity and well-being.

The disciplinary ecosystem in English has contributed to the toxic division between reading and writing, and these divisions have been deeply inscribed within our curricular structures. Reconfiguring injustices in our workplaces thus inevitably calls for curricular alterations in the distribution of rewards for specific kinds of tasks so that more non-disciplinary possibilities acquire professional recognition and status. Such possibilities cannot materialize if the curriculum is identified only with the principles of disciplinarity. Even progressive, as well as conventional efforts to reconfigure the discipline are often deeply linked to a paradox or contradiction that may seem to fly in the face of good sense. In times of economic contraction, budget restraint and the exploitation of part-time labor, one can understand the drive to shore up the discipline, to make disciplinary English stronger by more rigorously defining its subject matter and more precisely identifying its subdisciplines. Academics seek, that is, to resist further administrative budget cuts and loss of tenure track faculty by resorting to the traditional mechanism of resisting market forces: disciplinarity. If we could just define our objects more precisely and our methods more specifically, such disciplinary integrity should justify our continued preservation, if not expansion. If we could appear less "soft" as intellectual dilettantes and more "hard" as knowledge producing researchers vital to the culture and the economy, then the sharpness of our rhetoric will have more powerful political effect in staying the course against the market pressures. At least that's the dream of modernity. And some-times, in strategic places at the right time, it has the desired effect.

But here's the problem. The academic versions of disciplinarity simply work better for some other disciplines, especially the sciences where disciplinary specificity and rigor can have direct market conse-quences in terms of securing more grants, public funds, and corporate endorsements for such research. The "better" the discipline, the better able it is to attract private corporate grants and funding agencies, and administrators have not lost sight of this handy rule of disciplinary accounting, especially in public education. Intellectual discipline thus leads to financial discipline as certain kinds of work get commodi-fied into exchange value, and it does so in English as well, except in significantly intensified ways. Under the terms set by the longstand-ing disciplinary split between literature and composition, the former having disciplinary power to produce the new, and the latter being squeezed into the preservation of minimal standards serving the elite, virtually any form of disciplinary tightening will enhance the power of the literary/cultural/composition research specialists over the sea of low-paid temporary composition instructors. And administrators may, perversely speaking, love the consequences of such disciplinary "enhancements." They can see in the very principles of the disciplin-ary system the justification for "cheap teaching" (Bousquet, "Waste Product" 99). Because disciplinary research in the humanities does not generally produce short-term revenues, maintaining large numbers of full-time English researchers is costly. To management's good fortune, however, writing, the one marketable skill that everyone needs, gets staffed by less-disciplined, part-time employees. And our very disci-plinary history verifies that that's exactly how we have done things from Child's moment and the inauguration of English A on down: composition workers have floated literature's boat for much of the one-hundred-twenty-five-year history of the modern university.

Historically devalued by disciplinary criteria favoring literature, writing is now called for by market forces as a "skill" necessary for any corporate task. We've hardly skipped a beat from the days of English A when Hill's version of "managerial rhetoric" based on mechanical recipes of style for the gentlemanly classes gets recast as a mechanical skill and drill ready to serve capital's flexible needs for more "infor-mation" on the way to profits. Indeed, flexible accumulation favors separating writing into smaller, independent units or programs, free

is prof writing first?

of the imposing size of English departments, so that the smaller unit can then be more quickly fine-tuned to shifting market needs, whether towards electronic forms of literacy, professional writing, technical writing, or business writing. Disciplinarity has nicely greased the skids for this kind of exploitation because its powerful divisiveness shatters the grounds for professional solidarity. Since writing has rarely benefited from disciplinary privileges, administrators can justify the hiring of less than fully disciplinized, part-time employees because "that's the way the discipline works." We will always be very hardpressed to argue that more disciplinary rigor and specialization will heal the wounds that our disciplinary history has in fact produced. As Bousquet explains, "the disciplinarization of composition, marked by a great blossoming and new vitality in rhet-comp scholarship, has been accompanied by the near-total conversion of composition work to a system of flexible managed labor" ("Introduction" 5; see also Harris 55). Under these conditions, disciplinary divisions only serve to weaken broader forms of professional solidarity.

As composition theorists have been arguing for years, teaching writing and reading at any level calls for all the skills, resources, lore, and knowledge of a wide range of activities and practices, even though some forms of disciplinary criteria may not highly honor such work. Writing is one of the most complex activities known to humans, partly because it crosses all disciplinary borders, mixes modern, non-modern, vernacular, and street literacies, so that any effort to stabilize these plays of difference will inevitably shortchange in sometimes costly ways the complex set of practices, theories, and performances called for in verbal and textual acts.

Solidarity of labor across our different tasks calls for highly experienced individuals to work at all the tasks of teaching, writing, and research, and in the links among those activities, not just in the disciplinized arenas of specialized research. There's more than enough work to go around here, and none of them needs to be, in principle, the dull drudgery represented by Parker's inaccurate metaphor of the "unflowering desert." Narratives of teaching and cross-cultural encounters, avant-garde happenings, multimedia explorations of pedagogical experiences, publication in non-academic venues, for example, all should be evaluated with care equivalent to that given disciplinary endeavors, even though the former activities are often not amenable to disciplinary standards of measurement, since they may eclectically adapt in *ad hoc* ways different objects, methods, and forms of argumentation that mix such areas as creative writing, literary and cultural analysis, and composition theory. As Steven Mailloux has argued: "A multidisciplinary coalition of rhetoricians will help consolidate the work in written and spoken rhetoric, histories of literacies and communication technologies, and the cultural study of graphic, audio, visual, and digital media" (23). As I suggested above, "coalition" is a good word because it ought to register not just as an intellectual linking but as a political alliance and professional solidarity tied to collective bargaining. In order for such coalitions to happen, however, it will have to go beyond disciplinary identities and specializations not by negating them, but by recognizing that such a broader spectrum of intellectual and rhetorical practices will never be fully sustainable under strictly disciplinary criteria of evaluation.

There are also political and intellectual reasons that smaller "disciplinary" units (such as writing, literature, or cultural studies) cut their group members off from the potential support of their peers when they become institutionalized across departmental barriers. So long as the modern departmental bureaucracies survive (and I suspect they will be around for quite a while), we have to understand that the departments are not disciplines, but convenient arrays of associated paradigms with quite porous as well as conflicting institutional borders linked to a wide range of non-disciplinary activities. Within the solidarity of a field which can be rhetorically represented in some pretty forceful articulations about the reading and writing of cultures, we can more successfully form coalitions, fusions, links between subdisciplines and the surrounding arena of non-disciplinary activities. Specifically trying to break large departments into smaller departmental units based on compartmentalized subfields of knowledge and methods plays easily into the hands of management, especially when we package, commodify, and represent our work in disciplinary terms that further enables the "outsourcing" and "downsizing" of our limited resources.

Of course, short-term gains to such a strategy can and sometimes do accrue, as evidenced by the familiar enough history of literary elitism and condescension to compositionists. The long-term consequences of such elitism will eventually cast literary separatists into what James J. Sosnoski has called the "underworld of the university system" (29), a kind of inversion of the writing ghetto brought about because there is little in the long-term economic future to sustain literary privileges when global capital has little need for national identities fostered by the study of literary traditions. The aesthetic and the political, the literary and the rhetorical, the textual and the extra-textual are deeply entwined, and their disciplinary separation has been costly. At the same time, it is crucial that the subject matters of composition, rhetoric, writing have their rich cluster of disciplinary paradigms, just as the literary people do, and the past thirty years of scholarship by compositionists has clearly invented such a terrain. Yet the point is that disciplinarity itself will simply not serve to integrate those differences in productive ways. As I have argued elsewhere (*Knowledge Contract*), administrators out to cut budgets are the only ones to gain from the internecine warfare among competing subdivisions. In the end, disciplinary isolation disrupts solidarity and makes any small unit or program more vulnerable to administrative surveillance (see Bartholomae).

Any significant reform of English studies therefore calls for an integration of writing and reading activities more fully than most of what we have yet seen in the design of English curricula. North offers one of the few models for what he has called the "fusion" option for re-invigorating English studies, and I share his assessment that without the hard work of rebuilding the subdisciplinary splits that have characterized the history of the profession, we won't even be able to "begin the negotiations that might result in substantive change" (237). Besides healing the disciplinary splits within the field, this kind of broader institutional reform aims not only to legitimize emergent kinds of non-disciplinary academic work, but to recognize many practices that are already taking place but that have been systematically devalued such as narrative, creative writing, radical forms of pedagogy, electronic and community literacy projects, nonacademic publications, multimedia composing, and others. Such practices may always be challenges to, and in tension with, strictly disciplinary forms of academic research, which is as it should be so long as disciplinary research does not continue to get preferential treatment.

While the current crisis of English studies has been most commonly seen as evolving out of a need to expand the objects and methods of the discipline, my argument calls for the more fundamental task of altering the strictly hierarchical role of academic disciplinarity itself in determining the range of institutionally authorized labor practices of English professors (see Mahala and Swilky). While critical forms of expository argumentation under the conditions of disciplinary discourse remain deeply humane practices when they serve the interests of social justice for more people, it is also the case that "disciplinarity" has never provided suitable evaluative criteria for *all* the work we perform in the humanities. It will be best to see the range of tasks carried out by English professors along a horizontal spectrum from disciplinary to non- or post-disciplinary practices. Such a shift calls for different kinds of evaluative criteria appropriate for different kinds of work, and those differences must not be seen as necessarily subordinate to disciplinary methods of evaluation. This argument therefore raises large questions about the material processes whereby certain kinds of professorial labor get legitimized and authorized within our specific institutions. The production of cultural value in academia has proceeded according to the supremacy of disciplinary practices to the exclusion of other modes of accountability.

My more ambitious claim, then, is that, in the case of English and the humanities at least, we may have reached the end of the 125-year history where the dominance of the disciplinary models of the knowledge contract should continue to be the exclusive measure of academic performance and curricular design. This involves more than just expanding the borders of the canon or becoming increasingly interdisciplinary, no matter how vital and inevitable such practices may be to the overall project of curricular transformation, mainly because such expansions can be carried out without altering the fundamental principles of disciplinary selectivity. Some of the most innovative, exploratory, and vital tasks performed by English professors become systematically devalued as the purview of the academic underclass, exploited under the very disciplinary conditions designed to protect them. Although economic exploitation of part-time and temporary instructors has affected all departments, disciplinary divisions between reading and writing have deeply exacerbated internal class struggle within the field of English.

There's a lot of dynamic work going on in the profession of English studies besides the winning performances of the disciplinarians. If our concern for reforming English studies resonates with a commitment to equitable labor conditions, this chapter is a cautionary tale with a potentially happier ending. Instead of worrying that things are "shaky" from a disciplinary perspective, we can imagine them as flexible and adaptable within our larger professional spheres so as to better meet the needs of more users. There are possibilities for retooling evaluation practices and re-visioning humanities labor as running across a spectrum of disciplinary and extra-, non-, or post-disciplinary activities that need not be measured according to the predominant disciplinary yardstick. And the human labor involved in these expanded curricular and evaluation practices calls for a "rhetoric of solidarity" (Bousquet, "Composition" 12) throughout our professional ranks as we re-imagine the activities of reading and writing our cultures for a more sustainable future.

WORKS CITED

Appadurai, Arjun. "Diversity and Disciplinarity as Cultural Artifacts." *Disciplinarity and Dissent in Cultural Studies*. Ed. Cary Nelson and Dilip Parameshwar. New York: Routledge, 1996. 23–36.

Applebee, Arthur. *Tradition and Reform in the Teaching of English: A History*. Urbana, IL: NCTE, 1974.

Baron, Naomi S. *Alphabet to Email: How Written English Evolved and Where It's Heading*. New York: Routledge, 2000.

Bartholomae, David. "Composition, 1900–2000." *PMLA* 115.7 (2000): 1950–954.

Berlin, James A. *Rhetoric and Reality: Writing Instruction in American Colleges, 1900–1985*. Carbondale, IL: Southern Illinois UP, 1985.

—. *Rhetorics, Poetics, and Cultures: Refiguring College English Studies*. 1996. West Lafayette, IN: Parlor Press, 2003.

Bernstein, Charles. *Content's Dream: Essays 1975–1984*. Evanston, IL: Northwestern UP, 2001.

Bérubé, Michael. *Public Access: Literary Theory and American Cultural Politics*. London: Verso, 1994.

Blair, Hugh. *Lectures on Rhetoric and Belles Lettres*. 1783. Ed. Harold F. Harding. 2 vols. Carbondale, IL: Southern Illinois UP, 1965.

Blitz, Michael, and C. Mark Hurlbert. *Letters for the Living: Teaching Writing in a Violent Age*. Urbana, IL: NCTE, 1998.

Bousquet, Marc. "Composition as Management Science." Bousquet, Scott, and Parascondola 11–35.

—. "The Rhetoric of 'Job Market' and the Reality of the Academic Labor System." *College English* 66.2 (2003): 207–28.

—. "The Waste Product of Graduate Education: Toward a Dictatorship of the Flexible." *Social Text* 20.1 (2002): 81–104.

Bousquet, Marc, Tony Scott, and Leo Parascondola, eds. *Tenured Bosses and Disposable Teachers: Writing Instruction in the Managed University*. Carbondale, IL: Southern Illinois UP, 2004.

Bové, Paul. *Intellectuals in Power: A Genealogy of Critical Humanism.* New York: Columbia UP, 1986.

Campbell, George. *The Philosophy of Rhetoric.* Ed. Lloyd F. Bitzer. Carbondale, IL: Southern Illinois UP, 1988.

Connors, Robert J. *Composition-Rhetoric: Backgrounds, Theory, and Pedagogy.* Pittsburgh: U of Pittsburgh P, 1997.

Crowley, Sharon. *Composition in the University: Historical and Polemical Essays.* Pittsburgh: U of Pittsburgh P, 1998.

Downing, David B. *The Knowledge Contract: Politics and Paradigms in the Academic Workplace.* Lincoln: U of Nebraska P, 2005.

Faigley, Lester. *Fragments of Rationality: Postmodernity and the Subject of Composition.* Pittsburgh: U of Pittsburgh P, 1992.

Foucault, Michel. *Discipline and Punish.* London: Allen Lane, 1977.

Gee, James Paul, Glynda Hull, and Collin Lankshear. *The New Work Order: Behind the Language of the New Capitalism.* Boulder, CO: Westview Press, 1996.

Graff, Gerald. *Beyond the Culture Wars: How Teaching the Conflicts Can Revitalize American Education.* New York: Norton, 1992.

—. *Clueless in Academe: How Schooling Obscures the Life of the Mind.* New Haven, CT: Yale UP, 2003.

—. *Professing Literature: An Institutional History.* Chicago: U of Chicago P, 1987.

Graff, Gerald, and Michael Warner, eds. *The Origins of Literary Study in America: A Documentary Anthology.* New York: Routledge, 1989.

Harkin, Patricia. "Child's Ballads: Narrating Histories of Composition and Literary Studies." Shumway and Dionne 21–37.

Harris, Joseph. *A Teaching Subject: Composition Since 1966.* Upper Saddle River, NJ: Prentice-Hall, 1997.

Harvey, David. *The Condition of Postmodernity.* Oxford, UK: Blackwell, 1990.

Hill, Adams Sherman. New York: American Book Company, 1895.

Hoskin, Keith W. "Education and the Genesis of Disciplinarity: The Unexpected Reversal." *Knowledges: Historical and Critical Studies in Disciplinarity.* Shumway and Dionne 271–304.

Kamuf, Peggy. *The Division of Literature or The University in Deconstruction.* Chicago: U of Chicago P, 1997.

Kent, Thomas, ed. *Post-Process Theory: Beyond the Writing Process Paradigm.* Carbondale, IL: Southern Illinois UP, 1999.

Kitzhaber, Albert R. *Rhetoric in American Colleges, 1850–1900.* Dallas: Southern Methodist UP, 1990.

Leitch, Vincent B. *American Literary Criticism from the 30s to the 80s.* New York: Columbia UP, 1988.

Mahala, Daniel, and Jody Swilky. "Remapping the Geography of Service in English." *College English* 59.6 (1997): 625–46.

Mailloux, Steven. "Disciplinary Identities: On the Rhetorical Paths Between English and Communication Studies." *Rhetoric Society Quarterly* 30.2 (2000): 5–29.

Messer-Davidow, Ellen, David R. Shumway, and David J. Sylvan, eds. *Knowledges: Historical and Critical Studies in Disciplinarity.* Charlottesville: U of Virginia P, 1993.

Michael, John. *Anxious Intellects: Academic Professionals, Public Intellectuals, and Enlightenment Values.* Durham: Duke UP, 2000.

Miller, Susan. *Textual Carnivals: The Politics of Composition.* Carbondale, IL: Southern Illinois UP, 1991.

Miller, Thomas P. *The Formation of College English: Rhetoric and Belles Lettres in the British Cultural Provinces.* Pittsburgh: U of Pittsburgh P, 1996.

Nelson, Cary. *Manifesto of a Tenured Radical.* New York: New York UP, 1997.

North, Stephen M., et al. *Refiguring the PhD in English Studies: Writing, Doctoral Education, and the Fusion-Based Curriculum.* Urbana, IL: NCTE, 2000.

Ohmann, Richard. *English in America: A Radical View of the Profession.* New York: Oxford UP, 1976.

Owens, Derek. *Composition and Sustainability: Teaching for a Threatened Generation.* Urbana, IL: NCTE, 2001.

—. *Resisting Writings: (and the Boundaries of Composition).* Dallas: Southern Methodist UP, 1994.

Readings, Bill. *The University in Ruins.* Cambridge: Harvard UP, 1996.

Reid, Ronald F. "The Boylston Professorship of Rhetoric and Oratory, 1806–1904: A Case Study in Changing Concepts of Rhetoric and Pedagogy." *Quarterly Journal of Speech* 45.3 (1959): 239–57.

Russell, David. "Institutionalizing English: Rhetoric on the Boundaries." Shumway and Dionne 39–58.

Schell, Eileen. *Gypsy Academics and Mother Teachers: Gender, Contingent Labor and Writing Instruction.* Portsmouth, NH: Boynton/Cook Heinemann, 1998.

Schell, Eileen E., and Patricia Lambert Stock, eds. *Moving a Mountain: Transforming the Role of Contingent Faculty in Composition Studies and Higher Education.* Urbana, IL: NCTE, 2001.

Scholes, Robert. *The Rise and Fall of English.* New Haven, CT: Yale UP, 1998.

Schroeder, Christopher, Helen Fox, and Patricia Bizzell, eds. *ALT DIS: Alternative Discourses and the Academy.* Portsmouth, NH: Boynton/Cook Heinemann, 2002.

Shumway, David R. *Creating American Civilization: A Genealogy of American Literature as an Academic Discipline.* Minneapolis: U of Minnesota P, 1994.

Shumway, David R., and Craig Dionne, eds. *Disciplining English: Alternative Histories, Critical Perspectives.* Albany, NY: SUNY P, 2002.

Sirc, Geoffrey. *English Composition as a Happening.* Logan: Utah State UP, 2003.

Sosnoski, James J. *Modern Skeletons in Postmodern Closets: A Cultural Studies Alternative.* Charlottesville, VA: U of Virginia P, 1995.

Winterowd, W. Ross. *The English Department: A Personal and Institutional History.* Carbondale, IL: Southern Illinois UP, 1998.

Yood, Jessica. "Writing the Discipline: A Generic History of English Studies." *College English* 65.5 (May 2003): 526–40.

6 Embracing the Conflicts: An Argument Against Separating Writing Studies from English Studies

William P. Banks

As I sit here revising this essay, my "new mail" notice pops up to let me know that yet another English department is splitting, this time at DePaul in Chicago. In the written voice of the author is a weariness, a recognition of prolonged struggle, and mostly, a clear sense of relief that, perhaps finally, all that struggle will be over; that while there will be much work ahead, it will be good work, invigorating work, exciting and nurturing work. The act of creation. And it occurs to me that I've seen all this before—as a faculty member at Georgia Southern University (GSU) when the English department split in 1998 to become the Department of Writing and Linguistics and the Department of Literature and Philosophy.

In fact, the last hundred years have seen a number of such separations of Writing (capitalized here to suggest a coherent discipline/department) from English. In my current department at East Carolina University, I have watched as a slightly different divorce has begun to emerge, though this time I was fighting against it as a small group of very senior literature and creative writing faculty attempted to cast composition and rhetoric, technical and professional writing, and linguistics out of the "English" department. During one town-hall meeting, in fact, we were metaphorized as rap music, somehow sullying the aesthetic ideals of Western (white) culture. It was odd to be so racially Othered—and ideologically telling, of course. And though that particular split did not happen, there are occasional rumbles, and every once in a while, I think I feel that DePaul faculty member's weariness and have begun to think, well, maybe we should just go and have a vibrant, powerful Rhetoric department of some stripe. To leave is very tempting.

Certainly, there have been no shortage of recent calls for a separation; we have had, separationists argue, at best a bad marriage, a relationship predicated on dysfunction. These calls for dissolution, while based often on valid and important arguments, rarely speak to the powerful possibilities that exist when rhetoric and composition remains part of English studies, or, as I'll argue below, helps to guide English studies toward a twenty-first century discipline rooted in civic engagement.

Invariably, separationist stories rest on, to use Laura Micciche's word, *emotioned* narratives about being "tired" of the arguments, "exhausted" by trying to make composition seem valid to colleagues in literary studies, as well as affirming the obvious value of not living in the shadow of an inattentive and at times abusive partner. As a compositionist in a sometimes hostile department, I know full well how frustrating it can be to continually rehash these debates. However, in this chapter, I begin by looking at prevailing separationist narratives and argue instead for the importance of rhetoric and composition remaining firmly planted in English studies departments. After all, avoiding conflict is the last place *rhetoric* needs to go—in practice or in theory—and calls for leaving English departments seem to come more from our exhaustion than from our discipline's primary commitments to transformation and change, forward-thinking moves that are *always already* circumscribed by conflict and negotiation. I'll then conclude with brief examples in which English studies broadly, and literary studies and composition specifically, benefit from our working together to refashion what it means to research and teach "English."

QUID ERGO ATHENIS . . .

Decisions to separate literary studies and writing studies, of course, have not developed *only* among faculty in English departments, as the separation at Georgia Southern University demonstrates. There, the initial shift came from the upper-administration, and even beyond that, from the Board of Regents and the state legislature, which leveraged monies in support of a late-1990s business-buzz-concept: *restructuring*. As Eleanor Agnew and Phyllis Dallas note in their contribution

to *A Field of Dreams,* the faculty suddenly found itself at a meeting
with the vice president of academic affairs and the dean of liberal arts
and social sciences in which the restructuring was a foregone conclusion; the only question was how to implement such a change (39–44).
Such a move from outside the department reminds us that these attempts at dissolution are not only or always about disciplinarity—nor
are these decisions always made by disciplinary experts. In fact, if the
chapters in *A Field of Dreams* offer any collective wisdom, it may be
that the decision to restructure or redesign a unit like English is utterly place- and history-based. The obvious problem here is that local exigencies do not necessarily translate disciplinarily; what affects
particular faculty based on particular faculty governance policies or
fiscal realities at particular universities (or state systems, for that matter) does not necessarily bespeak discipline-based needs, concerns, or
philosophies. In many ways, shifting Writing Studies out of English
has not been about the movement of a coherent and disciplined faculty
with a rich history and research agenda so much as about the bandag-
ing of a stress fracture.

   Let me offer a brief story of my own, more recent experience. In
my department, which currently houses over fifty tenured and tenure
track faculty and an equal number of non-tenure-track faculty, when
the conversation reemerges about the value of a split, the six rhetoric
and composition faculty and the six technical and professional communication faculty find ourselves in a strange place. A "natural" split
might be to move our twelve into a Department of Writing Studies or
a Department of Rhetoric; that makes sense based on disciplinary af-
filiation, research agendas, and history. But our new doctoral degree—
which, one could argue, was constructed (perhaps problematically) to
help mend fissures among the faculty and to involve as many disciplines as possible—is in "Technical and Professional Discourses," with
tracks in rhetoric and composition, technical writing, and discourse
studies. Our discourse studies faculty are, for the most part, affiliated
with the discipline of linguistics, but our faculty in cultural studies
and multicultural and transnational literatures are also involved. So
do we take half of the linguists with us? Do we take them all? At the
time, several linguists expressed their desire to go with us if we were
excised, if for no other reason than our research methodologies are
much closer to theirs than are those of the literature and creative writing faculty. And what of those members of the literature faculty who

see themselves as integral to the discourse studies tract of the PhD program and want to go with us? Likewise, the creative writing faculty see themselves more aligned with the study of literary texts and want to stay with literature even though they are, in practice, seemingly about the production of texts (see also Royer and Gilles 31–33). Do we take some of the literature folks with us and leave others behind? Do we force creative writing into a Writing Studies department against its will (which is technically not possible in our faculty manual)? Regardless, now we're not a disciplinarily solid group so much as a reinvention of the English department: a loose collective of faculty working in divergent traditions, who happen to get along at the moment. Curriculum-wise, we'd also soon have two sets of courses with lots of overlap and similarity.

I do not want here to disparage those experiments in *A Field of Dreams* or condemn them from my own vantage point. When I talk to my former colleagues at Georgia Southern, I hear that now, some ten years later, they've begun to heal the fissures and frustrations that remained even after the split; it sounds like it has become a wonderful place to teach and research. Recently, I sat down with the chair of Georgia Southern's department of Literature and Philosophy, and he waxed eloquently about the productive and focused work of their department. What started at GSU as an administrative directive seems to have worked out, some years later, in beneficial ways for both groups. What I do want to argue is that, despite their successes, these (often emotional) narratives of movement to new lands do not necessarily make explicit the conflicts that remain between teaching and research in rhetoric and composition, conflicts that seem both central to, and perhaps unavoidable in, our work as writing teachers/scholars/ researchers. In the move to form new *writing* departments and programs, there's been little made of what happens to the aspects of *rhetoric* that are not explicitly about the teaching of composition. Do these analytical methods, which focus on minority rhetorics, visual rhetorics, etc. "naturally" go to a writing department/program?

In their contribution to *A Field of Dreams,* Daniel J. Royer and Roger Gilles reference Tertullian's maxim *Quid ergo Athenis et Hierosolymis,* which they translate, "What has Athens to do with Jerusalem?" (34). They use it to reference the supposed conflict a colleague brought up in comparing a piece of short fiction and a business memo. But the assumption that forming our own department will somehow naturally solve these conflicts seems equally problematic to me when our own faculty and our own conferences have for years pondered the relationships between *rhetorical studies* and *writing studies*. In some brave new department or program we might create, we might ask a similar question to the one posed by Royer and Gilles's colleague: what has *writing* to do with *rhetoric?* And as important, how do we avoid becoming the "new boss" if we start our own departments, which must needs be about research and scholarship? What happens to teaching? And what do we do with the "service component" of first-year composition (FYC)? Do we merely replicate the models we know from English departments and allow our PhDs in Rhetoric (of all kinds) to teach primarily (or only) at the upper levels and in graduate courses?

RHETORIC AND CONFLICT: SOME THOUGHTS ON RHET-COMP'S "VALUE-ADD"

As a professor of rhetoric and composition, whose doctoral degree was earned at one of the few remaining integrationist English studies programs in the country, my own sense of our discipline is that we gain a great deal by remaining in the larger field of English studies, but more importantly, we offer tremendous scholarly and pedagogical service to our colleagues "across the aisle." While decisions to separate are valid and worth considering, I believe it's also worth considering more fully the important work we do by staying together. In the rest of this chapter, I'd like to focus on what I see as rhetoric and composition's inherent value in an English department, as one discipline in a vast "field of differences" (C. Harris) that can encourage productive conflict if we take a more active role in framing debates as they emerge. Ultimately, I think our students benefit from our decision not to cut and run, and, more appropriately in my own department, from the decision to fight back and claim rhetoric and composition's value in terms of history, pedagogy, and programmatic development.

First, to state what should be patently obvious: refusing to engage in thoughtful argument with our colleagues in literary studies, creative writing, and linguistics is antithetical to the discipline of rhetoric and its rich history in civic engagement and democratic process. It seems to me that we teach our students, in both first-year writing and advanced writing and rhetoric courses, to think broadly, carefully, and critically about the discourses that surround particular issues; we want them to engage in research that speaks not just their own already-calcified positions but which encourages them to think more broadly about their topics (see Lynch, George, and Cooper); we teach a process not just of document composition but also of thinking that values divergent points of view. And in our attention to *kairos,* we recognize that the "opportune moment" (see Thompson) for certain kinds of speaking/writing may need to be future-oriented; we may have to *create* those moments in our discourse rather than rely on some situation simply to emerge. In our pedagogies, we value a type of large thinking that we should not be afraid to engage in with our own colleagues. Yes, I'm tired too, of answering certain questions again and again, of seeing that many of my colleagues outside of rhetoric and composition do not understand even what I think of as the "basics" of writing and rhetoric pedagogy or scholarship. But I'm also wary of working only or primarily with colleagues who would quit asking about those "basics" because they'd assume the answers were already fully settled. In fact, rhetoric and composition has, in many ways, abandoned the empirical research projects that clued us in to those "basics" in the 1970s and 1980s (perhaps to our peril), even as we've increasingly embraced new writing technologies and contexts. When my colleagues outside my discipline ask me questions about composing processes, about invention and revision strategies that "work," I find that I have very little new research to share with them, not because I've not read it but because what's new is really about nuances of what we already know. There's important socio-political work going on with rhetoric right now, but very little of that work is being re-connected to compositional practices that are directly translatable to classroom practice. It's too easy to return to those foundational articles of the 1980s and say, "See, that's the answer." The reality is that our academic deans and vice presidents want this data too, and making our arguments at the local level first—in our own departments—and carefully marshalling our arguments there, prepares us for these larger campus-wide (and perhaps national) conversations about writing that we need to have. And in persuading our colleagues, we create a larger cadre of academics who support our causes at various campus-wide meetings and on various campus-wide committees. Beyond that, these questions should remind us how important it is to revisit those early studies and conduct them again, or new projects that explore past assumptions through the lenses of more recent innovations in writing and rhetoric. Existing in a culture that demands accountability can be a productive space to work, though I'll admit that it is a tremendous amount of work that many of our colleagues in literary studies do not seem to feel compelled to do.

In a larger framework, this same question was asked recently at *InsideHigherEd.com* in response to a report on the 2007 Conference on College Composition and Communication. The report, "From Service Function to Discipline" by Scott Jaschik, highlights what seems to him the emergence of a discipline from a group of service-oriented first-year writing courses. While I think Jaschik may have spoken a bit prematurely upon entering our parlor conversation, as the discipline of rhetoric and composition is not so recent, responses to the essay highlight what I'm addressing above. One response from Bob Schenck pondered what, if anything, rhetoric and composition had really offered the writing classroom that we didn't already know: "What is just one of the important new discoveries or advances that have improved writing instruction? I confess my own advice is not new—read a lot and write a lot. What's the new way?" In responses from disciplinary experts like Douglas Hesse, Valerie Balester, Kim Ballard, and Nick Carbone, we see how much our toes have been stepped on by Schenck, but I also read that folks don't really know. Or at least, the responses do not sound as though we have a confident and articulate response to that question. There is a sense in the responses that, without question, advancements have been made, but as Schenck continues to press, one begins to wonder, "Well, what progress have we made on composing processes themselves?"—which is the real question, and one that clearly functions to limit our discipline to first-year composition. In the end, it does sound, to an outsider, that aside from contributing a little vocabulary (phrases like "heuristic" and "discourse community" are made fun of, for example), we haven't developed much beyond "read a lot and write a lot." But of course, we have, even though writing and rewriting remain the central component of the class—and Balester's response noted, as well, the research that suggests that the simplistic link between reading and writing is unfounded. What shocked me about the conversation, however, is that folks were not very articulate in defending the discipline at all. In fact, the respondents seemed unable to reframe the debate from being about one course to being about the emergence of a discipline that is bigger than FYC. How do we defend such an attack on our work? Our discipline? Our pedagogies? Or is our work indefensible?

It is also worth noting that rhetoric and composition's place in English studies departments can function to remind us of our own past and how to improve what we've done, even as we invent new avenues for growth and change. FYC does much to hold us to a roughly one-hundred-fifty-year history of service and teaching in English departments, and there is much in how FYC is constructed and offered that makes English, broadly defined, want to hang on to it. For one, at many schools, the full-time enrollments (FTEs) it generates help fund other areas of English studies, even as the work inequities involved are ultimately exploitative of some cadre of faculty who teach primarily FYC. For another, it represents a fairly stable required curricular component; it's there to teach when other courses do not make and faculty need an extra class to make up their load. In fact, we could think of a number of reasons why FYC courses are "valuable" (if not valued) in English departments. (For a particularly compelling account of this state of affairs, see Sharon Crowley's *Composition in the University.*) But FYC is also the course that gives new faculty an introduction to the university and its students by offering, usually, the only space in an English department in which each faculty member works with a fairly random sample of incoming university students. Departments and colleges, like business, education and others, cannot make such a claim, nor do their faculty benefit from the reality of working with such a diverse group of students.

And despite the hard work of teaching FYC—and, at times, feeling as though our colleagues perceive rhetoric and composition only in terms of this particular service course—it is also a core space for educating not just our elected majors, but the entire campus about writing and rhetoric, key arts in a liberal education. In fact, in the last ten to fifteen years, we've seen increasing numbers of FYC courses turn to servicelearning projects and other forms of writing that more closely align FYC pedagogies with the rich history in rhetorical education or civic engagement (see Coogan; Mastrangelo and Tischio; Adler-Kassner; Cushman). At my own university, it has been the non-tenure-track faculty, in fact, who have led this charge. Many of our non-tenure-track faculty are area natives or, because of family or other regional commitments, have become heavily invested in the local culture. As such, many of them have been the first to adopt service learning pedagogies, and because of their connections to the community, they have been extremely well positioned to help students think critically about service-learning projects and the roles that effective communication plays in local (and at times national) civic work. And the majority of these non-tenure-track faculty do not have advanced degrees in rhetoric and composition; they are primarily traditional and multicultural literature students who spend their professional development hours becoming better writing teachers. I think our department is fortunate to have these teachers working with so many of our students. By keeping rhetoric and composition in the English department, my colleagues and I have been able to train many of our non-tenure-track faculty when they were graduate students and we continue to offer them professional development workshops after they have joined the faculty. Surely, separationists might argue, if rhetoric and composition left an English department, we'd have more control over the pedagogical components of these important courses. That may be true in some contexts, but we should also recognize that we would be turning out a large number of master's degree students in literature departments without, perhaps, *any* training in rhetoric and composition. How well will these students fare in job and/or doctoral school applications where teaching FYC is expected? How well will their future students be served?

Undoubtedly, the working conditions surrounding FYC, both at my university and at a host of others around the nation, represent some of the most egregious forms of labor exploitation at the university: massive mental and physical labor for low pay, rare and/or inconsistent health insurance and retirement benefits, and no job security. But I've also not seen any of the newly formed independent writing departments/programs that were able to secure a full complement of tenure track faculty to cover the teaching of FYC. Even the recent, progressive, and heavily-endowed writing program at the University of Denver has not found a way to teach its composition classes by tenured/tenure-track faculty. Rhetoric and composition's leaving English studies departments does not suddenly create monies where they did not exist, nor does it make college and university faculty and administrators suddenly think the work of teaching writing to first-year students is important enough to resource it adequately. Ultimately, what I fear happening is the replication of power hierarchies already existing in many English departments only under a different name: now, the privileged will be those doing research in rhetoric and teaching advanced writing and rhetoric courses, but a caste system seems to remain (see J. Harris; Moore; Schell; Bousquet, Scott, and Parascondola). In fact, I would argue that in this new department we might create, as long as research is the golden calf—and I'm certainly not arguing against the value of academic research and publication—what we're likely to see is a second stratification between those focused on pedagogical aims and those focused on research in rhetorical studies (what I'd call the analytical track in our discipline). The former group, which would probably involve those serving as writing program administrators, as well as those concerned about processes directly related to teaching writing—that group, I fear, would be seen as less theoretical, more "applied." Why do I think this? Perhaps because I hear these statements at national conferences from those working in rhetorical history, those working in minority rhetorics (like myself), and those working in computers and writing, just to name a few sub-disciplines of rhetoric and composition that may not be always directly or obviously tied to teaching writing. In some ways, I've come to wonder if we've not adopted many "converts" who have found that they can call their textual studies "rhetorics of x" and suddenly get jobs, when the texts they study and their epistemological connections eerily resemble the projects of literary studies. Which is not to suggest that these projects lack value, but in the absence of a clearer sense of our discipline, I do wonder what will happen to those who do teacher/ action research and focus on classroom practice and research in these brave new departments we're creating. And while the programs that we're developing outside of English departments may be led by smart and disciplined rhetoric and composition professionals, I wonder how much new knowledge will be developed by the hiring of primarily non-tenure-track faculty (post-docs from various areas of English studies or related fields, those with MFAs in creative writing and MAs in literature, linguistics, and/or composition studies). In the absence of a tenure system that values and encourages (perhaps demands) research and scholarship by *disciplined professionals,* how do these programs create more/better knowledge about our discipline?

Third, it seems to me that one argument particularly worth making in keeping divergent disciplines within English studies has to do with our pedagogical knowledge and research, and particularly what that research can mean to areas of English studies that often go unexamined in these talks, like English education. One of the key "value-add" components of rhetoric and composition has been its continued concern for pedagogical work and its disciplinary focus on literacy education even at the college level. While our colleagues in literary study, linguistics, and creative writing do a great deal of teaching, particularly at smaller colleges, I would argue that very few of them are engaged in systematic inquiry into the teaching of their subjects, particularly as projects that take the shape of participant-based or classroom/action research. At my own university, for those literature faculty who have found it difficult to get published in their fields, I have offered them copies of the journal *Pedagogy* and said, "Well, what about publishing here?" The look I get is hard to describe; this offering seems, I suppose, too foreign to think about. And the reality is that very few of my colleagues in literary studies and creative writing have ever been trained to do classroom-based inquiry; those research methodologies remain foreign to them. But we do this work in rhetoric and composition, and various qualitative and quantitative data collection and analysis methodologies are central to our research methods courses. I suppose it is a type of "service" work in English departments constantly to be the voice asking, "Yes, but what about the students?."—but this is certainly valuable work. It represents one of the significant impacts we are having on English departments at the turn of the century, and I have no doubt that English/literature majors are better for these conversations. One failure of disciplinarity may be the failure to re-envision one's work; embracing the conflicts that come with so many different disciplines in the field of English studies productively revises the discipline in powerful and important ways, ways that are themselves worthy of further research and articulation.

And then, of course, there's the problem of English education. Where does it go when we separate writing and reading? Middle and high school English teachers need to know a great deal of literature and they need to know a great deal about various kinds of writing. At some universities, the majority of English education has been turned over to colleges of education. And while these colleges may offer some powerful and important courses—and at two universities I've worked at, there was much more critical theory and critical literacy instruction going on there than in the English department!—our students benefit from exploring literary texts with the precision and expertise of literature faculty, even as they can benefit tremendously from rethinking traditional writing instruction by taking courses with writing faculty. At the very least, pre-service teachers should get to major in departments that offer them excellent examples of the kind of teaching they will one day do themselves. I'm sure my experiences with English Education majors are like those of many others. When I've taught methods courses, I've had a healthy dose of students who had previously enrolled in my advanced composition courses. In that course, we do a great deal of whole-class workshopping of texts, as well as a host of peer review activities and a series of rhetorically oriented workshops intended to develop their projects toward particular audiences and purposes. When we reach the point in the methods course where we read Nancie Atwell's *In the Middle* or other pedagogical texts, invariably a large group of students voice a common complaint: "Well, that's all good in theory, but it won't work in real classrooms, and certainly not with high school students." But those students who take my advanced composition courses have been quick to offer a divergent argument; because of their experiences with different pedagogies, they can envision how workshops, small group work, etc. can work at the middle and high school level. Rhetoric and composition has the chance to lead by example in these spaces, to serve as models for more effective pedagogies that engage multiple modes of thinking and doing. What I've noticed is that as these students report back to their other teachers, I have colleagues who begin to ask me questions and to consider my suggestions for revising their own pedagogies. I don't pretend to have all the answers, of course, but I'm very quick to offer my colleagues methods for asking these pedagogical questions in their own classrooms because these are the sorts of questions my training in rhetoric and composition has led me to.

Ultimately, it is in being *proactive* in English departments that we offer the greatest value. By framing the debates that emerge, and by carefully articulating our positions, we stand in better position to effect positive changes. I will not pretend that everyone who goes into rhetoric and composition emerges as rhetorically savvy; it would be nice to think so, but such simply isn't the case. Too often, rhetoric and composition professionals take jobs at colleges and universities or in regions that just aren't good fits; the scholars may be ultimately unable to communicate in the value systems in which their colleagues and students, as well as individuals in the community, communicate. When I hear colleagues complain about particular problems they're having with the "old folks" in their departments, which tends to mean with literature professors specifically, I wonder how much of this is their own lack of rhetorical savvy and how much of it is really that their senior colleagues are too entrenched to move. Most likely, it's a mixture of these two problems, but I worry that we project too quickly and accept little of the blame for our own inability to marshal the best arguments and to develop effective *ethoi* to achieve our goals. In some ways, I believe Bruce McComiskey and I are thinking along similar lines here. In his recent edited collection on English studies, McComiskey suggests that *identification* (from Kenneth Burke) and *articulation* (from Stuart Hall) provide a productive method for communicating our goals and productively healing the emotioned divisions that obtain between the various disciplines of English studies. McComiskey challenges us to find rhetorical methods for establishing *identification* with our colleagues and then *articulating* those connections in ways that do not put one group ahead of the other (40–43). Rather, the *connections* across the disciplines (which McComiskey sees as our *articulations*, à la Hall) can supply a method both for more carefully and fruitfully framing our internal conflicts but also more effectively framing our needs and interests as externally motivated. What results, for McComiskey, are "functional relationships" which "emerge most productively from external, not internal, exigencies and motivations" (47). In creating this metadiscourse about our field and its work, we are better prepared to link our research and teaching with important external concerns like community literacy projects, teacher-training initiatives like the National Writing Project, and others:

Functional relationships like these lead to the cooperative search for new resources, not the self-interested allocation of existing funds that have led many disciplines to leave English departments in search of more equitable administrative homes. National Writing Project sites, literacy centers, and young authors' conferences—just a few among dozens of possibilities—require a fundamental change in the ways the disciplines that constitute English studies are conceived, or, as Hall might say, "articulated." (47–48)

By taking our discipline seriously as one invested not merely in academic treatments of rhetoric, but in rhetoric in actual practice, we can think carefully about framing the debates both within our departments and external to them. In this way, rhetoric and composition provides a productive internal monitor for English departments, reminding our colleagues in other disciplines of our history in civic engagement and in helping to formulate the language that demonstrates the value of English studies in richer and more complex ways than happens in the discourses that make fun of our (far too increasing) esoteric and elitist ways.

SCENARIOS OF TRANSFORMATION

When Stephen North suggests a model of fusion in his book *Refiguring the PhD in English Studies,* like McComiskey, I find the practicality of such a move problematic. North saw this experiment as a way to bring "disparate elements together under sufficient pressure and sufficient energy to transform them into a single new entity" (73), yet I couldn't help but think of past melting pot metaphors in multicultural education. It seems to me that our differences, which are our strengths, get lost when *fusion* occurs. Likewise, McComiskey notes in the introduction to his recent collection on English studies that "if each course includes content from all of the disciplines, the curriculum might never extend beyond a basic level" (39). Certainly, there are levels of English studies courses where we might, indeed, foreground the interdisciplinary enterprise of our department, but I'm hesitant to think that this model should permeate all our courses and work at the undergraduate and graduate levels. What I'd like to offer here, instead, are a few necessarily brief "case studies" of the kinds of productive work that can happen when faculty work from an English studies perspective and allow for disciplinary knowledge to inflect their thinking about literacy education at the undergraduate level.

Rhetorical Literatures

One troubling problem for faculty to face when we decide that separation is the only course of action is what to do with texts I call "rhetorical literatures." By *rhetorical literatures,* I mean literatures that name their audiences (e.g., children's literature) or those which have functioned at the intersections of art and argument (e.g., African American literature, gay and lesbian literature, etc.). The texts in these courses usually fall outside of the traditional literary canon and, because they seem inherently to be culturally focused in some explicit way, function simultaneously to evince poetics and rhetorics that make them difficult to divide up among the disciplines in English studies. At a curricular level, where do these courses go in a split? And what of faculty working in African American rhetorics or queer rhetorics? Most likely, they teach "literature" courses from time to time, and include "literature" in their rhetoric courses, though I'd imagine they do so with the inflections that a rhetorical education has offered them. How likely will undergraduate curriculum committees be to approve virtually the same courses for two different departments? And beyond that, will rhetoric and composition departments need to get "approval" from English departments if they try to create courses that investigate certain traditionally literary genres from a rhetorical perspective?

I'd rather we embrace the pedagogical and research potential that emerges when faculty with primary and secondary interests are allowed to teach and research in ways that facilitate such overlaps. One method of strengthening a discipline, of course, is to narrowly specialize, but surely another is to ask broad questions about one's discipline and to see one's discipline in context. In English studies departments, there is room for such work. In my own case, I have been interested in children's and adolescent literatures since my undergraduate days. I also took graduate courses in these subjects at Illinois State University (one of the premiere research and teaching institutions for the study of children's and adolescent texts). And now, from time to time, I teach an undergraduate course in children's literature designed primarily for education and English majors. I don't teach these texts as "Great Books" because, given my rhetorical background, I see these texts as products of culture—novels, stories, and poems that have emerged at particular times and often evincing rather explicit arguments about what children are and should be; how gender, race, and sexuality should be understood by (i.e., taught to) children; and how the adults who teach these books or read them with their children should be encouraged to (re)produce certain types of reading subjects. In teaching the course, I foreground the rhetoricity of the texts and ask rhetorically oriented questions of what are ostensibly poetical texts. And in conversations with my colleagues trained in literary study, we see that we cover much of the same ground, though we call our projects by different names. Given the general concern for youth literacy that continues to pervade our cultural mindset, particularly the spate of recent books on the crisis of literacy for boys (see Fletcher; Newkirk; Pirie; Smith and Wilhelm), courses in children's and adolescent literatures will surely become an even more common staple of English departments and, I would argue, a more central project of rhetoric and composition and literature scholars. There is important interdisciplinary work to be done here.

More specifically, I recognize that the students who take my children's literature courses will not be "literature specialists" or any other type of specialist that our disciplines seem far too invested in reproducing. Rather, they will be, primarily, language arts teachers; they will work with all the language arts to varying degrees and the artificial separations we create at the university will neither make sense to them nor be relevant to them when they go into their own classrooms. And while I recognize that these students would benefit tremendously from doing close readings of texts, they also benefit from doing *different* readings of texts and from being asked to think in broad ways about literacy. When I teach this course, I require a picture book project of the students as a way to embrace the various aspects of English studies that they will be able to use later in their own classrooms. We spend time reading Molly Bang's *Picture This,* a picture book that both demonstrates and critiques visual rhetorical theories of production and design even as it offers the students ways for talking about visuality and intention. Then the students choose a poem written (ostensibly) for adults and they re-purpose that poem into a picture book for which they create the art and design. The art, of course, might be drawing or the use of layered shapes, pictures from magazines, or paintings— anything that works for them to get the message of the poem across to readers. Recent books produced by students have used Whitman, Frost, Dickinson, Angelou, Walcott, and others. Most notably, one student chose Elizabeth Bishop's "Visits to St. Elizabeth's," a poem she chose quickly because she liked the "House That Jack Built" refrain and assumed it would be a simple poem to illustrate. After working with the poem, line by line, to illustrate it, she began to realize what the poem was about and worried it was too dark for children, so she thought of her project as an illustrated poem for adults. Whether she was right or not about the poem's appropriateness for an audience matters less than that she was asking that question and using specific examples from the text to support her claims. This project works at the intersections of traditional rhetoric, visual rhetoric, literary study, technical writing, and linguistics as students are required to process disciplinary-specific issues from all of these disciplines in order to do the work itself. In the end, the student's reflection on the project demonstrated how she pulled from all these disciplines to do the work, and she wrote several paragraphs about how this project would help her to think about the intersections of disciplines in English studies as she constructed learning projects for her own elementary school students.

Projects like these, while not appropriate, perhaps, for every class, also speak to the problem of what we will do as we've expanded our curriculum from traditional literary studies, which is itself an historical anomaly of the recent past, to a curriculum that embraces not only rhetoric and composition and linguistics but areas of literature that are more obviously rhetorical in nature. In discussions of separation, the nuances of our work have rarely been a focal point, but it is in these nuances that we see our disciplines expanding and growing. Dismissing that work seems exactly the wrong direction in which to move.

English Studies Seminars

Despite my previous concern that North's "fusion" model seems problematic as a curriculum-wide enterprise, I have seen a version of it work quite well at Illinois State University, where the English department made the turn to an integrationist English studies model in the 1980s. When I was there from 1999–2003, the department rather successfully required two courses for undergraduate English majors: English 100 and 300, the former an "Introduction to English Studies" and the latter a "Senior Seminar." These courses served as bookends to the major, and left the students with an otherwise totally elective curriculum. Likewise, these courses were all taught by tenure track and tenured faculty, on rotation. To me, this seemed to have a number of benefits. For one, the faculty who taught the courses—if they taught them as they were intended—were given continued renewal in the complexities of English studies. In teaching English 100, for example, a faculty member in a particular discipline would spend time putting together readings and other materials from the other disciplines in the department in order to "introduce" beginning majors to the broad range of inquiry projects undertaken by the different faculty of the department. Often they would invite their colleagues or graduate students in various programs to be guest speakers, as well, in order to offer more nuanced discussions for students from disciplinary experts. As this move helped new students to think expansively about English studies and their own options of study, so too did it encourage faculty to stay connected outside their narrow areas of specialty and to make links between their own current research to other areas of English studies. This course, over the years, served to "discipline" new faculty in the department into the English studies model, even as more senior faculty felt the need to talk to younger faculty on new lines and investigate how to include emerging disciplines into the curriculum. While students did not receive an *expert* knowledge of any individual English studies discipline in the course—and I can't imagine we'd really expect college sophomores to have such a knowledge—they did gain an awareness of the kind of department they were joining as English majors. It seemed to me at the time that this course created a mostly win-win situation for students and faculty alike, even though, from time to time, individual faculty would abuse the course to make it part of their current pet research project.

Another benefit accrued to faculty when they taught English 300, the capstone seminar for the major. Taken by students in their senior year of study, English 300 offered a curricular space for holistic reflection by asking students to think critically about the courses they had taken as part of their individuated experiences in the English department. Students in English 300 prepared a senior portfolio of the writing they had completed as part of the major; in the portfolio, students were required to revise a previous essay and extend the conversation by incorporating more critical theory, the goal being to help students prepare a complex project for use in graduate school applications or to have them seriously rethink previous arguments after some time had passed. Students also created an analytical essay that explored the intersections they had made in English studies, foregrounding the (dis)connections they had made across several classes. While some critiqued the fact that students did not necessarily do this meta-reflective work in all their courses, I think that holding that activity until the students had completed most of their coursework makes sense; essentially, the students now had a group of papers and projects and experiences that they could put back under the microscope and examine through a different critical lens. This project required students to articulate *for themselves* what their undergraduate degree in English meant, and how they had personally come to understand the various disciplines in English studies.

While beneficial for students, I'd argue that this course, like English 100, also actively re-educated faculty in important ways. As faculty read and responded to the students' revised and new projects, and as they worked to construct a course that would foreground reflective and critical thinking independent of a particular text, author, or critical school, faculty were forced to re-articulate for themselves the connections among the various disciplines in English studies, even as they were able to gain respect for the types of projects and experiences that students were having in courses and with teachers from throughout the department. On numerous occasions, I overheard faculty asking their colleagues or graduate student instructors (who taught some sophomore-level courses) about assignments they had given that seemed really effective to the faculty now seeing them for the first time because of teaching English 300. These were curricular conversations that rarely happen in our closed-off courses and hectic teaching and research lives. And they created important spaces for faculty to rethink and possibly enliven their own pedagogies. These are conversations that benefit faculty, certainly, but in the end they benefit our students in that their professors work actively to eschew solipsistic pedagogies and positions. Such faculty are better able to respond to a variety of students and their divergent interests. This path serves to preserve English departments rather than see them go the way of Classics and other shrinking majors that have lost the ability to connect to and excite undergraduate students.

CONCLUSION: DISCIPLINARITY AT THE EXPENSE OF PEDAGOGY?

Ultimately, as a scholar who began with two degrees in literary studies before pursuing a specialization in rhetoric and composition, I recognize that we all share a pedagogical connection. We are, in some way or another, all engaged in the pedagogical project of literacy education. For some of us, that type of literacy may look like what E. D. Hirsch et al. have proposed as a type of "cultural literacy" (one which Alan Bennett's recent Tony Award winning play *The History Boys* mocks with smart abandon); for others, it has to do with the interconnectedness of critical reading and writing; for still others, the project has made significant turns to visual and technological literacies that move beyond traditional alphabetic and print-based literacies. But these projects are, in the end, all about literacy: the coding and decoding of texts, broadly conceived, in various ways and for various purposes, in specific and identifiable contexts. That alone should offer a method for our thinking together productively about the work we do.

Separation will be a win-win situation for everyone: no more arguments, no more fighting over resources, teaching what you want, getting credit for the research you do—these are the sometimes illusory appeals of separation. New fences, with magically greener grasses. And for those who teach more than a narrow sense of their discipline, I've heard it argued that there's always the option of cross-teaching. This is one of the first lines of argument that proponents of separation will offer to colleagues who would rather stay together. And, I'm sure, it could be true. But I'd ask us to think about the last time we taught a rhetoric course in the communications department? When Communications split from English in the early twentieth century, I'd imagine there were suggestions that faculty could cross-teach courses and be involved in interdepartmental research and inquiry. Yet the machine of disciplinarity and departmental politics on campus works very hard to prevent such work. There are questions of FTEs and who gets credit and how we evaluate work "outside the department" in tenure and promotion materials. English departments are, certainly, at a crossroads, but this space offers us a powerful moment to rethink what our curricular goals are. In making smart choices, we have the potential to outlast faddish moves to render each of our projects or interests into a "department" of its own. In powerful ways, departments too often create compartments into which students and faculty get stuck and out of which the system makes it virtually impossible to escape.

In the end, most of us have a you-me problem. Not disciplinary conflicts but conflicts between particular people who have trouble thinking expansively about their own work or generously about the work of others. And solving a you-me problem by drawing new departmental boundaries or departmental dissolution is the ultimate "local" issue: it solves the problems that a very few people have with a very few other people, but does virtually nothing to promote knowledge, research, scholarship, or intellectual (and dare I say it, interpersonal) growth. I would argue that we work harder to model productive inquiry and intellectual curiosity for our students and our communities by starting that work in our own departments. Ultimately, we have much to gain by working together, by having intelligent and productive arguments, and by taking the time to process where our real problems are and are not. In this way, we model the value of English studies to our students for thinking and communicating broadly, complexly, and generously. There are certainly much worse enterprises to be involved in.

WORKS CITED

Adler-Kassner, Linda. "Service Learning at a Glance and Recommended Re-
    sources." *Reflections: A Journal of Writing, Service Learning, and Commu-
    nity Literacy* 1.1 (2000): 28–29.

Agnew, Eleanor, and Phyllis Surrency Dallas. "Internal Friction in a New In-
    dependent Department of Writing." O'Neill, Crow, and Burton 38–49.

Atwell, Nancie. *In the Middle: New Understanding About Writing, Reading,
    and Learning.* Portsmouth, NH: Heinemann, 1998.

Bousquet, Marc, Tony Scott, and Leo Parascondola, eds. *Tenured Bosses
    and Disposable Teachers: Writing Instruction in the Managed University.*
    Carbondale, IL: Southern Illinois UP, 2004.

Coogan, David. "Service Learning and Social Change: The Case for Mate-
    rialist Rhetoric." *College Composition and Communication* 57.4 (2006):
    667–93.

Crowley, Sharon. *Composition in the University: Historical and Polemical Es-
    says.* Pittsburgh: U of Pittsburgh P, 1998.

Cushman, Ellen. "The Public Intellectual, Service Learning, and Activist
    Research." *College English* 61.3 (1999): 328–36.

Fletcher, Ralph. *Boy Writers: Reclaiming Their Voices.* Portland, ME: Sten-
    house, 2006.

Harris, Charles B. Personal interview. 28 July 2000.

Harris, Joseph. "Meet the New Boss, Same as the Old Boss: Class Conscious-
    ness in Composition." *College Composition and Communication* 52.1
    (2000): 43–68.

Jaschik, Scott. "From Service Function to Discipline." *InsideHigherEd.Com.*
    23 Mar. 2007. 4 Apr. 2007 <http://insidehighered.com/news/2007/03/23/
    cccc>.

Lynch, Dennis A., Diana George, and Marilyn M. Cooper. "Moments of
    Argument: Agonistic Inquiry and Confrontational Cooperation." *College
    Composition and Communication* 48.1 (1997): 61–85.

Mastrangelo, Lisa S., and Victoria Tischio. "Integrating Writing, Academic
    Discourses, and Service Learning: Project Renaissance and School/Col-
    lege Literary Collaborations." *Composition Studies* 33.1 (2005): 31–53.

McComiskey, Bruce, ed. *English Studies: An Introduction to the Discipline(s).*
    Urbana, IL: NCTE, 2006.

Micciche, Laura. *Doing Emotion: Rhetoric, Writing, Teaching.* Portsmouth,
    NH: Boynton/Cook, 2007.

Newkirk, Thomas. *Misreading Masculinity: Boys, Literacy, and Popular Cul-
    ture.* Portsmouth, NH: Heinemann, 2002.

North, Stephen M., et al. *Refiguring the PhD in English Studies: Writing, Doc-
    toral Education, and the Fusion-Based Curriculum.* Urbana, IL: NCTE,
    2000.

O'Neill, Peggy, Angela Crow, and Larry W. Burton, eds. *A Field of Dreams: Independent Writing Programs and the Future of Composition Studies.* Logan: Utah State UP, 2002.

Pirie, Bruce. *Teenage Boys and High School English.* Portsmouth, NH: Boynton/Cook, 2002.

Royer, Daniel J., and Roger Gilles. "The Origins of the Department of Academic, Creative, and Professional Writing at Grand Valley State University." O'Neill, Crow, and Burton 21–37.

Schell, Eileen E. "Toward a New Labor Movement in Higher Education: Contingent Labor and Organizing for Change." Bousquet, Scott, and Parascondola 100–10.

Smith, Michael W., and Jeffrey D. Wilhelm. *"Reading Don't Fix No Chevys': Literacy in the Lives of Young Men."* Portsmouth, NH: Heinemann, 2002.

Thompson, Roger. *"Kairos* Revisited: An Interview with James Kinneavy." *Rhetoric Review* 19.1–2 (Fall 2000): 73–88.

Welch, Nancy. "'And Now that I Know Them': Composing Mutuality in a Service Learning Course. *College Composition and Communication* 54.2 (2002): 243–63.

7 Transforming Fragmentation into Possibility: Theory in the Corporate University

Matthew Abraham

THE HAZARDS OF SPEAKING UP AND OUT

As an academic of color who has studied and worked within predominantly white institutions for the last ten years, speaking up for the importance of maintaining equity within the university and speaking out against institutional injustices has never been a problem for me. The consequences for doing so, however, have been costly in terms of psychic stress, time, and effort. Nonetheless, these experiences have made me who I am, confirming in my mind the importance of going it alone when others refuse to join you in a struggle that you know to be absolutely right.

Despite the professional hazards that often prevent most academics from challenging patterns of abuse based on academic rank, political viewpoint, race, ethnicity, gender, sexual orientation, age, and disability that are so clearly evident in today's academic institution, I have sought to speak truth to power—even when it has been clear that those in power are neither interested in nor listening to anything I have had to say.

While directly facing the unfortunate legacies of the past is often considered the best way to confront the circumstances and perceived injustices of the present, and while it is well recognized that those who refuse to learn useful lessons from the mistakes of the past are often doomed to repeat them, the academic institution—and, as I will argue, the English department more specifically—has been somewhat oblivious to understanding the role it has played, and continues to play, in perpetuating and sanctioning *de facto* discriminatory practices. While this is a bold claim, one that will be fiercely resisted by many, it has to be understood as being made in response to what is often posited as the fundamental purpose of the university: to preserve dominant culture and to transmit dominant values. While surely it is the case that the university does more than this, as it represents a complex intersection of competing concerns and interests, one should not lose sight of how the structure of the university maintains a commitment to preserving hierarchy and social stability.

As is so often the case, conformity, silence, and complicity, rather than confrontation and controversy, seem to be the ruling orthodoxy within the academic institution, the English department, and American culture at large. Some have described my tendency to speak up and against such seemingly naturalized orthodoxies as a sort of suicidal impulse, a desire for self-immolation in an irrational mocking of power and the powerful, a need to demonstrate the utterly arbitrary nature of the constraints silencing even the possibility, much less the realization, of transformative action. As a former department chair of mine once noted: "A courage of this sort and a willingness to declare political allegiances are unusual in an untenured assistant professor." What was so unusual about this willingness to declare political allegiances? It seems that I "sought out upper-level administrators to talk about sensitive and potentially explosive issues of race in the department," that my "intellectual life is firmly rooted in [my] political commitments," and that I "bring those commitments to bear on the everyday life of the department, often working quietly, behind the scenes, to move colleagues in the direction that [I] believe the department needs to go." Perhaps a little background will explain why I do these things.

After witnessing some small scale abuses of power as a graduate student, and a very large-scale abuse of power several years ago as a temporary faculty member at a state university in Pennsylvania, I've come to appreciate the ironies of institutional life; often questioning the absurd and petty political fiefdoms that have almost, but not quite, destroyed the "life of the mind" in English departments and, perhaps, the university at large. No amount of theory or theoretical reflection will reverse this tendency, only strong political commitments guided by a deep awareness of the academic's responsibility to the larger public—and the pressing problems it faces—will make academic work relevant again.

Whether academics in the field of rhetoric and composition will choose to forego the pitfalls of the naked careerism that has undermined the sustainability of literary study in the corporate university may very well determine the size—as well as the relevance—of the contribution writing instruction and rhetorical analysis will make in the future. A radical departure from, and a radical re-evaluation of, current trends within the field with respect to the use and deployment of theory will have to occur. As this chapter will demonstrate, the message could not be much clearer: a change of course is in order. As Karen Kopelson argues in "Sp(l)itting Images: Back to the Future of Rhetoric and Composition," the field has reached an impasse in dealing with the theory/pedagogy split. As graduate students seeking to enter the field find themselves constrained by the pedagogical imperative which requires them to make their projects as applicable to the teaching of writing as possible, one notices a distinct tension between those who "do" theory and those who "do" writing. This tension represents the possible undoing of the field, as Kopelson warns, because it represents the setting up of warring camps around who actually "does" Rhetoric and composition, undermining the very reasons many students came to the field in the first place—to find a pragmatic, professional outlet for their political ideals.

As the fierce fight for academic capital—so very sought after through theoretical reflection—has intensified within the academy, so has the amount of "theoretical production" within rhetoric and composition; representing, in my mind, a betrayal of intellectual responsibility as this type of production, which meets the needs of academic capital, acts to contain controversies that very much need to be exposed. Whether seeking to compete with our literature colleagues in producing impenetrable and seemingly unreadable prose—which in fact, is often left unread—or continually aligning ourselves with hip theoretical movements and their French expositors, Mas'ud Zavarzadeh and Donald Morton write in *Theory (Postmodernity) Opposition: An "Other" Introduction to Literary and Cultural Theory*, our "protective" pedagogies and the theories that undergird them continue to

> insist that the best way to teach is to provide the novice learner with established knowledges and to avoid disputes which may create confusion for [her]. The rule is

> broken, of course, only when the "controversial" itself
> has already been normalized and turned into a routine
> and canonical point of argument. (1)

As Zavarzadeh and Morton go on to claim, "what is still at stake in
the dominant academy is exactly the (careerist) desire for canonization
and the containment of controversy" (2). In other words, theory—
even supposedly radical social theory—can be "defanged" and made
to serve oppressive social practices within the corporate university.
However, Zavarzadeh and Morton find that "[r]adical theory deploys
critique to investigate the conditions of what exists now in the name
of a non-oppressive and non-exploitative future and thereby opens up
a productive social space beyond the oppressive present without mea-
suring all 'directions' towards the future in terms of a doctrinaire 'utopian' blueprint" (2).

While Zavarzadeh and Morton identify how theory and controversy are contained by and within the academic institution, it is important to note that controversy threatens the very well being of faculty
and administrative units. In turn, the removal of controversial people
and their ideas stands as an unacknowledged consequence of the academic guild structure and the production of academic knowledge. As
Jeff Schmidt points out in his *Disciplined Minds,* subservience to an institutional hierarchy rather than intellectual ability is the most prized
attribute of the professional within the modern institution (universities, corporations, etc.). While this may appear as a bold and provoca-
tive claim, one need look no further than some recent controversies for
empirical evidence. I'll begin with my own experience, as experience
grounds theoretical reflection.

At a state university in Pennsylvania where I was as employed as a
temporary faculty member during the 2003–2004 academic year, the
English and theatre arts department had no women of color on the
tenure track. Only one person of color, quite recently, had achieved
tenure within the department. I along, with two women (one of color)
taught 5-3 loads as temporary faculty. All of the full professors in the
department were white. This particular university is the least diverse
of the fourteen universities within the state system.

Although this university possessed at the time an African American university president and an equity officer (as an assistant to the
president), per capita the number of faculty of color fell far below the
number of students of color on the campus. This was an issue of real

institutional attention, and with this backdrop I have described, it is easy to recognize the intense concern that was expressed in May of 2003 when one of the finalists for one of two tenure -rack positions in rhetoric and composition at this University turned out to be a white, male creative writer with friends on the search committee.

I had been ranked as the top candidate for this search, so I was devastated when the administration decided to cancel the position because of the threat of impending litigation, instigated by internal candidates who felt slighted by the fact they were not offered campus interviews. These candidates' suspicions were well warranted in this case. The white, male candidate held no qualifications in rhetoric and composition, expressed a lack of interest in conducting rhetoric and composition scholarship during his interview, and found himself ranked ahead of eminently more qualified candidates by a search committee eager to give him the job. This candidate, who had labored as a temporary faculty member for about four years and had established close personal relationships with English and Theatre Arts (ETA) department faculty members, had apparently been guaranteed a job.

The department's core leadership consists of five older, white men seemingly bent on maintaining control of hiring and promotion. The rhetoric and composition search was one of many searches in the last twenty years, in my estimation, that has been undermined within the department because of this pernicious good 'ole boy system that has prevented any sort of meritocracy from flourishing. This search represented the quintessential, paradigmatic example of "whiteness as property," as the improprieties of the search were covered up by administrative discourses: "Due to changing needs in the English and Theatre Arts Department, the position for which you applied has been cancelled. We regret any inconvenience that this may cause you. Thank you for your understanding." Changing needs, indeed! Covering one's institutional sinecure against litigation necessitates such ridiculous evasions. At this point, consider Zavarzadeh and Morton's reflection on how the teaching of controversy, or in my case the exposure of institutional controversies, is necessary, but can be avoided through bureaucratic discourse and the evasions of the purveyors of theoretical discourse:

> The teaching through controversy is all the more urgent now [at this historical moment] because some others who write and speak about literary and cultural the-

ory, about politics and pedagogy today, seek to render "ideas" unthreatening by trying to cordon off the classroom from the contestations of the social and by seeking to make it a site of purely cognitive awareness. (37)

Challenging such promoters of a dominant, institutional commonsense has long been my goal as a teacher and scholar, particularly with respect to issues of race and the institution.

After the Outrage

One can see how whiteness circulates quite normally within academic institutions without being recognized as such. In each case, the advancement of white interests is viewed as entirely "normal," even if this advancement seriously breaches well-defined institutional protocols and guidelines. Often these guidelines are breached so arrogantly, and in such wanton disregard of institutional mandates, that it is amazing "whites only" signs aren't hung over some university English departments. One colleague at this state university in Pennsylvania confided to me that, when the first person of African descent was being considered for a faculty position in the department about six years ago, another faculty stated quite bluntly, "Do we really want a nigger on the staff?"

When racial Others move into previously white-dominated labor spaces, there is a contraction of power at the institutional level which suggests that the institutional investment in whiteness should be protected as an unarticulated institutional goal. In his *Confronting Authority: Reflections of an Ardent Protester,* Derrick Bell writes:

> I have seen otherwise honorable faculty members engage in the most unscrupulous, underhanded conduct to avoid hiring or promoting individuals they did not wish to see admitted to their ranks. They have lied, maligned character, altered rules, manufactured precedents, and distorted policies. I am talking here about candidates for admission or tenure who are white, not minorities, candidates with impressive academic credentials, and the authors of traditional scholarly work. (75)

The high-sounding ideas and language of academe (merit, academic integrity, equity, etc.) which provide an ironic cover for the types of behavior that Bell describes above, take an even more insidious complexion when they are applied to scholars of color. Bell continues, "When the candidate is not a white man, and either has non-traditional qualifications or departs from the traditional in scholarly subject matter and approach, the opposition can be as fierce as it is illogical and unfair" (75).

Bell's brand of theory, critical race theory, is desperately needed within rhetoric and composition. In spite of initial efforts to bring critical race theory into rhetoric and composition, much more needs to be done, particularly as "rac[e]-ing" the institution and the field might yield significant theoretical coin. These insights might be discomforting, perhaps highlighting the deep corruption of the academic guild system, but they are vitally necessary at this historical moment.

THEORY IN RHETORIC AND COMPOSITION

As a graduate student and an academic of color who has been through the struggles and challenges of the job market, I've wrestled with the conflicting professional identities the discipline of rhetoric and composition seem to require and value. On the one hand, it is claimed that theoretical knowledge and theorists are central to the development of the field. On the other hand, this theoretical knowledge must show ready pedagogical application or risk being placed in "the critical theory—off limits" section of the field. As one senior scholar recently remarked to me, theory is used in rhetoric and composition like oregano is sprinkled on a pizza: it is used to bolster empirical and pedagogical claims just as oregano is used to bolster flavor.

The word *theory* comes from the Greek *theoria* or "spectacle" and, if the ancient sense of the term can be applied here, theory refers to an individual or group perception that has gained widespread acceptance or public sanction. For the purpose of this chapter, I am going to adopt a ridiculously simple definition of theory. Theory is the way we "talk the talk" about transcending the conditions under which we labor while fantasizing that we are persuading those who hold power and influence over us—without suffering any repercussions for doing so—that there is a better way to conduct the business of institutional work. In other words, theory allows us "to think otherwise," to imagine what our environments might be like if we weren't so alienated, oppressed, and—most importantly—so obedient. However, we can't escape our individual beliefs and assumptions in this moment of epiphany that we might call "theoretical reflection" because our beliefs and assumptions give shape and form to knowledge claims, including theoretical claims. Within the English department everyone claims to do theory and, consequently, no one does theory. The term "theory," then, has lost substantive content; it has been de-referentialized.

In his remarkable book, *The University in Ruins,* Bill Readings traces the historical transformation of the university as it has moved from an institution based on the principle of reason, to its refashioning as an institution committed to defending national culture, to its more modern form as an institution of excellence. Excellence, within the economy of transnational corporations, is another de-referentialized term that completely lacks substantive content, acting as an empty signifier to take the shape demanded of it by a bureaucratic structure committed to optimum performativity and economic output. Within the University of Excellence, the cash-nexus acts as the symbolic real that translates or connects knowledge production to the demands of capital.

Theoretical knowledge—the most privileged form of academic production—provides the basis for inquiry, discovery, and application. Unfortunately, the term "theory," like "excellence," has been so de-referentialized within the University of Excellence that everyone claims that the work they are engaged in is theoretical or that the work they do makes them working—albeit unrecognized—theorists. This has particularly troubling consequences for rhetoric and composition as a young field because—if all distinctions between what is particularly special about rhetoric and composition are broken down and become meaningless—then there is the danger that there is nothing all that special about what we do, contributing to the belief that anyone can teach writing or administer a writing program.

Although we have moved far away from simply being a service discipline, we clearly have not convinced others—and perhaps not ourselves—that rhetoric and composition is real intellectual work. The fact that we have poached heavily on other disciplines like literary criticism, philosophy, and linguistics for the construction of a knowledge base in composition theory, rhetorical theory, and empirical methods clearly does not mean that we don't have a field that is truly our own. We claim to be experts on the writing process and the administration of this process within academic institutions. Consequently, we claim that we understand that process better than any other field. But at-

tempts to make rhetoric and composition more theoretical or to claim
the name "theorist" for various types of work within rhetoric and composition may have negative effects.

In his 2003 *College Composition and Communication* review of
Shirley Rose and Irwin Weiser's *The Writing Program Administrator
as Theorist*, Gary A. Olson identifies what he calls a disturbing trend
in rhetoric and composition whereby terms such as *theory, rhetoric,*
and *process* have been collapsed to such a degree that they no longer
have a specific or useful meaning. For the editors of the book, a theorist is "someone who develops theory or adapts/adopts/tests theory as
a way of conceptualizing, organizing, explaining, analyzing, reflecting on, and interpreting experiences and specialized knowledge gained
through experience or observation" (Rose and Weiser 2). The different
types of theory showcased by the contributors in *The Writing Program
Administrator as Theorist* include, then:

- management and space theory
- existential phenomenology
- leadership theory
- postmodern theory
- ethical theory
- rhetorical theory
- genre theory
- archival theory
- network theory
- progressive theory

These attempts to demonstrate the applicability of these various types
of theory to WPA work come off, at least to me, as somewhat con-
trived because of the attribution of the term "theory" to any and all
types of reflection that take into account the complex interactions between people, power, ethics, and the management of resources. While
writing program administrators must certainly account for all of these
entities in their day-to-day activities, theory—as "a way of conceptualizing, organizing, explaining, analyzing, reflecting on, and interpreting experience and specialized knowledge gained through experience
or observation"(2)—does not, in itself, have any consequences for the
future of writing programs. A theory can only have the effects allowed
to it by the very conditions it would alter (Fish, *Professional* 58).

If the writing program administrator is now a theorist—in his or her reflection on competing needs within the English Department and across the university—the specific definition of "theory" or "theorist" loses all meaning. Why is such effort being expended toward re-describing administrative works as theoretical work? Perhaps this effort signals a failure within the English department to appreciate administrative work on its face as intellectual work. Weiser and Rose, then, probably envision themselves as refashioning this description through their edited collection. However, if the writing program administrator is a researcher and a theorist, or if writing program administration has theoretical and research components to it, the efforts to re-describe the WPA or to refashion what the WPA does will not necessarily make writing program administration intellectual work because theory is constrained by the very conditions that it attempts to transcend. The resistance to theory is the resistance within theory as Paul de Man once claimed. Stanley Fish likewise contends that

> A theoretical pronouncement is always an articulation of a shift that has in large part already occurred; it announces a rationale for practices already in force; it provides a banner under which those who are already doing what it names can march; it provides a visible target for those who have long thought that things are going from bad to worse. (*Doing* 155)

In contrast to Fish's stance, others believe that theory possesses strong implications for anti-establishment critiques, critiques that challenge the very foundations of a society's power structures and, more importantly, probe around for the constituting conditions of a dominant political configuration. In their volume *Theory as Resistance,* Morton and Zhavarzadeh claim that

> Theory is a critique of intelligibility. As a result of such a critique, readers in a culture become aware of the ways in which signifiers are always organized so that through them the world is produced in such a manner that its "reality" supports the "reality" of the interests of state power, gender, race, and the dominant classes. Through such a recognition, theory enables readers to historicize the "reality" of the ruling class that is presented in cul-

tural texts as being the universal reality of all classes
and thus to engage in ideological struggle. (53)

Historicizing the "reality" of the ruling class and analyzing its hegemony as a result of a particular arrangement and "reading" of cultural
texts disturbs the naturalness of dominance; consequently, the emergence of this dominance in cultural codes and practices results from
a continual struggle between competing groups. In contrast to Fish,
Morton and Zhavarzadeh conceptualize theory as possessing progressive and liberatory ends. These vastly different senses of theory's potential to effect change, or to simply reflect a change that has already
taken place, create tension between a discipline's participants. It is a
tension that is emerging within rhetoric and composition, particularly
between administrative and theoretical/historical areas of inquiry.

The success of rhetoric and composition as a field and of writing
program administration as a subdiscipline of rhetoric and composition can be attributed to the ability of both to adapt to the changing
conditions of the university in the environment of late capitalism. As
a discipline, we continue to struggle with the incongruous role that
rhetoric and composition occupies within the corporate university. In
the English department, in particular, we are witnessing the rise of the
new administrative and technologically savvy classes, and the decline
of specialties such as theory and cultural studies.

This is a reflection that is unlikely to win me very many friends,
but I think it's an admission that needs to be acknowledged and theorized about. Many of the leading lights in our field trained in literary
fields, for example, and perhaps came to the conclusion that the only
way they were going to survive in the English Department was as an
administrator. There is nothing wrong with that. New disciplines survive because they stipulate the doing of some task that cannot be done
by other disciplines. For example, if rhetorical theorists in rhetoric and
composition started claiming that their work is also administrative
work because Lacanian psychoanalytic insights can contribute to the
better operation of the English department and the first-year composition program, they would presumably not be doing anyone any favors.
In turn, the claim that writing program administration is theoretical
work or can use theoretical insights from existential phenomenology
does not really get us very far. As Lynn Worsham was quoted in Scott
McLemee's article, "Deconstructing Comp: The New Theory Wars
Break Out in an Unlikely Discipline," "Simply to collapse the work of

administration into the work of theory does everybody a disservice." McLemee's article suggests that Worsham is troubled by the fact that composition studies is now making "a fairly huge investment in the subject of writing-program administration." However, that fairly huge investment is simply a consequence of the changing economic realities of the academic institution.

Robert Samuels's 2002 article, "Žižek's Rhetorical Matrix" broaches this very problem. Samuels discusses a troubling trend in the job market with respect to theory. He suggests that

> Many of the graduate students doing theory in the last twenty years have wound up repackaging themselves as compositionists in a desperate attempt to gain employment. This economic process has helped to introduce theory into many writing programs from the bottom up. However, this infiltration of theory has often encountered the strong force of the service ethic, which works to undermine critical thinking in favor of the "practical" need to teach students how to write for their other classes and their future and their future employment. Every aspect of the system thus seems to work against the role of theory in the humanities. (330)

Although Slavoj Žižek, Thomas Rickert, and Janet Atwill provide spirited rejoinders to Samuels's article—two of them focusing on the specificity of Samuels's attack on Žižek—I don't think any of the three completely refuted Samuels's critique which, as I see it, views the undermining of critical thinking in writing programs and English departments as arising from a capitulation to the demands of the corporate university.

In conversations I've had with many younger faculty members in the field, I've become convinced that there is an anti-theory bias that currently pervades the field. It's almost as if those of us doing rhetorical theory have somehow betrayed our disciplinary allegiance by not being a card-carrying member of rhetoric and composition because we would rather read Paul de Man or Louis Althusser rather than the latest empirical study in composition. Indeed, Worsham attests to "a very chilly climate" that has been created for those who do theory (qtd. in McLemee). I contend that theory, or at least theory of the kind I really enjoy studying and putting into practice, has radically transformative effects. However, such theory—Marxist, Foucauldian, psychoanalytic—has been found to be "suspect" because it doesn't specifically advance composition aims, particularly the advancement of the field's disciplinary reach.

Such a sad state of affairs only undermines the progressive commitments so many of us hold dear. Perhaps a realization has sunk in: radical academics will be unable to live up to their theoretical commitments without calling into question the very lines of authority within the institution that protect faculty sinecure. The fancy phrase for this is "maintaining credibility" (i.e., talk the talk but don't walk the walk when it comes to critiquing your own institution). Yet, this desperate struggle to "maintain credibility" only contributes to the slow erosion of faculty power.

Real institutional and departmental change takes place when faculty members stand up against a university's and a department's exploitative labor practices in faculty or committee meetings, not when tenured professors publish yet another article on institutional critique in *College Composition and Communication*. No amount of theoretical reflection will allow us to avoid being a hypocrite on labor issues. I've seen way too much kowtowing and not enough resistance by faculty members and graduate students who have the theoretical ammunition to know better.

When you're faced with a real ethical dilemma, you won't need the musings of either Zygmunt Bauman or Emmanuel Levinas. Just listen to that voice inside telling you to do the right thing. Such a resistance politics is unlikely to win you very many friends in high or low places but it's certainly better than a gregarious tolerance for the way things currently stand in our institutions. Capitulating to a self-imposed censorship because of a fear of professional repercussions only contributes to silence, complicity, and a feeling of helplessness.

If we lose control of our institutions and departments, we have only ourselves to blame. As James Porter et al. write in their 2000 article, "Institutional Critique: A Rhetorical Methodology for Change," "We made 'em, we can fix 'em. Institutions R' Us" (611). However, I don't think—as Porter et al. claim—that institutions are re-written through rhetorical action but instead through real action that has rhetorical components. Such real action might entail confronting a colleague who has proclaimed *in theory* that graduate students should be more empowered but then votes in committee to exclude the graduate students from a meeting that discusses their interests. If theoretical commitments are what we use to advance our professionalization and to gain tenure, let's call them pseudo-commitments for the sake of not confusing them with the real work of figures such as Paulo Freire and Noam Chomsky.

Even a remote familiarity with the disciplinary history of rhetoric and composition reveals a past filled with marginalization and struggle that is a central part of its lore. The field advanced its disciplinary aims by confronting the realities of university education within the United States in the 1970s, realities that many in English departments seemed incapable of facing because of their investment in a white male, upper middle class paradigm: student populations from a diverse range of backgrounds, entering the university for the first time, presented new pedagogical challenges that required paying serious attention to the aims of higher education and the role of literacy and writing in the fulfillment of those aims.

While many English literature faculty seemed to deny the developing reality within U. S. universities—and in many instances actively resisted it—rhetoric and composition's pioneers focused on helping this new student population to become better writers. Rather than putting their heads in the sand and ignoring the new conditions of the postnational, soon-to-be-international corporate university, the field went to work, as it were. New times demanded new measures: rhetoric and composition performed this accommodation in a pioneering fashion.

In the year 2009, however, one begins to sense a flagging in our resolve as worn-out clichés and feigned dissent against the corporatization of the university seem to corrupt the one-time sincere efforts of this field's founders. Everyone is, of course, a "critical pedagogue," "a resisting intellectual," "a WPA who is also a theorist." We talk the talk in certain intellectual domains, but don't "walk the walk" in our *praxis*. Success, it seems, has spoiled what was once so endearing about the field's mission: its commitment to serving the university's student constituency rather than solely our own professional development and advancement.

While the two certainly go hand in hand, rhetoric and composition's capitulation to the demands of management (particularly in the instance of the WPA), has undermined our commitment to what James Berlin called "critical citizenship"(140). As many in the field

have made their work explicitly apolitical so as to avoid being impli-
cated in public controversies; ironically, this avoidance has made us
blind to what may very well lie at the heart of the intellectual mission
and downright mundane: our role as educators—I say educators because that's what we are before we're rhetoricians or teachers of literature—seems to demand finding the most controversial subjects in the
American public sphere, bringing them to our students' attention, and
seizing the opportunity to demonstrate the instrumental role rhetoric
and rhetorical positioning play in these controversies.

No task seems more urgent than to help our students become cit-
izen-critics capable of analyzing the American public sphere from a
critical/rhetorical standpoint. From such figures as Julien Benda to
Chomsky, intellectual responsibility entails a dogged pursuit of corruption and scandal wherever either might exist within the academic
guild structure or the larger public. By using what Mary Louise Pratt
termed the "contact zone" as a pedagogical heuristic, we can better
understand the "social spaces where cultures meet, clash, and grapple
with each other, often in contexts of highly asymmetrical relations of
power, such as colonialism, slavery, and their aftermaths as they are
lived out in many parts of the world today" 34). Writing, as a rhetoric
of resistance, allows for a transcendence of the conditions that stifle
human life, particularly in instances where we, as academics, are complicit in creating the conditions responsible for such dehumanization.
In his 1995 *JAC* interview with Gary A. Olson, Jean-François Lyotard
states that "writing is the capacity to resist the network of exchanges in
which cultural objects are commodities, and maybe to write is precisely to avoid making a book (or even a small paper or article) a commodity, but rather to oppose, to resist the simple and naïve exchangeability
of things in our world" (394). Such resistance writing requires avoiding the facile and embracing the difficult; more importantly, it means
usurping the most difficult social hegemonies of the present time.

A great deal of effort has been expended in rhetoric and composition to understand the direct relationship between composition teaching and its role in either enforcing or resisting the conditions of social
and political domination. Tackling this very question, naturally, invites a battle because it forces a real assessment of the institutional role
that composition teachers play, and that assessment often clashes with
a professional identity frequently described as "value orientation."

While not every teacher of composition would describe herself as an "organic intellectual," she often positions a set of concerns that are quite different from those professed by her economically driven departmental, university, or perhaps legislatively, defined role. While this personally constructed role, as a transformative or resistant intellectual, resonates well with a self-congratulatory sense of the composition teacher as an active social agent within the corporatized university; it overlooks how composition, as a discipline, upholds legal and curricular mandates about the institutional and citizen-subject. Challenging these mandates will require forsaking the "easygoing collegiality" with which so many of us are very familiar:

> One of the acts that faculties find it hardest to forgive is uncollegiality. If not for the code of silence entailed by that decorum, we would all have a more candid set of analyses of the warfare that drives the internal life of academic departments, harms careers, sours the life of the mind, and intoxicates teachers for hours when speaking off the record. Nothing is more striking, in fact, than the disparity between the sheer number of hours dedicated to maneuvering behind the scenes (or sizing up the maneuvers of others) and the relative absence of studies of the mechanics of such warfare in published articles on pedagogy, curriculum, and high-sounding matters like "professionalism." (Brennan 234)

While Timothy Brennan finds cultural studies to be "the subdiscipline best suited for conducting the candid analyses" ("Meanwhile" 234), I think rhetorical study, or what Steven Mailloux has called "rhetorical hermeneutics" (97), might be most appropriate for dealing with the bad-faith of our discipline in its attempts to intervene within the public sphere. The composition classroom presents the opportunity to conduct a candid analysis of the academic bad-faith that pervades the corporatized university. Indeed, our students are often better at sniffing out our cowardice than either we or our colleagues are. Just as academic faculty interpellate their students, students have an interpellative role in shaping the faculty.

The interpellative function of the composition classroom, and its direct connection and accountability to institutional mandates and legislative dictates, has been remarkably under theorized. What happens to a curriculum proposal, for example, when it moves from the departmental to the university committee level and then to legislative consideration? How do considerations of political economy condition the development of the curriculum?

Can we really occupy an institutional role and space while challenging institutional "conditions of possibility"? Chomsky has contended that institutions will not program themselves for self-destruction by allowing individuals—who, in some sense, are committed to exposing the institution's roots through their critiques—to survive (*Manufacturing*). Indeed, those who survive and advance within the institution are those who internalize what the institution values: stability, growth, hierarchy, the state, etc. The establishment and maintenance of an institutional hegemony ensures that "that which cannot be true is not true." Sealing the institutional space as a hegemonic space requires laying clearly defined but perhaps unarticulated ground rules that agents never explicitly fess up to believing (see James Sosnoski's *Token Professionals, Master Critics*).

Theory, or any theory worth studying or implementing, should create crisis within a set of institutional constraints that mask oppressive social practices. In this sense, a worthwhile theory should expose deeply entrenched interests, ones that often pass as the dominant commonsense, upsetting those who unconsciously practice hegemony. The commodification of theory within the posthistorical university, and the a-politicization of academic life, constitutes a serious threat to rhetoric and composition's future as a coherent discipline. That theory, as a reflection on practice, has been extended to writing program administration is not in itself a surprising or disturbing development; in fact, the development of the posthistorical university, as developed and explained by Readings in *The University in Ruins*, would have probably predicted this development, pointing out that it is consistent with the broad flattening and political "defanging" of the social science disciplines(i.e., theoretical projects that threaten the very foundation upon which the university system rests) will, simply as a matter of logic, be discouraged and consciously avoided. As many astute observers have pointed out (Fish and Chomsky), a serious academic program for explicitly training public intellectuals, who would be trained to address contemporary social issues, has not developed because the academy supports the legitimization of, not a confrontation with, the dominant culture. In this sense, academic knowledge relies on and is shaped by the dominant culture. John Brenkman, in his *Culture and Domination,* writes:

> Culture does not stand above or apart from the many other activities and relationships that make up a society, including the socially organized forms of domination, exploitation, and power pervasive in our own society and its history. Granted, cultural practices foster social solidarity and collective identity. But that does not keep them from participating in social divisions and exclusions. (vii)

While Brenkman's reflection may be true, challenging the dominant culture—the one that sanctions what happened to me at that state university in Pennsylvania—necessitates finding ways to make theory dangerous and disruptive once again; regrettably, one does not have to look very far to see the worst effects of "institutionalized" theory.

WORKS CITED

Atwill, Janet. "Rhetoric and Institutional Critique: Uncertainty in the Postmodern Academy." *JAC* 22.3 (2003): 640–45.

Bell, Derrick. *Confronting Authority: Reflections of an Ardent Protester.* Boston: Beacon, 1994.

Berlin, James A. *Rhetorics, Poetics, and Cultures: Refiguring College English Studies.* 1996, West Lafayette, IN: Parlor Press, 2003.

Brenkman, John. *Culture and Domination.* Ithaca, NY: Cornell UP, 1987.

Brennan, Timothy. "Meanwhile, in the Hallways." *Class Issues: Pedagogy, Cultural Studies, and the Public Sphere.* Ed. Amitava Kumar. New York: New York UP, 1997.

Fish, Stanley. *Doing What Comes Naturally: Change, Rhetoric, and the Practice of Theory in Literary and Legal Studies.* Durham: Duke University Press, 1989.

—. *Professional Correctness: Literary Studies and Political Change.* Oxford: Oxford UP, 1995.

Kopelson, Karen. "Sp(l)itting Images; or, Back to the Future of (Rhetoric and?) Composition," *College Composition and Communication* 59.4 (2008): 750–80.

Mailloux, Steven. "Re-Marking Slave Bodies: Rhetoric as Production and Reception." *Philosophy and Rhetoric* 35.2 (2002): 96–119.

Manufacturing Consent: Noam Chomsky and the Media. Dir. Peter Wintonick. 1993. DVD. Zeitgeist Films, 2002.

McLemee, Scott. "Deconstructing Comp: The 'New Theory Wars' Break Out in an Unlikely Discipline." *Chronicle of Higher Education.* 21 Mar. 2003. 18 Aug. 2008 <http://chronicle.com/free/v49/i28/28a01601.htm>.

Olson, Gary. Interview with Jean-Francois Lyotard. *JAC* 15.2 (1995): 391–410.

—. Rev. of *The Writing Program Administrator as Theorist: Making Knowledge Work.* Eds. Shirley Rose and Irwin Weiser. *College Composition and Communication* 54.3 (2003): 499–502.

Pratt, Mary Louise. "Arts of the Contact Zone." *Profession* (1991): 33–40.

Porter, James E., Patricia Sullivan, Stuart Blythe, Jeffrey T. Grabill, and Libby Miles. "Institutional Critique: A Rhetorical Methodology for Change." *College Composition and Communication* 51.4 (2000): 610–42.

Readings, Bill. *The University in Ruins.* Cambridge: Harvard UP, 1996.

Rickert, Thomas. "Enjoying Theory: Žižek, Critique, Accountability." *JAC* 22.3 (2003): 627–40.

Rose, Shirley K, and Irwin Weiser, eds. *The Writing Program Administrator as Theorist.* Portsmouth, NH: Heinemann-Boynton/Cook, 2002.

Samuels, Robert. "Žižek's Rhetorical Matrix: The Symptomatic Enjoyment of Postmodern Academic Writing." *JAC* 22.2 (2002): 327–54.

Schmidt, Jeff. *Disciplined Minds: A Critical Look at Salaried Professionals and the Soul-Battering System that Shapes their Lives.* Lanham, MD: Rowman, 2000.

Sosnoski, James. *Token Professionals, Master Critics: A Critique of Orthodoxy in Literary Studies.* New York: SUNY P, 1994.

Zavarzadeh, Mas'ud, and Donald Morton. *Theory (Postmodernity) Opposition: An "Other" Introduction to Literary and Cultural Theory.* Washington: Maisonneuve P, 1991.

Part III

Curricular Design

8 The Purpose of the University and the Definition of English Studies: A Necessary Dialogue

Marcia A. McDonald

In the daily work of higher education, the goals and needs of departments often clash with the goals and needs of a university. These clashes occur over hiring, promotion and tenure, budgets, curriculum, academic policies, and special programs, to name a few. The ubiquity of these clashes helps sustain the master narratives about "evil administrators" and "renegade faculty." Many faculty members in English departments have stories about administrative "plots" to suppress the voices of critics, and many administrators have complaints about English faculty being *a priori* against administrative actions, even those that benefit English departments. What if we imagine these clashes as opportunities for dialogue rather than for the perpetuation of narratives of opposition? What might a dialogue between the university and English studies produce about definitions and purposes?

Although this dialogue takes place in some form on every campus virtually every day, it is usually a subtext to the main task of solving a problem. Beyond the local level, these discussions of definitions and purposes take place for the most part in separate spheres: the "purpose of the university" among administrators, legislators, foundation heads, and national higher education organizations, and the "definition of English studies" among faculty in the subdisciplines of English studies, and in the humanities in general. I propose to bring these discussions together, looking for points of resonance and overlap, and considering the implications of each for the other.

What is at stake for each party in this dialogue? Universities need to make responsible and strategic choices about the use of resources, and these choices depend upon some stability in definitions of study and departmental organizations. Departments need to articulate the purposes of their course of study in recruiting students and in faculty and policy decisions. Because of the ubiquity of general education courses often housed in English departments, these courses and programs have the most at stake in the "purpose of the university" discussion. Likewise, the "purpose of the university" stands the best chance of being enacted through learning experiences that are widely required. I will conclude by proposing an integrated curriculum for English studies as a curriculum that can both help enact the broad purpose of the university and provide English with a rationale for a central position within the university.

THE PURPOSE OF THE UNIVERSITY

The current discussion about the purpose of the university centers on the issue of "education for democracy," or as it is also called, "education for civic engagement" or "education for citizenship" or "democratic liberal learning." The key assumption underlying this discussion is that the university needs to serve a goal external to itself, and external to the expansion of knowledge for its own sake. This is not new. In the tradition of American higher education, its early claimants were Benjamin Franklin and Thomas Jefferson. John Dewey's 1916 book *Democracy and Education* provides much of the philosophical groundwork for current claims. To a basic point that "[s]ince a democratic society repudiates the principle of external authority, it must find a substitute in voluntary disposition and interest; these can be created only by education" (87), Dewey adds a deeper point:

> A society which is mobile, which is full of channels for the distribution of a change occurring anywhere, must see to it that its members are educated to personal initiative and adaptability. Otherwise, they will be overwhelmed by the changes in which they are caught and whose significance or connections they do not perceive. The result will be a confusion in which a few will appropriate to themselves the results of the blind and externally directed activities of others. (88)

Dewey's words here have a prophetic ring; one thinks of Robert Kegan's perception that we are "in over our heads" in our efforts to cope with contemporary crises (6, 335). Thus, one of the challenges to higher education is to shape students' "voluntary dispositions" and strengthen their "personal initiative" in the interests of democratic society.

In the last decade or so, various ideas and agendas have converged to emphasize the purpose of the university as an institution engaged in education for civic life. These include federal legislation (itself a response to political agendas), foundation and association goals, university initiatives, and research and pedagogical projects. These particular agendas respond to a widespread perception of a crisis in civic society. This crisis is signaled by declining interest in politics and civic issues among college students (Mann 263), increasing population diversity intensifying linguistic and cultural divides, a widening gap between rich and poor, and a fragmenting of neighborly society (highlighted in Robert Putnam's study vividly entitled *Bowling Alone*). The scenario of civic decline calls into question whether the democracy in the United States is genuine or a lost ideal, replaced by polarized politics, capitalist corruption, and consumer mentalities.

Responses to this scenario of civic decline came and continue to come from both within and without the university. Federal legislation establishing the Corporation for National Service linked funding for college to students' work in the fields of literacy and provided grants for university-community collaborations (Gladieux and King 169). The United States Department of Housing and Urban Development offers grants for large-scale university-community collaboration "designed to build the capacity of local communities to solve their own problems" by tackling those problems in partnership with urban universities (1). That these programs have been sustained through shifts in political power in Washington may speak to their ability to represent both "a thousand points of light" and a domestic incarnation of the Peace Corps.

Private granting agencies, likewise, called for universities to propose projects to address civic needs. In an influential whitepaper first issued in December, 1997, Russell Edgerton, then Director of Education for Pew Charitable Trusts, concludes that higher education must "engage the public's agenda" (15) or risk becoming irrelevant to the two major issues confronting the nation: "how to earn our national living in an increasingly interdependent, global economy" and "how to renew our social, political, and cultural life in the face of unprecedented change and a growing accumulation of unsolved domestic problems" (9). Indeed, "If the nation is coming unglued, as ours seems to be today under the onslaught of the mass media and commercialism, colleges and universities can—and should—lean hard into the wind and become a force for social renewal" (50). What Edgerton proposes is for the university to be a counterweight to contemporary social problems and commercial culture (50).

The university is not exactly a student to be tutored by the federal government and private foundations about its mission. Many universities have as part of their founding missions civic involvement as an aspiration for students. Three university presidents and the president of the Education Commission of the States initiated Campus Compact in 1985, believing "colleges and universities [are] vital agents and architects of a diverse democracy, committed to educating students for responsible citizenship" (Campus Compact). Scholars and academic associations formulated arguments for the civic function of the university, and numerous publications and conferences address this topic. Three key features of "education for democracy" or "civic education" or "democratic liberal education" can be culled from this decade-long discussion: diversity, pragmatism, and values. For the sake of establishing working perspectives on these three features, I will cite a particular discussion of each from the national discussion.

The Association of American Colleges and Universities (AAC&U) has identified diversity as the center of "education for democracy." Over a decade of work, including partnerships with disciplinary organizations, has produced strategies for reorienting higher education to "education for democracy" by highlighting diversity of participants, of subject matter, and of means of education. Given the patterns of re-segregation in public schools and persistent patterns of segregation in housing, the college years for many students will be their first extended experience living and working with a diverse population. Thus, the AAC&U contends, because "Democracy [. . .] depends for its effectiveness on the fullest possible engagement of all the human talents and perspectives within a society," universities have an opportunity and an obligation to strengthen students' resources for functioning in a diverse, fully participatory democracy (*Drama* xx). To do this, universities must conceive of themselves as "authentic public spaces," not as private enclaves (*Drama* xxii).

A second dimension of "education for democracy" is pragmatism. Scholars link the emphasis on "education for democracy" in the 1990s to the philosophical pragmatism of William James, John Dewey, and others, and to the formation of a particularly American university (Orrill xvi–xxi). One reason the "education for democracy" initiative has been so widely accepted is its "applied"—i.e., pragmatic—dimension: students may change jobs or careers, but they will not change their need to live in community. Therefore, developing the skills to function effectively in civic settings is not only useful for each student personally but also necessary for perpetuating a democratic political system. Bruce Kimball's version of "pragmatic liberal education" identifies seven key qualities, three of which are directly related to matters of democracy: education must be "multicultural"; "promote the commonweal and citizenship"; and "promote the formation of values and the practice of service" (47). Not only does a "pragmatic liberal education" help inculcate dispositions towards tolerance and inclusiveness, but it also emphasizes skills of critical reasoning, clear communication, collaborative work, and problem-solving, skills common to a range of college curricula.

It is rare to find a university statement of purpose that does not invoke the "value" of civic engagement and community involvement. Indeed, the current version of the "education for democracy" discussion has compelled universities to consider how they translate the general language of their vision statements into specific learning experiences. The authors of *Educating Citizens: Preparing America's Undergraduates for Lives of Moral and Civic Responsibility* argue that "it is preferable for colleges and universities to examine the values they stand for and make conscious and deliberate choices about what they convey to students" (Colby et al. 11). Colby et al. locate varied examples of the implementation of this value-laden civic education in large and small universities. They identify successes and good first starts to support claims that a university should educate each student to become "a morally and civically responsible individual" who "recognizes himself or herself as a member of a larger social fabric and therefore considers social problems to be at least partly his or her own" (17).

The key components of diversity, pragmatism, and values are effectively summarized by the AAC&U's one-page, 1998 "Statement on Liberal Learning." The AAC&U is intentional about linking education to social responsibility, a link highlighted in these excerpted passages:

A truly liberal education is one that prepares us to live responsible, productive, and creative lives in a dramatically changing world. It [. . .] fosters a well-grounded intellectual resilience, a disposition toward lifelong learning, and an acceptance of responsibility for the ethical consequences of our ideas and actions. Liberal education requires that we [. . .] explore connections among formal learning, citizenship, and service to our communities.

Because liberal learning aims to free us from the constraints of ignorance, sectarianism, and myopia, it prizes curiosity and seeks to expand the boundaries of human knowledge. [. . .] It embraces the diversity of ideas and experiences [. . .]. To acknowledge such diversity in all its forms is both an intellectual commitment and a social responsibility [. . .].

To put the current articulation of the purpose of the university in perspective, I want to place the AAC&U statement against a formulation familiar to those in English studies: John Henry Cardinal Newman's *Idea of a University*. His eloquent summary of the benefits of a university education includes a social goal: "it aims at raising the intellectual tone of society, at cultivating the public mind, at purifying the national taste, at supplying true principles to popular enthusiasm and fixed aims to popular aspiration, at giving enlargement and sobriety to the ideas of the age, at facilitating the exercise of political power, and refining the intercourse of private life" (125–26). Newman connects these social effects of a university education to its primary purpose of cultivating the individual: "It is the education which gives a man a clear, conscious view of his own opinions and judgments, a truth in developing them, an eloquence in expressing them" (126). Newman's powerful treatise recognizes an educated individual's influence on society; however; his call for this liberal education is rooted in its goodness for the individual and for the Catholic Church. The call today, as typified by the AAC&U statement above, is significantly different—it is through the realization of a social purpose that an educated individual truly knows himself or herself to be educated. Newman's university-educated individual is a restraining influence on society: his language of "purifying," "fixed aims," "sobriety," and "refining" places the university-educated individual above the public at large. The AAC&U language is about "free[ing] from constraints," "explor[ing]," "expanding," "embrac[ing]" ("Statement on Liberal Learning"), a different kind of social orientation than Newman envisioned, and a reflection of the "idea of the university" in the twenty-first century.

There are dissenting voices and contrary views in the discussion of the university as the province of "education for democracy." In a critique of Colby et al.'s book, Stanley Fish makes the case that "democratic values are not academic values," and he raises the valid question about how we know when we have achieved anything called "education for democracy"—the academy is not equipped to measure this achievement (C5). Bill Readings in *The University in Ruins* finds that "the story of liberal education has lost its organizing center" (10); into that vacuum has come the corporate university. Readings believes an alternative to the corporate university can emerge if the university relinquishes the claim to be "a model of the ideal society" and instead becomes a place "in which it is possible to think the notion of a community otherwise, without recourse to notions of unity, consensus and communication" (20). Readings does not have confidence in the contemporary, market-driven university to do the kind of civic restorative work envisioned by Russell Edgerton, the AAC&U, and others. Yet, he sees this "posthistorical" (6) moment for the university, when it has lost its function of transmitting a national culture to its students, as a moment when it can become "one site among others where *the question of being-together is raised*" (20). Although in this essay I will work seriously with the claims for civic revitalization as a function of the university, I want to raise Readings's critique of the market-driven university, because universities face the challenge of distinguishing between fulfilling a social mission because it is a legitimate mission, and fulfilling a social mission because it is a competitive advantage. Indeed, with the *U.S. News & World Report* ranking top schools in "Programs that really work," including Service-Learning, Writing in the Disciplines, and First-Year Experiences, the key pedagogies associated with "education for democracy" have a marketing sparkle ("Programs").

What I have outlined here as the current understanding of the purpose of the university is not something that has been inscribed on the consciousness of the university solely by external forces. Internal projects of faculty and departments have been pursuing the links to social issues for some time. In English studies, the expansion of the canon since the 1960s represents an effort to bring traditionally marginalized voices into the curriculum. The various "studies" areas, many of which have relationships to English departments, have long struggled to balance competing public and academic agendas and have often called the university into question in regard to its public role. The more recent service learning movement has a nationally-recognized voice and following in English studies (Zlotkowski; Deans). However, at present, I think the university–English studies dialogue is restricted to particular areas (service learning, for instance) and triggered by local causes. For the long term health of both the university and English studies, we need to broaden this discussion.

THE DEFINITION OF ENGLISH STUDIES

When we consider the shape of English studies in recent years, we face a dilemma simply characterizing "English": literature? composition and literature? literature in English only? theory? cultural studies? creative writing? literacy and linguistics? And should it be the Department of English Studies or the Department of English? While open intellectual territory can be stimulating, the current fluidity in definitions of English studies challenges departments needing to retain some institutional and disciplinary shape. A scholarly community depends on a common language and shared areas of inquiry. The resources for sustained intellectual inquiry are for the most part within the university. The university depends on some stability in definition in order to distribute those resources with confidence in their usefulness. Likewise, the presentation of a course of study requires faculty consensus about knowledge and skills for students to acquire and a conversation for them to join—assuming that an undergraduate major invites students into a conversation they will engage in beyond college.

What adds an edge to these intradisciplinary dialogues is the perceived weakening in the status of English studies in the university curriculum. The Report of the ADE Ad Hoc Committee on the English Major contextualizes the decline in English degrees awarded between the 1960s and the late-1990s within other trends, including cyclical patterns of enrollments in liberal arts majors, expansion of opportunities for women, changes in teacher licensure requirements, and the impact of changing demographics on higher education (Schramm et al. 68–91). This report cautions against attributing enrollment shifts to curricular content, but the authors note that programs that undertake "periodic curricular review and reform" that "strengthen[s] curricular cohesiveness" are likely in the best position to attract majors (86). The report emphasizes that numbers alone do not measure the strength or quality of the English major (85), though it notes that enrollment numbers factor into administrative decisions about resources (68). The report also makes the important point that what may be perceived as fragmentation may actually be healthy curricular diversity (69). My contention is that a dialogue between English studies and the university may be a way to cohere this healthy diversity, to stave off curricular and administrative fragmentation, and to help the university think critically and pragmatically about its purpose.

One of the most significant internal debates on both a disciplinary level (e.g., what constitutes "English studies"?) and an institutional level (e.g., how do we organize to make "English studies" happen?) focuses on the relationship between composition and literature and the relationship of each of these to cultural studies and theory. As we enter the twenty-first century, in an interesting reversal of ranks, composition—the discipline often taught by marginalized faculty with unmanageable workloads—"represents a world of hope" (Bloom, Daiker, and White 277); literature, on the other hand, "does not have much of a public rationale for itself" (Bérubé 32), despite its legacy of prominence within English departments. I think Bérubé's comment about the status of literary study points to why composition has optimism about its future. Despite nagging inequalities in faculty status and the complexities associated with its "gatekeeper" role in the university, composition has multiple public roles. Many of these are aligned with broader university missions. In contrast, the study of literature seems to have lost its public rationale. Once the core of the teaching of Western humanities in required courses, now literature is often found as an option on a humanities menu within a distributive general education program (Graff, *Professing* 171).

Those who analyze the current state of studies in English often blame theory or cultural studies for the decline in the status of literature (Levine 1–4; Scholes 28; Spellmeyer 127–36). One of the main charges against theory is that it has no moorings in what constitutes a "relevant" education—contemporary theory destabilizes knowledge and authority and thus undermines agency and action. Cultural studies generally fares better in these critiques, whether understood to be the legacy of a nineteenth-century poet-critics (Graff and Robbins

422–24), or a product of contemporary political critique (Graff et al. 29–30). Neither heritage makes contemporary cultural studies palatable to all; Levine sees a threat in making literature "indistinguishable from other forms of language" and "merely another part of the culture" (2), and Readings sees cultural studies as having been deployed as "the discipline that will save the University by giving it back its lost truth" (18). Whether cultural studies might be the old "humanities" on a steroid of theory or a new field created by the expansion of the canon and the influence of cultural materialism, it is a significant component in the definition of English studies.

When we turn to composition, we find a healthier internal dialogue than literature—if by "healthier" we mean that scholars in composition studies appear to be debating multiple directions for development as opposed to survival as a discipline. Indeed, the "world of hope" in Bloom, Daiker, and White's previous comment actually refers to the act of "conceiving, constructing, changing any field" (277). The possibilities for composition's future range from common cause with education for work and civic life (Berlin, "English" 223), to an immersion in community-based learning (Deans), to a focus on "Writing" (North 202), to a concern with literacy (Yagelski 6–12), to a liberation from required freshman writing (Crowley 241–43), to name a very few of the many proposals (Bloom, Daiker, and White; Gere). Composition may have this abundance of futures because, as Gere notes, "questions about the nature of discourse, writing, and subjectivity emerge from mutually defining stances" as various disciplines inquire into the nature of discourse, reality, and subjectivity (4). Berlin finds that, historically, the "college writing course [. . .] responds quickly to changes in society" (*Rhetoric* 5). Needless to say, composition benefits from the perception, largely external to composition itself, that writing skills are marketable, useful, and transportable from context to context, including from the academy to the workplace.

However, simply to propose that composition rescue literature or keep it on life support is to miss an opportunity for dialogue with agendas at play beyond departmental walls. Before presenting my own proposal, let me review four proposals for English studies alongside the key ideas of diversity, pragmatism, and values from the "education for democracy" discourse. The four versions I will use are representative, not definitive, directions for English studies currently under discussion: Michael Bérubé's proposal for "literatures in English"; Shirley

Brice Heath's proposal for a community-based writing and literature; Kurt Spellmeyer's proposal for a renewed aesthetic-historical teaching of literature and interdisciplinary writing; and Jonathan Culler's proposal for a general-education focus to English studies.

Bérubé characterizes the choices for literary study, or English, as four: "cultural studies and eventual doom-by-duplication; literary studies and eventual doom-by-irrelevance; cultural studies and prosperity with the nascent professional-managerial class; literary studies and prosperity with everyone who wants to study the aesthetic uses of language" (25–26). His proposal, however, is not for one of these four, but for a curriculum "center[ed] [. . .] on the global ramifications of the world travels of the language first spoken on the British Isles" (32). The strength of writing in the curriculum may erode the place of both literary studies and cultural studies, but a "literatures in English" program offers cultural studies fused with a literary curriculum: "whereas the original institutionalization of the literature curriculum, in the United Kingdom and the United States, had clearly served the purposes of nationalism and particularism, a 'literatures in English' curriculum explicitly presents nationalism not as an assumption but as an object of interrogation" (31). Bérubé's curriculum would provide the diversity, the critical skills, and the texts for exploration of values called for in an "education for democracy," and in its interrogation of nationalism, the kind of fruitful critical dialogue I envision emerging between English studies and the university. However, in looking for a solution to the literary studies/cultural studies divide, Bérubé does not include writing. Without finding a way for writing to be a part of this English studies program, Bérubé loses a significant strategy for bringing literature and cultural studies together and for finding a pragmatic way to interrogate the values and concepts of nationalism, language, gender, that these literary texts invite.

Heath imagines that a different curriculum will require a different structure for the work of English studies—and the work will not always take place within the university:

> [Colleges] will first build networks [. . .] to job opportunities, community-based organizations, and health-delivery systems. Within these networks, they will link communication skills, oral and written, to a host of needs—social, aesthetic, personal, as well as vocational. [. . .] Would-be writers and readers in

> some classes selected for aesthetic and personal expres-
> sion will receive the benefit of instructors' guidance
> in choosing materials and composing their own poet-
> ry, stories, and dramas. Reference skills, editing skills
> for would-be publishers, and aids to journal keeping
> and poetry techniques will be the norm within such
> groups who see their involvement with literature for
> its aesthetic and personal functions, with no illusion
> about direct transfer to job skills. (236–37)

Heath's proposal for a significant departure from the conventional structures of university English studies programs responds to the continuing marginalization of students based on class and ethnicity and the marginalization of the "gateway" writing courses. She advocates a direct relevance of education to productive work and a need to disillusion literary study from the claims that it offers "transportable" knowledge and skills. In the real world of jobs and securing a viable career path, literature as "cultural capital" is not particularly useful. It is, however, a source of aesthetic pleasure and should be treated as such. Heath's proposal is similar to programs that seek to locate education in the community, rather than in the classroom. Truly, students in programs like these have the opportunity to practice the arts of democracy and community building in a direct way; they have a pragmatic education and the opportunity to explore questions of value and meaning in the ample writing she envisions. Yet, could a rich, experiential program like this one be strengthened with some form of "cultural capital," be it literatures in English or cultural studies?

Spellmeyer, like Heath, advocates a program in English that does offer "attention to the problems [students] will have to address, and the skills they will need in order to improve on our common life" (245). However, his rationale is quite different. Based on a critical narrative of "The Trouble with English," a chapter title in *Arts of Living*, Spellmeyer proposes a reinfusion of historicism in the teaching of literature: "I want my students to find connections for themselves between the writer's work and the crises of the day, and between the writer's time and their own. And once students find these connections, they will have carried out the most essential work of the arts, whether or not their activities qualify as 'literary'" (168). These connections of arts to life make the arts, particularly literary art, a means "to transform our passive politics by first changing the character of the private life"

(220). To do this, literature needs to be freed from theory and critical perspectives that make it solely an object of analysis. Spellmeyer argues that it is possible to read literature in the academy directly, without theory, and through that to gain a sense of agency and purpose and ultimately a democratization of culture. Though he sees the possibility for the reading of literature in the academy to be a challenge to "passive politics," his proposals for the new aesthetic-historical reading of literature could be significantly enriched by some direct link to the community. It is not clear how this reading will be a direct challenge to "passive politics" if its implications remain theoretical. In his "Postscript" to *Arts of Living,* Spellmeyer offers his richest vision for the future of English studies: the interdisciplinary first-year writing course. This course, as taught at Rutgers and as described by Spellmeyer, has students addressing directly the challenges of the present and explicitly supporting them in exploring how "to think and to act in ways beyond the imaginings of most of their professors" (246).

Finally, Culler offers several ways of "Imagining the Coherence of the English Major." He concludes with a proposal for framing the major in terms of processes of analysis, which "include literary and rhetorical analysis, historical analysis, social analysis, cultural analysis, cognitive and moral analysis, and the practice of writing" (92). These varieties of analysis identify English studies as "comprehensive" and "central" to intellectual inquiry, thus making English studies a form of general education (92). However, the reliance on analytical practice leaves little room for other ways of thinking about and exploring literature and for using writing as a means to learn. Although general education goals are most often the place that a university seeks to enact its master narrative, Culler's version of English studies would have few direct ways of engaging a master narrative of education for democracy other than the cultivation of individual analytical practices and the discussion of questions.

I hope that the review of these four perspectives shows the possibility of a dialogue—a genuine dialogue that enriches both the university and the discipline. Admittedly, I find each of the four proposals outlined above wanting in relationship to some aspect of the "education for democracy" focus of the university. It is entirely possible that each of these proposals, reframed in terms of the "education for democracy" discourse, could respond to and critique that discourse. My test of the value of this discourse for English studies is in the curriculum that I propose: a curriculum that presents composition/writing and literature/culture as interrelated acts in the field of language. English studies can offer students an opportunity to explore traditional understandings of knowledge and aesthetic experience and to construct knowledge of self and world by linking the local and global, the personal and social.

The "fused" version of English studies provides grounding in disciplinary knowledge defined by composition, literature, and cultural studies; a disciplinary organization; and a relevance to life in a democracy. Instead of dividing the aesthetic and critical, the rhetorical and cultural into separate courses, or separate tracks, or dominant positions within a major, an English studies curriculum should seek to bring its broad and fluid disciplinary stream into focus within individual courses as well as the program of study. My proposal has sympathy with Scholes's desire to "put students in touch with a usable cultural past" and to "help students attain an active relationship with their cultural present" (104). It is comparable in philosophy to Berlin's concepts ("English" 223–25), except that it seeks to bring together literature and composition. It has considerable consonance with Spellmeyer's conception of interdisciplinary composition and literature without theory, though with more direct ties to the community. My proposal is similar to Alan W. France's proposal in "Dialects of Self: Structure and Agency as the Subject of English," though with a different grounding. Citing Newman, France sees his curriculum as suitable for "anyplace [. . .] still subscribing to the traditional mission of liberal arts education: Cultivating the intellect as 'its own proper object'" (151). I have tried to imagine a curriculum growing out of a dialogue between the "education for democracy" project for the university and the carnival of disciplines encompassed in English studies that would cultivate the life of the mind and the life in the world.

What would this look like? While not all courses would "fuse" the strands of English studies, a core of courses within the major should do this, and they might look like these: In a "First-Year Reading and Writing" course, college students mentor elementary students in reading and writing, paralleling the college students' own task of expanding their reading and writing skills. The function of literacy within social contexts is a key subject for reading and writing assignments. In an upper-level course "Victorian Literature: Progress and Community," students explore the question of what happens to community in the face of technological revolution. By paralleling the depiction of the industrial revolution in key novels with local experiences of bringing technological change to economically disadvantaged populations, students have the opportunity to parallel the concerns of the Victorians about industry, technology, and community with the technological changes of our present and to consider how the novel functions to interrogate these changes. An upper-level course titled "Immigrant Voices: Literature and Writing" requires students to read literature and memoirs by immigrants and work with new immigrants on projects of writing narratives. Students analyze forms of expression that immigrant literature and narratives take, become partners in the crafting of such expressions, and reflect on their reading and service through journals, class dialogues, and sessions with the immigrant community members. A final example is a course that can be either introductory or advanced: at my university, this course is titled "Writing Nashville." In this course students explore an urban environment through their own writing and the writing of others. The class compiles a body of literature about Nashville that can then become its own subject of study about community and discourse.

These courses have been taught in some form by colleagues at my university. What kind of curricular frame could contextualize these courses? In what ways could students make connections to other English courses? Because all of these courses make use of composition, literature, and cultural studies, these courses require students to understand the theoretical dimensions of these particular discourses. Alongside critical theory, students need discussion of pedagogies, the institution of the university, and English studies as a discipline. I also think a "fused" curriculum works best in tandem with some "pure" courses in literary/cultural history, genre courses, and writing courses. The courses could be framed by introductory seminars and senior capstone courses. The courses could also be framed by a humanities focus, with courses on epistemology, aesthetics, and ethics linked to these offerings.

Pedagogies in these classes reproduce the goals of these classes. One of the main goals for students in the "education for democracy" framework is the achievement of a sense of self and a sense of agency. France proposes that this can happen through writing assignments that require students to "occasion serious intellectual inquiry into the formation of the self as well as the articulation of selfhood" (163). It is that "articulation of selfhood" that is part of recognizing agency. The other part of this project of acquiring agency is in action in the world; as Deans puts it, students "see themselves as participants *in* that world, not just spectators of it" (xi–xii). Students formulate a sense of self and agency through the direct engagement with the other, with difference. One point of that direct engagement is literature; another is culture, broadly construed; another is the other person and/or the other community. Ideally, a student would have frequent opportunities for all three of these engagements with difference and the opportunity to make and explore the meanings through writing.

These classrooms are deliberately de-centered, and the community component provides an external frame of reference for the knowledge constructed by the student. This definition of an "engaged," community-oriented pedagogy results not from an *a priori* commitment to service or community-based learning, but results from thinking about these courses in light of the "education for democracy" project. There is no hope for even a beginning point for civic engagement without getting students authentically civically engaged. Responsibly used service learning pedagogies, with the emphasis on reciprocity with the community and reflection on the service experience, have been shown to be effective learning experiences (Giles and Eyler). All these courses are "writing intensive," but rather than considering writing as an "add on" for literature classes, these are actually writing and reading courses. The writing is not conceived as a vehicle for mastering and showing control over the meaning of a literary work, but as a means of making meaning, be it critical, analytical, creative, or expressive. All courses would use multiple modes of writing, particularly in relationship to literature.

All four courses engage the three components I have identified in the education for democracy dialogue: diversity, pragmatism, and values. They are effective for having both a context in theory and traditional studies of literature, culture, and writing, and a point of reference that is external to the discipline. First, students have a chance to connect these courses to learning in other courses that have ties to questions about culture, social, political, and civic life today. Second, students are invited to think about the relationship between knowledge and civic life—not something for the future but for the present. Third, students have a position from which to critique their experiences as English studies majors. Finally, by having a point of reference, a site of learning that is not solely the classroom, students have an opportunity to assess the role of the university in the community. The "education for democracy" framework is not to be approached uncritically—and by positioning the students outside the university for a part of their education, they have a point from which to observe the university in relationship to the community.

It is possible to construe this whole project of a fused curriculum as Bérubé's options three and four—using cultural studies and literary studies to make English studies popular. If we pull in John Guillory's analysis of English/cultural studies as the production of cultural capital for the nascent professional-managerial class, we do face the charge that we are substituting a new cultural capital comprised of literature and writing with some experiential learning for the traditional cultural capital comprised of cultural studies with some theory. If we frame the university in cultural materialist terms, indeed we may see a new project in any area as a reconfiguration of the university to the services of a professional-managerial class or to a convenient marketing strategy. As a counter to this limiting cultural-materialist box for English studies—and indeed all the liberal arts—as merely cultural capital for a managerial class, a fused writing/literature curriculum that has significant learning rooted in the community has the potential to destabilize conventional formulations of knowledge and to serve "the *counterweight* function in American society" (Edgerton 50). Both the often-invoked purpose of English to "serve" the needs of professional education and the language of cultural materialism that pictures English in service to master narratives deny English studies the potential of genuine efficacy in the context of the purpose of the university, and genuine efficacy in educating students to an authentic, critical agency within and without the university.

Against the materialist and "service" readings of the purpose of English studies, I want to put Dewey's version of the purpose of education cited earlier, emphasizing an education for "personal initiative and adaptability" necessary for students to cope with "the changes in which they are caught" (87–88). I take Dewey's formulation seriously because it seems all the more true in our age of internet, international communications, and instant messaging. Stanley Fish's argument that we cannot claim to educate beyond the academic is an appealing safety net. In accepting that safety net, however, we may imprison ourselves in a present that is violent and unjust, and we may lose the energy of one of the best-equipped institutions, and the rich, complex discipline of English studies, to address our collective problems. Nussbaum's call to the humanities is, I think, directly relevant to English studies:

> Our campuses educate our citizens. Becoming an edu-
> cated citizen means learning a lot of facts and master-
> ing techniques of reasoning. But it means something
> more. It means learning how to be a human being ca-
> pable of love and imagination. [. . .] That is not "po-
> litical correctness"; that is the cultivation of humanity.
> (14)

We simply have no choice but to risk the future of our discipline and our institutions of higher education for the sake of fashioning a true education for democracy.

Works Cited

Association of American Colleges and Universities. *The Drama of Diversity and Democracy: Higher Education and American Commitments.* Washington, DC: Association of American Colleges and Universities, 1995.

—. "Statement on Liberal Learning." Association of American Colleges and Universities. Oct. 1998. 1 Aug. 2008 <http://www.aacu.org/about/statements/liberal_learning.cfm>.

Berlin, James A. "English Studies, Work, and Politics in the New Economy." Bloom, Daiker, and White 215–25.

—. *Rhetoric and Reality: Writing Instruction in American Colleges, 1900–1985.* Carbondale, IL: Southern Illinois UP, 1987.

Bérubé, Michael. *The Employment of English: Theory, Jobs, and the Future of Literary Studies.* New York: New York UP, 1998.

Bloom, Lynn Z., Donald A. Daiker, and Edward M. White, eds. *Composition in the Twenty-First Century: Crisis and Change.* Carbondale, IL: Southern Illinois UP, 1996.

Campus Compact. "Campus Compact's Mission and Vision." *National Campus Compact.* 2007. 18 Aug. 2008 <http://www.compact.org/about/vision>.

Culler, Jonathan. "Imagining the Coherence of the English Major." *Profession* (2003): 85–93.

Colby, Anne, Thomas Ehrlich, Elizabeth Beaumont, and Jason Stephens. *Educating Citizens: Preparing American's Undergraduates for Lives of Moral and Civic Responsibility.* San Francisco: Jossey-Bass, 2003.

Crowley, Sharon. *Composition in the University: Historical and Polemical Essays.* Pittsburgh: U of Pittsburgh P, 1998.

Deans, Thomas. *Writing and Community Action: A Service-Learning Rhetoric with Readings*. New York: Longman, 2003.

Dewey, John. *Democracy and Education: An Introduction to the Philosophy of Education*. 1916. New York: Macmillan/Free Press, 1966.

Edgerton, Russell. "Higher Education White Paper." The Pew Charitable Trusts. 1997. 18 Aug. 2008 <http://www.pewtrusts.org/uploadedFiles/wwwpewtrustsorg/Reports/Miscellaneous/HIGHERED%20-%20White%20Paper.pdf>.

France, Alan W. "Dialectics of Self: Structure and Agency as the Subject of English." *College English* 63 (2000): 145–65.

Fish, Stanley. "Aim Low." *Chronicle of Higher Education*. 16 May 2003: C5.

Gere, Anne Ruggles, ed. *Into the Field: Sites of Composition Studies*. New York: MLA, 1993.

Giles, Dwight, and Janet Eyler. *Where's the Learning in Service Learning?* San Francisco: Jossey-Bass, 1999.

Gladieux, Lawrence E., and Jacqueline E. King. "Federal Government and Higher Education." *American Higher Education in the TwentyFirst Century: Social, Political, and Economic Challenges*. Ed. Philip G. Altbach, Robert O. Berdahl, and Patricia J. Gumport. Baltimore: Johns Hopkins UP, 1999. 151–82.

Graff, Gerald. *Professing Literature: An Institutional History*. Chicago: U of Chicago P, 1987.

Graff, Gerald, and Bruce Robbins. "Cultural Criticism." *Redrawing the Boundaries: The Transformation of English and American Literary Studies*. Ed. Stephen Greenblatt and Giles Gunn. New York: MLA, 1992.

Graff, Gerald, Janice Radway, Gita Rajan, and Robert Con Davis. "A Dialogue on Institutionalizing Cultural Studies." *English Studies/Culture Studies: Institutionalizing Dissent*. Ed. Isaiah Smithson and Nancy Ruff. Urbana, IL: U of Illinois P, 1994. 25–42.

Guillory, John. *Cultural Capital: The Problem of Literary Canon Formation*. Chicago: U of Chicago P, 1993.

Heath, Shirley Brice. "Work, Class, and Categories: Dilemmas of Identity." Bloom, Daiker, and White 226–42.

Kegan, Robert. *In Over Our Heads: The Mental Demands of Modern Life*. Cambridge: Harvard UP, 1994.

Kimball, Bruce A. "Naming Pragmatic Liberal Education." *Education and Democracy: Re-imagining Liberal Learning in America*. Ed. Robert Orrill. New York: College Entrance Examination Board, 1997. 45–67.

Levine, George, ed. *Aesthetics and Ideology*. New Brunswick: Rutgers UP, 1994.

Mann, Sheilah. "What the Survey of American College Freshmen Tells Us About Their Interest in Politics and Political Science." *PS: Political Science and Politics* (June 1999): 263–68.

Newman, John Henry. *The Idea of a University*. Ed. Frank M. Turner. New Haven, CT: Yale UP, 1996.

North, Stephen M. "The Death of Paradigm Hope, the End of Paradigm Guilt, and the Future of (Research in) Composition." Bloom, Daiker, and White 194–207.

Nussbaum, Martha. *Cultivating Humanity: A Classical Defense of Reform in Liberal Education*. Cambridge: Harvard UP, 1997.

Orrill, Robert. "Editor's Prologue." *Education and Democracy: Re-Imagining Liberal Learning in America*. Ed. Robert Orrill. New York: College Entrance Examination Board, 1997. xiii–xxvi.

Putnam, Robert D. *Bowling Alone: The Collapse and Revival of American Community*. 2000. New York: Simon and Schuster, 2001.

"Programs that Really Work." *U.S. News & World Report: America's Best Colleges*. 2003: 113–14.

Readings, Bill. *The University in Ruins*. Cambridge: Harvard UP, 1996.

Scholes, Robert. *The Rise and Fall of English: Reconstructing English as a Discipline*. New Haven, CT: Yale UP, 1998.

Schramm, Margaret, J. Lawrence Mitchell, Delores Stephen, and David Laurence. "The Undergraduate English Major." *ADE Bulletin* 134–135 (2003): 68–91.

Spellmeyer, Kurt. *Arts of Living: Reinventing the Humanities for the Twenty-First Century*. Albany: SUNY P, 2003.

United States Department of Housing and Urban Development. Office of Community Partnerships. "Capacity Building Efforts Empower Communities to Help Themselves." *COPC Central*. Summer 2003. 18 Aug. 2008 <http://www.oup.org/files/pubs/newsletter/COPCSummer03.pdf>.

Yagelski, Robert P. *Literacy Matters: Writing and Reading the Social Self*. New York: Teachers College Press, 2000.

Zlotkowski, Edward. *Successful Service-Learning Programs: New Models of Excellence in Higher Education*. Bolton, MA: Anker, 1998.

9 A Socially Constructed View of Reading and Writing: Historical Alternatives to "Bridging the Gap"

Lynée Lewis Gaillet

As composition emerges as a discipline concerned with literacy, technology, and social change, departments of English defining themselves by "literary rather than literacy studies" are fast becoming antiquated "classics departments of the twenty-first century" (Miller 33). This dichotomous relationship often described in English studies scholarship is avoidable. Rather than retreat to our separate (but equal?) corners, English department faculty need to explore ways in which our goals are similar. The reduction of a comprehensive view of rhetoric into modern, mutually exclusive departments of study (literature, writing, grammar, speech, philosophy, etc.) will only lead to further separation of the arts and sciences associated with rhetoric, evident in the current secession of writing instruction/study from traditional departments of English in colleges and universities across the country. The recent proliferation of historical studies addressing composition and rhetoric and the rise and formations of English departments helps us to understand the current rift between literature and composition—and the role cultural and civic concerns play in that separation—but much scholarly work remains to be done in order to "bridge the gap" defined by Winifred Bryan Horner and others in 1983.

A review of historical educational models outside traditional English departments reveals teaching plans based on the holistic integration of many areas of study now typically falling within the domain of English studies. For example, George Jardine, eighteenth-century Scottish academician, forged a unique model of language studies in

his logic and philosophy classes at the University of Glasgow by rejecting traditional theories of higher education and instead attending to
student needs. Examining the contributions of academic predecessors
like Jardine reveals how the goals of civic humanism, appreciation and
analysis of *belle lettres*, and the acquisition of writing skills share a symbiotic relationship within English studies.

THE TWENTIETH-CENTURY LIT/COMP DEBATE

The North American debate over the place of literature in first-year
writing instruction has a long history dating back to the turn of the
century when the Pedagogical Section of the MLA questioned the relationship between reading and writing, asking, "Was good reading
alone sufficient to develop good writers, or was additional training
necessary? If so, what should be the nature of this training be?" (qtd. in
Stewart 20). A majority of participants recommended reading supple-
mented by good instruction in composition. The next year (1902), the
Pedagogical Section also questioned whether the teaching of composition should be "principally a practical business or whether it should be
authorship, the production of literature." Again, the majority of participants called for a resolution, a marriage of composition and literature (Stewart 20). However, the MLA's groundbreaking resolution was
not enacted. Not until 1983 with the publication of *Composition and
Literature: Bridging the Gap,* edited by Winifred Bryan Horner, did the
field see the theoretical and professional issues raised by the MLA at
the turn of the century thoughtfully considered in its scholarship. At
this time, scholars and teachers responded to the lit/comp issue because
of the "widening gulf between research and teaching in literature and
research and teaching in composition" (Horner 1). Literary study had
become the major preoccupation of our departments, and, thus, was
rewarded by tenure and promotion while the study and teaching of
composition was regarded as a peripheral activity, "a barely tolerated
stepchild" (Stewart 22). This gulf has been narrowed and supplanted
by other concerns in the last twenty-plus years, but the issue remains
unresolved over the role belletristic literature should play in writing
instruction, evidenced in controversies surrounding first-year writing
curricula, published debates in journals, and postings on listservs.

Ten years after the publication of *Composition and Literature,* Erika
Lindemann and Gary Tate's discussion of "Two Views on the Use of
Literature in Composition" appeared in the March 1993 issue of *Col-*

lege English, spawning renewed interest in the debate. Tate and Lindemann addressed issues raised in Horner's work, questioning the purpose of writing instruction and that of education itself. I'm oversimplifying a bit, but in general the 1990s scholarship concerning the role of literature in first-year writing courses can be divided into two (rather reductive) camps: the view of writing instruction as a "service" course for the academy and the community at large, valuing academic and workplace modes of writing vs. the view of writing instruction as a "humanist" course, focusing on the intrinsic value of writing as an expression of ideas. In arguing against including literature in a writing course, Lindemann claims that composition classes should provide "guided practice in reading and writing the discourses of the academy and the professions" (312). As a spokesperson for this group of scholars, Edward P. J. Corbett explains that they fear

> literature is so attractive to the typical English teacher
> and can be made so attractive to students that it often
> turns out to be a distraction from the main objective
> of a composition course, which is to teach students
> how to write the kind of utilitarian prose they will be
> asked to produce in their other college classes and later
> on in their jobs. (180)

Most writing program administrators (WPAs), those who supervise teaching assistants and adjuncts, find this concern still valid. Consider this common scenario: my institution employs approximately one hundred teaching assistants annually to teach first-year composition— most of these apprentice teachers are pursuing advanced degrees in literature, not rhetoric/composition. Understandably, they want to share their passion for literary analysis with their students, a desire often in conflict with the established learning outcomes for our institution's first-year writing courses. When denied both extensive training in composition instruction and the opportunity to teach what they know, these new teachers become disillusioned, threatened, and often subversive in curriculum design matters. Ultimately, students, teachers, and writing programs suffer by ignoring these teachers' frustrations.

On the other side of the 1990s debate are scholars who believe that literature and composition are intrinsically connected. Anthony Petrosky succinctly defines this position:

> [O]ne of the most interesting results of connecting
> reading, literary, and composition theory and peda-
> gogy is that they yield similar explanations of human
> understanding as a process rooted in the individu-
> al's knowledge and feelings and characterized by the
> fundamental act of making meaning, whether it be
> through reading, responding, or writing. [. . .] Our
> theoretical understandings of these processes are con-
> verging [. . .] around the central role of human under-
> standing—be it of texts or the world—as a process of
> composing. (26)

I see the validity of this position and embrace the humanist philosophy
of education; however, the majority of writing instructors (particularly
in large institutions where inexperienced instructors or adjuncts teach
the bulk of first-year writing courses) are new to composition theory
and pedagogy while viewing themselves as accomplished reader-crit-
ics. These teachers often lack the experience, education, and interest
to engage in Petrosky's view of instruction. This dichotomous relationship is frustrating for both teaching supervisors and instructors
alike, often resulting in either vast differences between individual sections of the course as teachers independently develop curriculum and
pedagogy according to their own interests, or rigid instruction (often
uninformed) dictated by a prescribed text and syllabus mandated by
the department. In supervising large numbers of teaching assistants
interested primarily in literary studies, I've become increasingly em-
pathetic over the years with writing specialists who advocate secession
from traditional English departments and those who favor abolishing
first-year writing instruction in favor of writing across the discipline
approaches to writing. However, I don't see either of those alternatives
offering sustainable solutions to the (often oversimplified) plight of
English departments, which now often include the study of literature,
composition, technical and professional writing, cultural studies, creative writing, and secondary education.

   In seeking solutions or bridges to span the widening "gaps" in
educational philosophies and practices within multifaceted English
departments, it becomes increasingly obvious that we must look for
shared departmental and institutional concerns, adopt overriding goals
rather than building bridges, nurture symbiotic relationships with related disciplines and non-academic communities. In *Composition and/*

or Literature: The End(s) of Education (2006), edited by Linda S. Bergmann and Edith M. Baker, contributors explore the schisms between literature and composition instructors, suggesting ways the two disciplines might join forces rather than simply forge a bridge. Insightfully, many contributors recommend (among other pedagogical theories and strategies) that instructors adopt a philosophy of civic engagement and emphasize the reading process rather than the study of literature in beginning first-year classes. This work holds great promise, but the overall results are less than satisfying despite the forward-looking and philosophically sound recommendations of select contributors, in part because the tone of the work ultimately stresses the existing schizophrenia found between the two disciplines rather than focusing on potentialities for revisioning first-year instruction. In particular, readers and reviewers find the book to be extremely one-sided. As reviewer Melody Heffner explains, "According to Mary T. Segall, whose essay closes the book, students are the 'missing voices' in the conversation, but one could also argue that the exclusion of literary scholars constitutes another group of missing voices." The debate continues between the two camps.

A HISTORICAL PLAN FOR INTEGRATING READING, WRITING, AND CRITICAL LITERACY

As a discipline, we often neglect to search for historical educational models outside of English studies, a twentieth-century configuration. Many of these earlier teaching plans offer concrete examples of ways to incorporate civic engagement and to blend reading/writing skills in introductory courses. Beyond our own relatively new field of study exist interdisciplinary examples of enlightened curriculum—often based on cultural and social circumstances foreshadowing in limited ways our own educational climates, students' needs, and multi-faceted departments. Consider, for example, the work of late-eighteenth-century professors of moral philosophy working in the British cultural provinces. In hopes of preparing both local citizenry and university students for better jobs and improved social standing, these professors included the study of English literature, composition, and rhetoric in their college courses—and also in public lectures delivered to citizens interested in social, political, and economic advancement. The study of English literature and lessons in communicative competence offered students a means to personal advancement and skills necessary for civic engagement. Thomas Miller explains, "critical literacy begins with the ability to imagine alternatives, and one way to foster the civic imagination is to teach literature that challenges expectations, makes other experiences knowable, and thereby calls established conventions into question" (41).

Viewing the aims of contemporary English departments in terms of civic rhetoric offers possibilities for revitalizing the study of literature, and allowing composition to break free of the shackles of "skills course" definitions. According to Miller, "[a]s we develop rhetoric and writing into a subject of study, we need to reassess the modern distinction between the arts and sciences that underlies the reduction of literature to nonutilitarian, nonfactual discourse" (41). Teachers adopting a civic philosophy better understand the natural connections between reading and communicative competence (both writing and speaking). Most importantly, students receiving a civic education are fully equipped to enter the public sphere as informed citizens interested in advancing the common good. Historical models of class designs illustrate ways we might (re)envision twenty-first-century English studies curriculum to include philosophies of civic humanism and unify our often divergent areas of study.

In the late–eighteenth-century Scottish universities, we see the emergence of interdisciplinary course designs that prefigure and encompass subjects housed within contemporary English studies departments. In response to changing student needs and cultural/political factors, professors began addressing rhetoric, economics, and ethics while promoting "a conception of language that emphasized the moral value of the study of aesthetics" in their introductory courses (Court 14). For example, Adam Smith—the famous economist—was also Chair of Moral Philosophy and Logic at Glasgow University from 1751 to 1764. During his tenure teaching the moral philosophy class, Smith modified the traditional course curriculum, merging his thoughts on literary criticism with his interests in ethics and economics. Court explains, "The philosophical rationale behind his case for the formal study of English literature was closely connected to his thoughts on 'sympathy' and his argument for the education of the 'good man' (the 'good bourgeois') and 'studious observer'" (12). Smith essentially revised the course curriculum to enable students to link their personal interests with public concerns. For example, Smith believed that the formal study of literary characters' ethical and unethical behavior—

based on "close textual examination and interpretation"—would lead students "to share experiences and feelings over time through a process of associative, imitative identification that naturally approved good acts and deplored evil ones" (Court 12). Smith's influence on curricula typically falling under the auspices of present day English studies is noteworthy. However, Smith's greatest influence in this area is perhaps seen in his students' contributions to rhetorical theory and practice. Hugh Blair and George Jardine, both famous professors of moral philosophy in their own right, codified Smith's changes to Scottish rhetorical education. Blair's treatment of belletristic rhetoric is well documented in the scholarship; however, Jardine's integrated reading and writing curriculum merits further attention.

Jardine offers a model for appropriating Blair's (now famous) interest in belletristic literature in an innovative pedagogy that responds to social and cultural concerns. The following comparison of Jardine's teaching plan with ecological/writing across the curriculum approaches to writing instruction suggests potentialities for contemporary text selection and pedagogy. While belletristic literature was preferred and available during Jardine's day, contemporary teachers might achieve similar results by adopting other available and currently powerful texts—political speeches, 9/11 reports, films and documentaries, advertising, technical reports, websites, etc.

Why Study Jardine?

From his published letters, his work *Outlines of a Philosophical Education* (1818, 1825), and his unpublished letters and lecture notes housed in the Glasgow University Library, we find that George Jardine, Professor of Logic and Philosophy at the University of Glasgow, Scotland, from 1774 to 1824, stressed the value of reading English literature and composing written assignments to help students acquire skills necessary to participate in society. Jardine believed that by integrating writing instruction with the study of English literature, his students would become critical thinkers, improve their communication skills, and learn to write well in other classes. Echoing civic humanism of the day, Jardine's primary educational goal was to prepare his students to compete for better jobs and act locally. Perhaps Jardine adopts belletristic literature as the primary texts in his course because those materials were published and readily available, and also because the eighteenth-century Scottish universities were recently committed to introducing students to the formal study of English literature. A closer examination of his educational theories and practices, however, reveals strong consideration of the blending of rhetorical engagement with student needs.

Maureen Goggin suggests that from a pedagogical perspective, teachers and scholars often view literature as "an object of contemplation in literature classes and one of utility in composition classes" (146). In Jardine's conduct of the first philosophy class at Glasgow, we find a teaching plan offering an alternative to the geopolitical trope of the bridge between composition and literature—a trope that "emphasizes separation and difference" (Gere 617). For Jardine, reading and writing are not separate tasks or disciplines linked by bridges of what Gere labels "good will" and "mutual interest" (617), but rather intrinsically connected epistemic skills.

Jardine's community-based plan for what we call peer-editing and peer-tutoring, and his insistence that his (often rustic and ill-prepared) students study and appropriate "correct English" to succeed in business incorporates socially constructed definitions of reading and writing. Jardine realized the importance of creating a sense of community in his classroom to help his students from diverse educational, social, and cultural backgrounds compete with English students for jobs but also to prepare his students for rhetorical engagement within their own local communities. Jane Peterson urges us to "admit that the original question about the place of literature in freshman composition identified an inappropriate starting point" (314). She encourages us to "displace this spatial metaphor so the field may be freed to think in other, more effective, ways about literature and its relationship to composition" (Goggin 148). The integrated teaching theories and practices of eighteenth- and nineteenth-century Scottish rhetoricians, exemplified by Jardine, shed light on how we might answer Peterson's challenge. Writing instruction and the study of literature should not be treated as mutually exclusive disciplines. Both areas of study are critical in promoting civic humanism and encouraging students to become community intellectuals—worthy educational goals for the twenty-first century as well.

In *Outlines of a Philosophical Education* (1818, 1825), a treatise written for teachers, Jardine explains the "pedagogical potentialities" within the existing Scottish system of general instruction—a system of education that Jardine defended against the specialized instruction found at Oxford and Cambridge. In part two of *Outlines,* Jardine fully described his practical teaching plan designed to help prepare his Scottish students for full participation in British society. His revision of traditional educational goals led Jardine to merge existing studies, to borrow across the disciplines, and to revamp methods of instruction to include reading and writing instruction. Upon taking over the first-year philosophy class at Glasgow, Jardine quickly realized that both curriculum and traditional pedagogy in the Scottish universities were outdated—for both students and the communities they served. As a result of his own observations, which reflected public opinion, Jardine radically revised his class to include student-centered practice in composition and the study of English (rather than Greek and Latin) literary models.

JARDINE'S "ECOLOGICAL" MODEL OF WRITING AND READING INSTRUCTION

In "Three Views of 101," Erika Lindemann describes three ways of approaching first-year writing instruction: (1) writing as product—a content course centered in texts, (2) writing as process—expressivist courses grounded in self discovery, and (3) writing as system—courses based on "ecological models," stressing the social context in which all writers work. Jardine's philosophy of composition instruction in many ways exemplifies contemporary models of "writing as system," a view based on Marilyn Cooper's 1986 ecological model of writing instruction. Yet, he grounds his pedagogy in the belletristic approach to language study of his day. Jardine's philosophy class foreshadows and influences many of the same goals and pedagogical strategies typifying our current community-focused composition classes, but the study of what we call "imaginative literature" is central to Jardine's curriculum in part because the texts were readily available and the study of English literature was in vogue. His teaching practices and principles provide an historical model for us to study as we continue to examine the relationship between literature and composition—and the potentialities of civic rhetoric within a unified lit/comp pedagogical plan. The ecological model is now known by a variety of names within WAC scholarship, but I am citing Lindemann's description of Cooper's clearly delineated, early description of this first-year writing philosophy as a foundation most compositionists recognize as the basis for subsequent course designs. A comparison of the two pedagogical approaches illustrates ways in which Jardine's models might address contemporary concerns within English studies.

As described by Lindemann, "The ecological model suggests that, if students learn the systems and conventions characterizing particular discourse communities, they can successfully participate in and eventually even alter these communities" (296). Likewise, Jardine was attempting to prepare his Scottish students, who in many cases were socially alienated and economically disenfranchised, for full participation within British society. He viewed the study of language (through reading and writing) as the means whereby his students could gain access to economic success:

> [In] every period of education, from first to last, the study of language, including, of course, the formation and expansion of those associations which connect thought and feeling with verbal signs, whether as used by the orator, the poet, or the philosopher, gives full scope and exercise to all the intellectual endowments,—calls into play the imagination, the memory, and the judgment—and gives birth to those rapid processes of thinking, speaking, and writing, which distinguish the accomplished scholar and the intelligent man of business. (*Outlines* 213–14)

To improve their employment opportunities, Jardine encouraged his students to acquire an understanding and appreciation of "correct, chaste and graceful English style" (*Outlines* 489). He finds it reprehensible that in the British educational system of his day, Greek and Latin "are taught in their most minute parts, and occupy a great portion of the time allotted for study [. . .] while the language we ourselves speak and write receives comparatively little attention" (*Outlines* 219). By adapting his course of study to address more practical concerns and introducing his students to the language, grammar, style, ornamentation, and rhetorical figures of English literature, Jardine believed his students improved their own intellectual powers of reasoning and self expression. To that end, Jardine insisted that students study "good models in poetry, eloquence, and history" and learn the "proper method of reading, and of imitating these models" (*Outlines* 218). Through analysis and production of a wide variety of texts (avoiding expressivistic essay topics) Jardine's students gained academic English literacy. For Jardine, the goal of a liberal arts education was to equip the student with the ability to assimilate new knowledge and "to make that knowledge completely his own, by improving the faculties of his understanding" (*Outlines* 275). Jardine's novel teaching plan included traditional lectures, student reading, and—of equal importance—writing instruction and assessment.

Current community-based courses encourage the study of invention, arrangement, and style to determine a particular discourse community's conception of principles of good writing. As Lindemann explains, students must study texts to "understand the community's culture, what subjects it finds worth writing about, how readers and writers relate to one another, what value people place on experience, observation, interpretation, speculation, objectivity, and so on" (298). Jardine first instructed his students in the history of the English language, the grammar and syntax of the language, and stylistic choices and "diversity" based on the "character and talents of individuals, or of nations" (*Outlines* 220–21). In "writing as system "courses, students also study texts of a discourse community to determine the range of flexibility within such concepts as audience, purpose, and style; "[s] tudents come to understand that 'good writing' requires making effective choices in juggling the demands of a task, a language, a rhetoric, and an audience" (Lindemann 298). Jardine introduced his students to English literary models, as representative texts of the British discourse communities in which they wished to participate. Adopting the composition genres categorized by Francis Bacon—(1) memory or historical compositions, (2) reason or philosophical treatises, and (3) imaginative fiction—Jardine explained that these divisions are arbitrary: "there is no composition, under any one of these three heads, which could possibly be executed without the use of all the three faculties" (*Outlines* 221–22). Jardine teaches that each kind of composition integrates itself with others in the way the mind integrates certain operations of reason, emotion, and the will in the production of a composition.

Both views of writing instruction under consideration share a belief that writing is epistemic—that "English 101 can introduce students to some disciplinary assumptions about using language to make knowledge" ("Three Views" 297). To this end, Jardine (like many of his contemporaries) introduced his students to criticism, "the set of rules [. . .] directing what ought to be done and what ought not to be done, and thereby founding, upon the basis of principle, a distinction between good and bad taste" (*Outlines* 234). As Jardine's students study criticism of a discourse community, they begin to find their place in it. He insists that students first read the model essays without assistance from the critics in order to develop their own opinions of taste; then they compare their thoughts and feelings regarding the piece with "those which bear the stamp of authority and of established taste" (*Outlines* 235). Otherwise, Jardine believes the students will adopt the critics' opinions. The primary object of introducing the study of criticism "is to afford to his pupils, from the various sources which reading and reflection have opened up to him, the means of forming for themselves a standard of taste" (*Outlines* 237).

According to Lindemann, "Teachers adopting the ecological model attempt to forge their English 101 classes into a community of writers. [. . .] Community, collaboration, and responsibility are the watchwords" (297). This description characterizes Jardine's teaching plan as well. He believes that the writing students find most useful in college is the kind that prepares them to enter the work force and improve their local communities. He argues that by participating in collaborative-learning settings, students develop interpersonal traits and skills "indispensable at once to the cultivation of science, and to the business of active life" (*Outlines* 394). Jardine believes collaborative work should be an integral part of every classroom because it patterns workplace discourse. Although never explicitly using terms such as "community" and "social context," Jardine fosters collaborative work among his students by creating a sense of community and responsibility within the classroom. In Jardine's plan, all students participate in the peer learning procedures of the class, and all students are responsible to each other under the rules of participation. Unless they adhere to the rules of the community and remain loyal and respectful to each other, the students will be banished from involvement within the community of their peers and denied any advantage associated with participation:

> Such as are found to disobey these injunctions are considered as academical traitors, viewed with contempt and reproach and, if the fact be proved against them, they are subjected to a forfeiture of their privilege [. . .] and deprived of the honours which they themselves may have otherwise deserved. (*Outlines* 390)

Like ecological models of writing instruction, Jardine's teaching plan "reinforces the principle that students really are writing for one another, for the class-as-discourse-community, which will eventually judge their work" ("Three Views" 299). Jardine goes so far as to compare the rules governing the interaction of his students to public communities and suggests that "it would be well for the public if laws of higher authority were as regularly observed, and as seldom violated" as they were in his classroom (*Outlines* 371).[1]

Lindemann explains that in evaluating student writing, some teachers "emphasize communal standards for good writing, standards developed in the context of the English 101 class itself" and claim "with proper training, students can be as capable and conscientious as teachers in evaluating student writing responsibly" ("Three Views" 298–99). Similarly, Jardine designed a plan of peer review whereby students were responsible for examining each other's themes according to his detailed instructions. He claims that by encouraging students to assume responsibility for the academic progress of each other, teachers will foster a notable increase in self-worth and group pride of the students, while also preparing students for responsible participation in society (*Outlines* 374). In regard to the students' marking of themes as compared to his own evaluation, Jardine frequently found justification to prefer the judgment of the students (*Outlines* 393).

Admittedly, Jardine was working in a culture and time fundamentally different from our own, but his integration of reading and writing instruction—combined with his training in civic humanism at the hands of Smith—results in a seamless course design requiring no disciplinary bridge. Jardine's primary motivation for curriculum revision was a desire to produce effective, educated citizens. Jardine himself was committed to community and university service; he was a public/ community intellectual worthy of his students' emulation. Jardine's course was tremendously successful at the University of Glasgow, and his use of writing as an epistemic tool and a method of assessment was adopted by Scottish professors from a range of disciplines, including math and physics (Davie 17).

IMPLICATIONS

For many teaching assistants in my department—both rhet/comp and lit trained—civic rhetoric philosophies and service-learning pedagogies provide the theoretical and pedagogical avenues for blending disciplinary concerns, institutional goals, and teacher/student interests in general education courses. For tenure track English faculty and administrators, the possibilities and potential of civic rhetoric are far greater. In *Scholarship Reconsidered,* the Boyer Commission asks, "Can America's colleges and universities, with all the richness of their resources, be of greater service to the nation and world? Can we define scholarship in ways that respond more adequately to the urgent new realities both within the academy and beyond?" (3). Adoption of philosophies of civic rhetoric provides avenues for refiguring and blending responsibilities defined by the traditional triumvirate of research, teaching, and service and breathes life into traditional English studies. Responding to the Boyer Commission Report, the recently reconfigured Carnegie ranking criteria for colleges and universities, and the growing body of scholarship addressing faculty responsibilities, *Teaching, Research, and Service in the Twenty-first Century English Department: A Delicate Balance,* edited by Ray Wallace and Joe Hardin, fully explores ways in which English faculty can integrate institutional demands and disciplinary interests, in conjunction with cultivating their roles as community intellectuals. Many of the contributors to this collection suggest avenues for "bridging" and merging disciplinary differences within our departments as well.

The abundance of recent scholarship addressing public literacy and public intellectuals (see works by Ellen Cushman, Christian Weisser, Elizabeth Ervin, Thomas Deans, Jeffrey Grabill) combined with an emerging "ethics of care"—made all too real post 9/11 and amidst global terrorism—usher in a climate for renewed interest in rhetorical engagement and interdisciplinary studies. Rather than creating bridges between disciplines, civic humanism in the form of rhetorical engagement and service learning offers an umbrella for a wide range of interests typically housed in the college of arts and sciences. The adoption of civic rhetoric philosophies and pedagogies within the arts and sciences curriculum often culminates in service-learning projects and internships that promote ethical awareness and responsibility, while offering students concrete avenues for employment—reminiscent of the eighteenth- and nineteenth-century Scottish moral philosophy classes based on civic humanism and the acquisition of communicative competencies. In both cases, the study of community-based texts (literature included) and writing instruction are crucial, inseparable endeavors. Our task, then, is not to build better bridges between disciplines and divisions, but rather to seek larger, encompassing philosophies for what we do in English departments, colleges of arts and sciences, and universities.

NOTE

1. For a full discussion of Jardine's plan for peer review, see Gaillet's "An Historical Perspective on Collaborative Learning." *JAC* 14.1 (1994): 93–110.

WORKS CITED

Bergmann, Linda S., and Edith M. Baker. *Composition and/or Literature: The End(s) of Education.* Urbana, IL: NCTE: 2006.

Boyer, Ernest L. *Scholarship Reconsidered: Priorities of the Professoriate.* Lawrenceville, NJ: Princeton UP, 1992.

Cooper, Marilyn. "The Ecology of Writing." *College English* 48 (1986): 364–75.

Corbett, Edward P. J. "Literature and Composition: Allies or Rivals in the Classroom?" *Composition and Literature: Bridging the Gap.* Ed. Winifred Bryan Horner. Chicago: U of Chicago P, 1983. 168–84.

Court, Franklin. *The Scottish Connection: The Rise of English Literary Study in Early America.* Syracuse, NY: Syracuse UP, 2001.

Evidence, Oral and Documentary, Taken and Received by the Commissioners Appointed by His Majesty George IV. July 23rd, 1826; and Re-Appointed by His Majesty William IV, October 12th, 1830; for Visiting the Universities of Scotland. Vol. II. University of Glasgow. London: W. Clowes and Sons, 1837.

Gere, Anne Ruggles. "Composition and Literature: The Continuing Conversation." *College English* 51 (1989): 617–22.

Goggin, Maureen Daly. "Literature." *Keywords in Composition Studies.* Ed. Paul Heilker and Peter Vandenberg. Portsmouth, NH: Boynton/Cook, 1996. 145–50.

Heffner, Melody. Rev. of *Composition and/or Literature: The End(s) of Education,* edited by Linda S. Bergmann and Edith M. Baker. *Composition Studies* 35.1 (2007) <http://www.compositionstudies.tcu.edu/bookreviews/online/35-1/Heffner%20Web.html>.

Horner, Winifred Bryan. *Composition and Literature: Bridging the Gap.* Chicago: U of Chicago P, 1983.

Jardine, George. "Correspondence of Professor Jardine with Baron Mure." *Selections from the Family Papers Preserved at Caldwell.* Ed. William Mure. Paisley: Gardner, 1883.

—. "Lectures to the Logic Class at Glasgow University." MS Gen. 166. University of Glasgow Manuscript Library, Scotland, 1783.

—. "Lectures to the Logic Class at Glasgow University." MS Gen 737. University of Glasgow Manuscript Library, Scotland. 1793–94.

—. "Letters to Robert Hunter." 12 Sept. 1765 to 30 Oct. 1810. MS Gen 507. University of Glasgow Manuscript Library, Scotland.

—. *Outlines of a Philosophical Education, Illustrated by the Method of Teaching the Logic, or, First Class of Philosophy in the University of Glasgow.* Glasgow: A&J Duncan, 1818. 2nd ed. Edinburgh: Oliver and Boyd, 1825.

Lindemann, Erika. "Freshman Composition: No Place for Literature." *College English* 55 (1993): 311–16.

—. "Three Views of English 101." College English 57 (1995): 287–302.

Miller, Thomas. "Rhetoric Within and Without Composition: Reimagining the Civic." *Coming of Age: The Advanced Writing Curriculum.* Ed. Linda K. Shamoon, Rebecca Moore Howard, Sandra Jamieson, and Robert A. Schwegler. Portsmouth, NH: Boynton Cook/Heinemann, 2000: 32–41.

Peterson, Jane. "Through the Looking Glass: A Response." *College English* 57 (1995): 310–18.

Petrosky, Anthony. "From Story to Essay." *College English* 33 (1982): 19–36.

Report Made to His Majesty by a Royal Commission of Inquiry into the State of the Universities of Scotland: Clowes, 1831.

Stewart, Donald. "Some History Lessons for Composition Teachers." *The Writing Teacher's Sourcebook.* Ed. Gary Tate and Edward P. J. Corbett. New York: Oxford UP, 1987. 16–23.

Tate, Gary. "A Place for Literature in Freshman Composition." *College English* 55 (1993): 317–21.

Wallace, Ray, and Joe Hardin. *Teaching, Research and Service in the Twenty-First Century English Department: A Delicate Balance.* Lewiston, NY: Edwin Mellen, 2004.

10 On the Border: Theorizing the Generalist

Matthew T. Pifer

Concern has arisen in recent years regarding the job preparation of English PhDs. Increasingly, new PhDs are taking positions at small colleges and universities that require skills not fully reflected in their education. In the professional literature, this concern has been articulated in terms of a crisis, which has been characterized by debates addressing issues ranging from the disenchantment caused as the number of tenure track positions shrink in the face of increased enrollment, to the chronically deplorable working conditions experienced by part-time and adjunct faculty, and to the struggles faced by full-time faculty as they attempt to respond to changing curricular demands and heavier teaching and research loads in increasingly underfunded departments. These debates include not only a concern for how and why PhDs are being prepared but also a broader concern for the future of higher education as universities become increasingly privatized and, as Stanley Aronowitz notes, "faculties [are transformed] into a casual labor force" and educational excellence is measured almost exclusively in terms of utility, marginalizing those qualitative aspects of an education that are not easily quantified (160). In this essay I argue that a theory of the generalist can help us mitigate this crisis, avoiding the often self-serving rhetoric of dismay and anxiety that tends to dominate it, and begin to refigure the professional opportunities that are already present in it. Indeed, a theory of the generalist connects discussions about curriculum or structural changes to the development of educational aims, or what John Dewey refers to as a purpose:

> [The formation of a purpose] involves (1) observation
> of surrounding conditions; (2) knowledge of what has

happened in similar situations in the past, a knowledge obtained partly by recollection and partly from
the information, advice, and warning of those who
have had a wider experience; and (3) judgment which
puts together what is observed and what is recalled to
see what they signify. (69)

THEORETICAL FRAMEWORK

Dewey's heuristic describes a three part approach that I use in this
effort to articulate a theory of the generalist. Dewey suggests that
any reform in or refiguring of education requires a clear sense of the
situational context, which is composed of the current difficulties facing the reformers and how those difficulties relate to the history of
the discipline. No change can or should be thought to emerge from
a vacuum, and any decision on reform needs to emerge from the dia-
lectic between past practices and contemporary needs. This approach
keeps reforms from becoming mere fashionable reactions, and ensures
that those reforms that are made evolve through broad debate. My approach is founded on these principles.

Rather than articulating a theory of the generalist and then applying it to the realities facing English studies, I feel it is best to work in the
other direction, analyzing how new PhDs are prepared, how that preparation figures in their professional identity, and how both inform the
collaborative practice that has become the norm, the expected form of
exegesis, in the field. The three areas I have selected for analysis are the
points of rupture—those categories defining the debates and disconti-
nuities—that inform the lattice composing the generalist framework.
(1) *Preparation* relates realities of the job market to ideas regarding
curricular reform and how these justify and promote generalism; (2)
professional identity explores the tendencies in scholarship and how a
generalist framework can bring these efforts into conversation; and (3)
practice examines how a generalist framework might affect day-to-day
teaching. These areas do not form a totality, but indicate the points of
contention through which English studies forms new knowledge and
promotes the kinds of collaborative practices that might transform the
discipline and the institution, interrogating Aronowitz's notion that
the best "preparation for the work of the future might be to cultivate
knowledge of the broadest possible kind" (13–14).

THE JOB MARKET

Even though I do not want to suggest that decisions about PhD programs in English studies do or should revolve solely around the veri-
ties of the job market, I do realize that these realities weigh heavily
upon the discipline's practitioners, who, among other ambitions, first
seek a job—a job which will make possible their subsequent social
and cultural contributions. Therefore, the market provides sometimes
subtle but often overt indicators of what knowledge and skills English
departments and, to a significant but fortunately lesser degree, their
institutions find valuable (at least worth offering a salary, even if that
salary does not include tenure or benefits).

It follows then that in preparing PhDs we need to take into account
the realities of the job market. As numerous sources have reported,
most new PhDs who secure a tenure-track position do so in departments at small colleges and universities (those non-PhD granting institutions). However, either securing a tenure-track job or a job at all is
uncertain. What it boils down to is that there are too few jobs to meet
the needs of an ever-increasing number of new and unemployed PhDs.
In *Refiguring the PhD in English Studies,* Stephen North describes the
corporate logic that has created this condition. He notes that the "erosion in the number of full-time tenure track faculty lines" (233) has
coincided with reductions in funding for English departments and increases in enrollments. This situation led the ADE Ad Hoc Committee
on Staffing to state in a 1999 report that "trends in PhD production,
PhD placement, and staffing of undergraduate courses indicates that
the opportunity costs and sheer human waste associated with graduate
education have increased dramatically since 1988 and are approaching
an unacceptably high level that forebodes serious difficulties for higher
education" (278). Current trends in the job market suggest that these
difficulties have indeed come to pass.

The results of this corporate logic have been described by MLA
and ADE *ad hoc* committees responsible for examining the state of the
profession. In the 2002 issue of *Profession,* the MLA Ad Hoc Committee on the Professionalization of PhDs reports that of the 2,548
job seekers in 2001–02, only 1,162 (46 percent) secured a tenure track
position (206). Supplementing these statistics are the findings of the
MLA Committee on Community Colleges, which in the 2003 issue
of *Profession* suggest a location for many of these elusive jobs: "As the
Final Report of the MLA Committee on Professional Employment pointed

out [in 1997], 'In the United States over 90% of English programs and most likely between one-half and two-thirds of the total number of professorial-rank appointments are located outside doctorate-granting institutions'" (164). Unlike the more coveted research positions at larger universities, these positions typically require professors to teach three, and often more, sections a semester (between nine and sixteen credit hours a term), including a heavy load of general education courses (sometimes referred to as service courses) such as first-year composition. These demands leave professors little time or energy to pursue the types of research projects many had expected to be the primary criteria for their professional advancement, those projects that would define their professional identity and ensure their success.

However, these statistics and the conclusions drawn from them are not all negative. Running counter to this rhetoric of crisis have been voices arguing for the professional possibilities that might be present in this so-called crisis. These voices tend to see change and reform as a more or less necessary process in any intellectual discipline and endeavor. Even a leisurely glance at history supports such an attitude (recalling, of course, that this history also documents that such reform has always been contentious for those involved). Taking a second look at the statistics compiled in the 1999 ADE report on staffing, one notes that in 1996–1997, 42 percent of "all undergraduate course sections taught" in doctoral granting institutions were first-year composition courses, most of which were taught by underpaid and underrepresented graduate-teaching assistants, part-time lectureships, and adjuncts (276–77). These statistics have been used to call attention to the deplorable state of adjuncts and teaching assistants in the discipline, but they also indicate that writing and the rhetorical issues associated with it are still central to any college curriculum. As James Berlin argues, "the materials and methods of all courses should be organized around text interpretation and construction [. . .] leading to a revised concept of both reading and writing as acts of textual production" (xxii).

When this focus on writing is combined with jobs that highly value teaching, we arrive at the nexus suggested in Berlin's description of the classroom: "I argue that the classroom should become the center of disciplinary activities" (xxi–xxii). What becomes binding among practitioners in this field, the place where their various discourses (research and writing) interact to create knowledge, is teaching. Teaching, and the teaching of writing, which is the "primary means of exchange" in nearly every discipline (North xiv), can be understood as, in effect, the methodology of the generalist.

PREPARATION

What the realities of the job market suggest is that what is valued in most new PhDs often runs counter to their graduate preparation. The MLA Ad Hoc Committee on Teaching notes in its report published in the 2001 issue of *Profession* that "Research, by and large, has focused on textual study from various theoretical perspectives. With few exceptions, neither the MLA nor individual scholars have concerned themselves with how such knowledge reaches students" (228). Most new PhDs, as follows from this observation, have been trained to focus on such textual study rather than on the kinds of teaching the job market demands, even if the market does so only implicitly. The committee goes on to state "in the strongest possible terms" that graduate programs, given the nature of the job market and changes in the discipline, need to link scholarly emphases to "teaching concerns in a range of instructional settings as well as in applications outside academia" (229). As this committee's findings make clear, and what the realities of the job market support, effective teaching will become more of a factor in tenure and promotion decisions. What the committee's conclusions suggest is that the teacher-scholar—another name for generalist—will, or at least should, define the professional values of an evolving professoriate, values that will benefit "not only the scholar but also the scholar's students, institution, and professional associations" (228). In essence, the unity of methods and knowledges suggested by the term "teacher-scholar" has the potential to bring disparate aspects of the institution into conversation.

In the professional literature one can find several possible programs providing the kinds of reform this committee recommends. To assist such reform, the committee on teaching suggests that the profession (1) reward effective teaching, making sure that it figures in decisions about "job security, promotion, and the selection of book prizes, publishing contracts, sabbaticals, and grants"; (2) promote scholarship in teaching, recommending that such scholarship be afforded more value in professional journals and be more visible at seminars and conferences; (3) establish teacher education to make "the value of our disciplines—of our scholarship and our teaching—known"; (4) reform graduate education to focus on the development of the "teacher-schol-ar"; and (5) improve working conditions, decreasing the "course size and class load" to ensure that scholarship is possible which will help, in this scheme, promote high quality teaching (233–37). To ground these conclusions in actual daily practice, I will examine examples from the 1997 issue of the *ADE Bulletin* in which a group of new PhDs reflect on their experiences at small colleges. The point underly-ing these reflections is that a need exists for a multidisciplinary type of professional preparation, with both academic and community-based elements. These elements should not be merely tacked on or cosmetic, but should be integral to the study of English as a discipline—a disci-pline that is defined by border crossings.

In "Crossing the Great Divide: From Manhattan to Montana," Danell Jones provides an apt description, and typical among these ac-counts, of the conflicted desires experienced by many new professors:

> Because a school like Rocky [Mountain College in Billings] cannot afford a large, diversified faculty, in-dividual professors must be able to cover enormous fields of knowledge. For instance, as the sole instruc-tor in British Literature at Rocky Mountain College, I was responsible for an area that would be covered at Columbia by some twenty full-time English pro-fessors. Not only did I teach the requisite Beowulf-to-Virginia-Woolf British surveys and first-year com-position courses, but I also taught beginning and ad-vanced creative writing, film studies, humanities, and environmental studies, all the while supervising hon-ors and independent studies projects on topics rang-ing from women in medieval literature to equestrian journalism. (42)

Jones's description illustrates the intellectual diversity expected of pro-fessors at often underfunded and, therefore, understaffed colleges, re-vealing also the anxiety and anger typically experienced by them as they realize that their teaching and research efforts are being under-mined by this workload. Jones states, "Although I had some remarkable students, some as bright as any at Columbia, my teaching assignments ranged far from my research interests, and class discussions rarely co-incided with my scholarly work. With luck and the indulgence of my colleagues, I might have been given a seminar in my field every other spring" (43). Jones refers to professors facing such a situation as "social servants," suggesting that professors at small colleges are expected to provide "services" to "customers" rather than facilitate students' acquisition of knowledge for its own sake.

In Jones's and the other accounts published in the *ADE Bulletin*, I am struck by what they seem to overlook, what, I imagine, they were never prepared to value. A better term for the kind of professor Jones outlines—one that explores the intellectual possibilities of this designation rather than solely its negative, consumerist aspects—might be "teacher-scholar," a term the MLA stresses, or "generalist," the term I prefer. If Jones had considered the generalist form of knowledge (one specialized discipline informing others) rather than its specialized, or cropped, form, she would have had at her disposal a more flexible framework for thinking of these frustrations as professional challenges. We can see how what Jones views as mere "service" invites a form of scholarship in which diverse kinds of knowledge and modes of inquiry are combined into an interdisciplinary curriculum.

If graduate students took degrees in what might be called "generalist studies," what would happen? The newly credentialed generalist might become what would pejoratively be referred to by administrators and less benevolent chairpersons as, say, a "utility player" (North 239). Lower pay and heavier workloads would then become institutionalized while graduate schools offering these programs, while marketable and profitable, would be touted as the vocational schools of postgraduate English education. I can imagine similar complaints being lodged by this new class of (now) fulltime professors as those currently expressed by adjuncts. One such complaint, collected in Michael Dubson's *Ghosts in the Classroom*, notes, "A part-time faculty member is paid typically one-fourth to one-third of what a full-timer gets for teaching a course, usually receives few or no fringe benefits, and has virtually no chance of ever getting sabbatical, tenure or promotion" (Naparsteck 58). If such a proposal were implemented, then the following academic class system might emerge: a generalist class would be seen as working for rather than with the specialist class.

Yet any theory of the generalist needs to be firmly grounded in concerns about preparation. Jones, Janet Gardner, and Eric Gadzinski suggest, in their articles collected in this issue of the *ADE Bulletin*, that PhD programs need to continue to prepare students more or less as they have been, or, regardless of the changes, ensure equitable preparation for all graduate students. These professors' stories indicate that preparing generalists or small college teachers would not require a complete overhaul of current curricula, but only a way of enabling the kinds of discoveries these professors describe. And at the core of these discoveries is the ability to apply specialized knowledge to diverse and often unexpected educational situations through teaching and scholarship. At the same time, however, simply maintaining the *status quo* because it is easier to do so, and leaving new PhDs to negotiate the realities of the job market on their own, not only does graduate students a disservice but also denies them the opportunity to grow and evolve as the nature of knowledge and the discipline evolves.

Programs in generalist studies that might be fashioned to address these concerns about the relationship between teaching, the pursuit of specialized research projects, and the often arbitrary demands of service, tend to fall into two categories: (1) those programs that are perceived as separate from or supplemental to the PhD curriculum; and (2) those that emerge from it as a unifying perspective. A program typical of the first type is described by Ed Folsom in the 2001 issue of *Profession:*

> If I were going to start a new English PhD program or try to revitalize an existing one, I'd set it up as a program for small-college teaching. Part of the program would involve summer seminars taught by small-college professors, who would be brought to campus to work with graduate students on how the profession works in a small-college setting. The program would recruit the best students from small colleges and send them back to small colleges—broadly educated in the field, theoretically sophisticated, immersed in the latest cutting-edge debates, eager to enter into those debates as time allowed, ready to carry out a full and satisfying and energetic professional life in a small college. (128)

The problem with Folsom's program, and those of its kind, is that it is divisive, perpetuating a professional underclass in which one sort of PhD is prepared expressly for so-called "teaching institutions" and another sort for "research institutions." Such programs might also undermine the academic futures of those colleges deemed "teaching institutions" by seeming to water down the degrees they grant. Yet Folsom's proposal highlights an important issue: the disparity between those who commit to teaching and those who focus on research. This disparity is in part what the MLA Committee on Teaching attempts to bridge in promoting teaching in the person of the "teacher-scholar."

However, the problem with programs constructed outside of an existing curriculum is that they are removed from the dialectical exchange that needs to inform them. Thus, they become, as we see in Folsom's example, tautological, teaching teachers to teach. A lack of interaction with the established system (an approach Dewey sought to avoid) leads to programs that become isolated totalities, unable to inform or interact with broader disciplinary practices. Programs like Folsom's have worked, but their effectiveness has typically emerged as they have migrated back into a relationship with other programs or academic systems.

North's fusion-based curriculum described in *Refiguring the PhD in English Studies,* on the other hand, provides a more useful model for bringing the broad expectations of most teaching jobs into conversation with similarly broad expectations for professional development. In this curriculum, North argues that "everyone involved must commit to locked-room negotiations; doctoral students must be afforded a major role in the deliberations as participants, not spectators; and the graduate faculty must be willing to renegotiate their disciplinary and professional status vis-à-vis one another and those doctoral students" (255). Had Danell Jones been involved in such a curriculum she may have been able to draw connections between her situation and recognized how her scholarship might have informed and been informed by it. For example, Jones might have given more value to her community work as a catalyst for curricular and institutional enhancements. Specifically, she might have been able to develop a service-leaning program, which could have involved the undergraduate students in applying their knowledge to situations present in the community. Such a program might have brought the department more status and funding, and elevated the school's visibility and usefulness within the surrounding community. As North notes, new professors are not always given opportunities to develop such programs. However, North's observations often apply primarily to larger, research universities; whereas at smaller colleges, such opportunities are often encouraged if not required as part of the job description (as Jones's experience suggests). Since most new PhDs who find jobs do so at small college programs, these might be the places to look for cross-disciplinary approaches to English studies—approaches that may be usefully replicated in the curriculums of larger schools.

PROFESSIONAL IDENTITY

How we prepare PhDs requires us also to recognize that the professional identity of instituting and providing such preparation needs modification. In this section, I provide some ways of framing this reconfiguration. First, we need to consider North's unsparing pronouncement:

> If the faculty's goal is *not* to replicate itself, but rather to prepare doctoral students for careers "doing the kind of lower-division teaching associated with the great experiment in social access that inspires American education," [. . .] how can the extant graduate professors hope to provide the training required? The simplest and harshest answer is that they cannot. (245)

North admits a few pages later that this is not exactly true, but current professors have no real incentive to change what they are doing to accommodate new modes of teaching, research, and service. Therefore, as I mention above, these changes will probably move from the bottom up, from smaller colleges and new professors to the larger schools and those professors who are more established. This situation is not as stratified as it may seem. As Gerald Graff points out in *Clueless in Academe,* most of these "highly visible" professors, he notes, already value cross-disciplinary, collaborative, or what I call generalist research projects. Indeed, academic publishing is making such generalism a necessity.

Central to refiguring English studies is a reevaluation of the role of scholarship, long considered the primary measure of professionalism in the academic life of professors. In "Scholarship Reconsidered: Ten Years After and the Small College," Jayne E. Marek discusses Franklin College's English Department's implementation of Ernest L. Boyer's procedures for assessing professionalism. Marek argues that "Ernest L. Boyer's study *Scholarship Reconsidered,* [. . .] initiated a profound shift in the ways professionals in higher education thought about and assessed academic life, particularly in terms of connections among teaching, learning, pedagogies, and varying forms of research and intellectual endeavor" (44). Boyer describes a "four-fold approach" for assessing scholarship: "'Scholarship of Discovery,' (new work, including creative productions as well as traditional, refereed, scholarly articles)"; "'Scholarship of integration' (interdisciplinary or disciplinary work placed in a wider context, including assessments or reviews of prior work in a field)"; "'Scholarship of application' (a service component, defined by Boyer as using professional skills for community development and problem solving)"; and "'Scholarship of teaching' (the means of bringing one's research and professional development into the classroom)" (46). In Boyer's scheme, scholarship becomes a unifying principal rather than merely one of several distinct professional activities. Effectively, scholarship is a methodology by which professional responsibilities, traditionally described as research, teaching, and service, can be connected to a coherent-educative objective. In this case, that objective is to integrate different disciplines into a broad, liberal arts curriculum—a curriculum, as I noted earlier, that might provide the best "preparation for the work of the future."

An obvious concern with the scheme Boyer describes, and any theory of the generalist, is that some fear it might undermine academic rigor and diminish the authority, indeed the validity, of the PhD. However, as Marek points out, "recent articles in the MLA's *Profession* point toward the increased value of generalist skills for crafting a career in today's tight marketplace. Additionally, many highly visible professors have expanded from their traditional specialties to include various interdisciplinary topics in their research and teaching" (53). Graff, one of these highly visible professors, has made a similar observation about generalist research: "Though research still rules, what counts as 'research' has changed dramatically over the last century in ways that elevate generality and downgrade specialism" (*Clueless* 117–18). This change in research has not emerged from a vacuum, but suggests a similar change in the nature of knowledge, and thus, what is expected from an education. Within this context, generalism no longer suggests inadequacy or "diffuseness" but rather indicates, as Marek notes, "a firm grounding in multiple areas of a field or in several fields" (52). This grounding makes possible the movement across disciplinary boundaries required for professors to make the "big, ambitious, interdisciplinary claims" Graff claims better socialize students "into academic culture" (79), and, it follows, teach others to make similarly impressive arguments in order to gain acceptance in the field.

Epistemologically, the generalist, as a professional category, approaches academic practice from a fundamentally different point of view. From it, as Boyer's scheme suggests, knowledge is produced among the intersections of disciplines and subdisciplines, rather than from sustained research in only one specialized field. North's fusion-based curriculum describes knowledge being created in this way. In his study of the writing produced by graduate students in the Albany PhD program, he analyzes writing in which meaning is negotiated from the mingling of dissimilar discourses, meaning which is built from the students' "perspectives as creative writers, [. . .] rhetoric and composition [. . .] and literary scholars" (98). Such "(re)combinatory" writings, as North refers to them, are present in most college curriculums, even if not as cutting edge as Albany's. Most English departments offer courses in technical writing (which combines writing and the sciences, such as engineering), courses with a service learning component (which combines writing and other disciplinary knowledge to community service), literature (which in most instances combines history with reading and writing), and creative writing (which combines writing and fine arts). Several other examples of such writing could be provided, but the point is that knowledge production, from a teacherly perspective, is rarely focused in a particular discipline. It is more often a dialectical pursuit between previously entrenched epistemologies.

Therefore, the work produced by generalists, in many cases, has a cooperative and often interdisciplinary feature. Thus it makes sense that new PhDs should be prepared to work among disciplines, to use diverse modes of inquiry in their research, which they should see as collaborative efforts not only among themselves and their colleagues but also among themselves, their students, and surrounding communities. This was the aim of Albany's Doctor of Arts program, a forerunner to Albany's current "Writing, Teaching, and Criticism" program, as North describes: "The aim of the version mounted by the English Department at Albany [. . .] was to produce well-rounded but also coherent generalists, people prepared primarily to teach undergraduates at two- and four-year colleges" (88). These generalists should be encouraged to think of scholarship, as Marek's report suggests, not as a solitary pursuit but as a methodology connecting teaching and scholarship to service and making it possible for each to inform the other.

In Lisa Ede and Andrea A. Lunsford's discussion of collaboration in "Collaboration and Concepts of Authorship," they describe the importance of this activity not only in conducting research and publishing but also in the reevaluation of "not only who we are but also what we do" (364). They state that "if we in English Studies are to meet the challenges [inherent in defining authorship, subjectivity, and professionalism], two conditions must obtain. First, we must make space for—and even encourage—collaborative projects in the humanities. But as we do so, we must address related professional standards and practices" (364). Collaboration is a means of moving across boundaries and building relationships between various kinds of knowledge, indicating how the generalist and generalist preparation can be justified. For, as Graff notes, "The problem is not the proliferation of studies that are so specialized that they can't communicate [. . .], but rather the existence of entities that [are] 'freestanding'—programs and courses that have potential interests in common but no means of coming together" (77). A theory of the generalist fills this gap, emerging there as a form of agency through which professional activities and curricular choices can work in concert to form a more coherent educational purpose.

PROFESSIONAL PRACTICE

The everyday practices of the generalist are defined by collaboration, which is a product of carefully managed disciplinary border crossings. Such border crossings are discussed by Graff in *Clueless in Academe*. In his analysis of the discontinuity between composition education and what students actually learn, Graff describes a "collaborative curriculum" that stresses interdisciplinarity as a way of making writing matter. Graff argues that composition should be more "centrally placed" in the curriculum because this course helps bring other courses and disciplines into conversation, and it is through these conversations that broader learning can be achieved—a form of education that more closely replicates the ways in which knowledge is actually created. In the example Graff includes, he describes the development of learning clusters for first-year students at the University of Illinois at Chicago. These clusters consist of three courses—"a freshman seminar taught by faculty members across the disciplines, a section of English composition, and a third course that fulfils general education requirements" (77–79). As with North's fusion-based curriculum, Graff observes that the "writing assignments of the composition course were especially important" (79), for it is through this course that the disciplines within a given cluster are brought into conversation and the various subjects learned. Writing in Graff's example, as in North's, is the primary mode of "exchange," the operation through which knowledge, traditionally closed off within disciplines, is created among the borders and various intersections of the disciplines.

In Graff's scheme, teaching is collaborative, requiring that faculty from different departments and disciplinary traditions unite to ensure that the different discourses are converging to help teach a specific subject. For instance, students might learn about critical reading and the elements of argumentation in their composition course and apply that knowledge in their efforts to describe or prove a hypothesis in biology. Both of these assignments might, then, inform discussions in a first-year seminar exploring the history of the natural sciences. We can see how such clustering might invigorate learning as the often frustrating progression from general education requirements to disciplinary specific courses is abandoned for a more integrated approach, one in which the disciplines and the various research pursuits they inspire inform each other.

Even though such collaborative teaching (which might lead to the kind of scholarship Boyer describes) does not appeal to everyone—some absolutely despise it, as Graff notes—it does more accurately enact, however, the collaborative practices common to the communication, management, and research aspects of most jobs. And though most of us in English studies enjoy the freedom of our private and often hermitic pursuits, we still depend on the work of others to inform them. Composition studies is one method and subject of research that has risen in importance (if not popularity), and, as has been noted, this field of inquiry, with its focus in bringing disciplines into conversation through writing and informed teaching, has the potential to shape the future of English studies.

CONCLUSION: THEORY OF THE GENERALIST

The theory of the generalist should be a tool for reflective practice, which is a mode of analysis implicit in Dewey's description of how best to form an effective educational purpose. The MLA Ad Hoc Committee on Teaching suggests the importance of such practice in their report published in 2001. Reflective practice, the committee claims, is "the operative term that best describes the attitude and activities that make teaching matter" (228). The act of teaching, as the fundamental professional activity for those committed to English studies, is also a subject and method of scholarship. Through teaching, the generalist "turns thought back on action and on the knowing which is implicit in action" (Schon qtd. in MLA Ad Hoc Committee on Teaching 228). In other words, through reflective practice the generalist turns teaching into an epistemology, a way of knowing that reveals how the various subjects of research ultimately impact, transform, mutate, and rupture the illusions of an audience (our students). If English studies seriously institutionalized this notion, then disciplines within and separate from it might come to learn and grow with each other, and, thus, more closely emulate the way knowledge is actually produced.

This idea is not new; it has been important to rhetoric for centuries, as the story of the Sophists, those much-maligned intellectuals of ancient Greece, suggests. They were a model for today's teacher-scholar, a little too committed to the verity of rhetorical performance for Plato's tastes, but aware of that one aspect of knowledge that demands reflection and imagination, contingency. They understood that "only provisional or probable knowledge was available to human beings" (Bizzell and Herzberg 22) and, so, were players in the contingencies (the regions where different discourses overlap) that defined the elusive nature of truth as a product of disciplinary interactions. For the Sophists, the operative phrase might be summed up as "we change" and, therefore, the nature of change, as a way of establishing a flexible coalition between different descriptions of truth, needs to be explored and encouraged. As the Sophists argued, to know "human nature" required a methodology that allowed socially constructed truths to come into conversation to create a more complete picture of how "humans" know (22). The theory of the generalist, as a frame for preparing, developing, and instituting dialectical learning into the curriculum, is based on this Sophistic methodology.

The lesson of the Sophists, and Plato's response, holds for us today. English studies will continue to evolve, and a theory of the generalist provides a way of exploring this reality. Therefore, we no longer need to talk of an English studies in crisis, especially if this seeming crisis is, in effect, a "chronic condition," as North mentions, that has and will continue to frame our discussions of the discipline. This talk of "crisis" is actually a way of describing change, which is really only another in a series of professional challenges. Discovering procedures for responding to these challenges—a task that should be enjoyable for us, while keeping the discipline intact—might be a useful project for future generalists.

Works Cited

ADE Ad Hoc Committee on Staffing. "Report of the ADE Ad Hoc Committee on Staffing: Executive Summary." *Profession* (1999): 275–81.

Aronowitz, Stanley. *The Knowledge Factory: Dismantling the Corporate University and Creating True Higher Learning.* Boston: Beacon, 2000.

Berlin, James A. *Rhetorics, Poetics, and Cultures: Refiguring College English Studies.* 1996. West Lafayette, IN: Parlor Press, 2003.

Bizzell, Patricia, and Bruce Herzberg. *The Rhetorical Tradition: Readings from Classical Times to the Present.* Boston: Bedford/St. Martin's, 1990.

Dewey, John. *Education and Experience.* 1938. New York: Touchstone-Simon, 1997.

Dubson, Michael, ed. *Ghosts in the Classroom: Stories of College Adjunct Faculty—and the Price We All Pay.* Boston: Camel's Back Books, 2001.

Ede, Lisa, and Andrea A. Lunsford. "Collaboration and Concepts of Authorship." *PMLA* 116 (2001): 354–69.

Folsom, Ed. "Degrees of Success, Degrees of Failure: The Changing Dynamics of the English PhD and Small-College Careers." *Profession* (2001): 121–29.

Gadzinski, Eric. "The Year of Living Dangerously; or, Not Just an Adventure, but a Job." *ADE Bulletin* 117 (1997): 35–37.

Gardner, Janet. "Trained in Theory, Hired in Literature." *ADE Bulletin* 117 (1997): 31–34.

Graff, Gerald. *Clueless in Academe: How Schooling Obscures the Life of the Mind.* New Haven, CT: Yale UP, 2003.

Jones, Danell. "Crossing the Great Divide: From Manhattan to Montana." *ADE Bulletin* 117 (1997): 42–44.

Marek, Jayne E. "Scholarship Reconsidered: Ten Years After and the Small College." *Profession* (2003): 44–54.

MLA Ad Hoc Committee on Professionalization of PhDs. "Professionalization in Perspective." *Profession* (2002): 187–210.

MLA Ad Hoc Committee on Teaching. "Final Report." *Profession* (2001): 225–38.

MLA Committee on Community Colleges. "Considering Community Colleges: Advice to Graduate Students and Job Seekers." *Profession* (2003): 164–71.

Naparsteck, Martin. "The Censorship of Part-Timers." Dubson 58–60.

North, Stephen M., with Barbara A. Chepaitis, David Coogan, Lâle Davidson, Ron MacLean, Cindy L. Parrish, Jonathan Post, and Beth Weatherby. *Refiguring the PhD in English Studies: Writing, Doctoral Education, and the Fusion-Based Curriculum.* Urbana, IL: NCTE, 2000.

Part IV

Kairotic Approaches

11 We Are (Not) One: Corrupting Composition in the Ruined University

Michael Pennell

[W]e believe that only serious action on a number of fronts will enable progress toward resolution of the economic, social, and educational problems posed by the inequitable and insufficient multitier job system that has developed in all too many institutions across the country. What we confront is therefore a crisis in the truest sense of the word: not just an "unstable condition" but a "turning point," which we hope will evoke significant transformations of the academic settings we inhabit.

—Sandra Gilbert et al.,
"Final Report of the MLA Committee on Professional Employment"

The Tipping Point is the moment of critical mass, the threshold, the boiling point.

—Malcolm Gladwell, *The Tipping Point*

In his book *The Moment of Complexity,* Mark C. Taylor, in a discussion of complexity theory, claims that "all significant change takes place between too much and too little order" (14). That place, Malcolm Gladwell might argue, is the "tipping point"—that elusive point between one pattern and another, between too much and too little order, between structure or organization and chaos or fragments. For Gladwell this phenomenon is illustrated through examples such as the spread of AIDS, the reemergence of Hush Puppies, and the rise in teenage smoking, while Taylor employs the concept in examining the shift from grid to network culture. But the concept of the tipping point also proves applicable to recent changes in institutions, ranging from automobile factories to schools of higher education—the places "we inhabit," according to the "Final Report of the MLA Committee on Professional Employment." For my purposes here, I will relate this concept to shifts occurring in the university in general and the field of English studies in particular.

Claims to the fragmentary state of modern (global) society are commonplace (Hardt and Negri; Taylor). Currently, this phenomenon is witnessed in the (arguable) withering of the nation state, through a rise in non-governmental organizations (NGOs), and through space-time compression and its influence on the global economy. This transition greatly impacts and reflects a change in the daily lived experience of people, witnessed in the rise of dislocated, outsourced, and nonstandard work and workers (Barker and Christenson; Carre et al.), the supposed decline in community and participation (Putnam), the growth of gated communities (Judd), and the rise in a support economy centered around individuals (Zuboff and Maxmin). The university, and institutions of higher education in general, are not immune to this trend and its postindustrial/global/network/postmodern rhetoric. Everyday more pieces of the university and formal education institutions are corporatized, privatized, franchised, or downsized, creating a new place within which teachers and students work—a place that is routinely praised by administrators and decried or feared by those in English studies.

But with this essay my goal is not to add to the lamentations aimed at globalization and its influence on education. Rather, I intend to explore this tipping point in higher education, and, in particular, the emergence of English studies as it parallels a transition in writing. What if we considered the university as a site within which those of us working in the field of rhetoric and composition, and English studies more generally, can employ as a means to reconsider the prominent themes in our field and the places within which we and students work? Before moving "beyond English" or "beyond the corporate university," we might move metaphorically through, and within, this fragmentary and wobbly state. It may be a state in which the university and those studying and teaching writing and rhetoric in this ruined university, to use Bill Readings's terms, might reconsider some rather transparent themes. I push at and explore two key concepts in/for English studies as it inevitably reaches this tipping point: corruption and non-place.

Arguing that as a field, English studies has relied for too long on generation, I introduce its counterpart, corruption, through its more recent application in the work of Michael Hardt and Antonio Negri, and through its more classical use in the work of Aristotle. However, the place where corruption might occur is not the university of old. Therefore, I apply Marc Augé's concept of non-place to the fragmentary university of today, contending that those pushing "beyond" English studies have not fully considered place. Finally, this essay will return to writing and the possibilities for a writing of corruption in the (non)place of the ruined university.

WRITING AS THE FUTURE OF ENGLISH STUDIES

The rise of the field of rhetoric and composition has prompted, or reflects, a definite shift in the aims of many English studies configurations. Recent considerations of the changing nature of English studies have relied on writing as the common element or glue in the disparate pieces. Interestingly, this call for writing (versus interpreting) as the unifying theme of the future English studies appears as "writing" itself is nearing, or traversing, a tipping point. In this section, I examine briefly the role writing plays in English studies and the limited pre-tipping point view of writing that these accounts employ.

In describing the rationale behind the State University of New York–Albany's new doctoral curricula, Stephen North asserts, "Any serious effort to alter graduate education in [English studies] [. . .] must be grounded in a refiguring of the role that writing plays in such education" (xiv). Rejecting the dissolution and corporate compromise options for English studies, North calls for and describes a fusion-based curriculum for English studies as a means to move beyond the age of "College English Teaching, Inc." (233). This curriculum centers on writing and its ability to forge connections between graduate students and faculty, leading to a fusion of disparate elements of English studies. In advancing the fusion approach, North claims that when operating as "the insistently hierarchical College English Teaching, Inc.," English studies has discounted one of its central "institutional wares," writing (235). In turn, the teaching of writing was and is relegated at many large programs to part time instructors and teaching assistants (see Bousquet, Scott, and Parascondola; Marshall).

North maintains that this discounting of the teaching of writing, and teaching in general, must be eliminated for any advancement of English studies institutionally. Generally, I agree with North's assessment of the discounting of writing and teaching and its detriment to the productive future of English studies. Further, North shows a consideration of economic shifts and the role such shifts have on English departments. However, North's focus on the labor of the teaching of writing ignores, for the most part, a consideration of the tipping point writing has endured of late. He fails to problematize fully "writing" as it has shifted from pen and pencil on paper to basic word processing to multimedia composing. Even within English studies, or more particularly rhetoric and composition, those who are "writing" the field have created online journals such as *Kairos: A Journal of Rhetoric, Technology, and Pedagogy; Enculturation;* and more recently, an online version of *Computers and Composition.* The scholarship these journals publish is not the same scholarly writing of even ten years ago. Clearly, those who are "writing" the field—faculty, graduate students, and undergraduate students—have pushed the boundaries of writing.

North is not alone in the attention he affords writing, as recent scholarship on the "work" of rhetoric and composition stresses writing as the linchpin to English studies. Susan Miller and Charles Bazerman in their individual contributions to *Rhetoric and Composition as Intellectual Work* pinpoint writing as central to rhetoric and composition and English in general. Although "such inquiry has no serious home of its own," writing studies is described as both important and central to English departments (Bazerman 32). Further, despite its nomadic characterization, writing is foregrounded by both Bazerman and Miller as central to the university. Bazerman, in "The Case for Writing Studies as a Major Discipline," goes so far as to label writing a "fundamental matter of the constitution of our world" (33). Thus, he suggests adopting a "life-span" perspective on writing in order to investigate the study of writing's location in the middle of "the history of human consciousness, institutions, practice, and development over the last five millennia" (36). This argument for the importance of writing and its study, and in turn, its disciplinarity, is expanded by Miller's depiction of "writing studies as a mode of inquiry" (41). Placing the production of texts (writing studies) in contrast with their interpretation (literary studies), Miller illustrates the varied and dynamic possibilities for research in writing studies. More than arguing for the importance of rhetoric and composition as a field, Bazerman and Miller attempt to reconsider the possibilities for a department, or for researchers and teachers, engaged in the study of literacy. Yet, both authors promote rhetoric and composition, or some version, as the appropriate place for studying writing and literacy. Rather than moving beyond writing, their goal is to strengthen the role of rhetoric and composition and those who practice it in the university—this, as the title of their collection indicates, is intellectual work.

Although not dealing with the economics of a ruined university explicitly, each of these arguments for the significance of writing addresses the call from the editors of the recent collection *Beyond English, Inc.*: "We need innovative, visionary, and collectively imagined possibilities for a vital English Studies in a technological, global economy" (Downing, Hulbert, and Mathieu 14). This collection provides a unique and overdue engagement with larger economic shifts and the role that those shifts play in the curriculum of English studies. Yet, in the call for innovative and visionary possibilities, allowing the field to move "beyond," there is still a rather limited focus on how we can "inhabit the university in the twenty-first century" (14). Thus, the essays, although accurately pinpointing the corporate influence on/in the university, do not thoroughly consider the writing that will allow the "we" to inhabit such a university. Whereas the previous engagements with the future of English studies placed writing at the centers of such futures, the contributors to *Beyond English, Inc.* do not show the same awareness of writing and its role in moving beyond. This is disappointing because, as Elspeth Stuckey and others have shown, any shift in the economy causes a concomitant shift in literacy, especially valid in light of the most recent economic transition where "literacy is the condition of postindustrialism" (Stuckey 19). And a shift in literacy must be reflected in any configuration of a viable English studies.

A focus on innovative approaches to writing and the possibilities that a visionary approach to writing can have for English studies is overdue. Yet, much of the work, such as in the previous examples, straddles a literacy and economic divide. So, the focus on writing of the former group must be united with the economic focus of the latter group. While North attempts a fusion of these aspects, he fails to consider adequately the complexities of writing. My claim is that we need to open our "writing" up to scrutiny. In the remainder of this essay, I will investigate a key metaphor to the field of English studies and the ways in which a reconsideration of that central metaphor may forge innovative connections within a ruined, but still relevant, university.

GENERATION AND CORRUPTION

I start with what has become transparent in our field: generation. As a field interested in the art of composition, of putting things together, we equally value generation, the act of producing, of bringing into existence. The ubiquity of this concept is witnessed in the seemingly endless directions to students to generate: we ask them to generate everything from paper ideas to thesis statements to drafts. Why it seems that each of the standard stages of "the writing process" centers around generation, whether the generation of "productive invention" and prewriting or of drafting and revising. Moreover, the field's annual flagship conference (the Conference on College Composition and Communication) promoted a theme for the 2001 conference of "composing community." Besides pushing the generative process underlying our work, the theme points to a place, a community, where our generation can occur. And, as a field, this generative ability manifests itself in our implicit and explicit importance in the university's role as producers of critical (i.e., good, citizens). We generate the citizens and workers necessary for our nation (see "A Nation at Risk" and "A Skills Gap" as examples; see Hull for a critique of such pronouncements).

North points to the success of writing as generation—writing is positioned as central to the fusion approach to English studies. Students, both undergraduate and graduate, rely on writing as a means to compose the field and to compose themselves as members of the field. In essence, these students use writing to generate the field. While North seems inclined to move beyond College English Teaching, Inc., and the institutional hierarchies replicated in College English Teaching, Inc. (the teaching of writing), he appears less inclined to investigate "writing," that is, how students write or what it means to write. The term is employed without much discussion, miscalculating, it seems, a general understanding of its meaning. North appears content to allow any investigation of writing to be engaged through the fusion enacted by the student as she constructs her education. And in the work of Bazerman and Miller, "writing" flourishes. This identical use seems to me more than mere coincidental word choice. As I sit in, essentially, a self-contained multimedia station in a campus computer lab, I wonder how many of us are "writing." That term lacks the complexity and range of activities occurring at each station. And, this lack of writing connects to our field's affinity for generation. Even a sampling of many textbooks within our field highlights the prevalence of "generation."

Our field has fostered generation as a concept central to how we identify ourselves and to how we present and teach writing. However, as the university grows more fragmentary and as rhetoric and composition finds itself in a university in, at the very least, transition, it may be a key moment to explore the overlooked other side to a rhetoric of generation: corruption. What if we let the tipping point tip, and see what new patterns and activities for college writers, our field, and "writing" may emerge? In their extensive work, *Empire,* Michael Hardt and Antonio Negri call for a return to a more classical vision of corruption. Although acknowledging its connection to morality in most current usage, they call for an understanding of corruption apart from "the perverted, that which strays from the moral, the good, the pure" (201). Today, we might find it hard to consider these contrary processes, especially corruption, outside of morality. What with the weekly headlines revealing yet another instance of "corrupt" business practices in corporate America and other organizations, it proves difficult to engage with the concept of corruption merely as a counterpart to generation.

Nonetheless, Hardt and Negri push the concept as reference to "a more general process of decomposition or mutation with none of the moral overtones, drawing on an ancient usage that has been largely lost" (201). In *Generation and Corruption,* also translated as "Coming to-be and Ceasing to-be," Aristotle outlines the universe and its bodies as constantly in a process of generation and corruption, of coming to be and ceasing to be. He writes, "coming together produces generation, their falling apart corruption"—moreover, these processes are "together and interlocking" (28). The *OED* presents Aristotle's definition of corruption as lost today; therefore, the dictionary contrasts a physical understanding of corruption with a moral understanding. In the physical definitions, corruption is presented as a counterpart to generation: for example, "the breaking up or decomposition of a body" and "dissolution of the constitution which makes a thing what it is." This involves seeing "ceasing to be" as an inventive process worthy of attention.

If we see corruption as de-generation, then it is also de-composition, or as Hardt and Negri say, it is "a moment of metamorphosis that potentially frees spaces for change" (201). This process of breaking up can be seen not only as excessive but also inventive, allowing for formerly ignored connections. Might we see that breaking apart as spaces for change, as spaces for accidental relations? The coming to be of generation highlighted in Robert Atwan's definition of convergence contains a viable although overlooked counterpart because just as there is coming to be, as Aristotle argues, there must also exist ceasing to be. And it is within the momentary "ceasing to be," that tipping point which English studies finds itself traversing, where invention, where different connections, where different writing, might occur. Although I am not advocating the abandonment of generation in English studies, clearly "writing" is much more than generation and requires a more nuanced and complex definition. Why not look at more sides of the writing coin?

THE NON-PLACE OF ENGLISH STUDIES

Rediscovering this concept of corruption is key today because of the shifting state of place in our and our students' lives. Moreover, it offers another way in which to address English's crisis of identity as depicted by North et al. In this next section, I will locate this concept of corruption in the university but not the university of old, rather the university as one of the growing number of non-places that create our lived landscape. In his work *Non-Places,* Marc Augé explores the growing number of locations in our lives that are intended as places of movement and exchange—airports, shopping malls, department stores, expressways. These non-places, Augé argues, are built around, and market in, excess—excesses of space and information. One might position the university and the classroom as non-places, centering around movement and excess. There is no shortage of movement and excess from morning to night in the hallways and classrooms housing writing courses at my institution. Seeing the university as a non-place is complicated, however, by Pratt and Hanson's claim that despite a proliferation of globalization rhetoric, including the recent campaigns waged by university administration, people live very local lives. We are bound to and influenced by our local places; at the same time, we influence these environments as we interact with them. So, the university presents a complex non-place composed of residents that may be transient but also intimately involved with the environment.

Further, and key for those of us working in rhetoric and composition, Augé claims, "The link between individuals and their surroundings in the space of non-place is established through the mediation of words, or even texts" (94). This mediation of words offers us ways in which we are to interact with the places. The traveler, writes Augé, sees signs on the highway, the same signs if the path is frequently traveled, resulting in an image of the place. The person's imagining of the place is mediated through the signs. These non-places are engaged with users through what Bolter and Grusin might term remediation—previously simple signs and media are remediated in new places with more recent media, resulting in excess and abundance (60). I recall when I was an undergraduate in the Upper Peninsula of Michigan, frequently driving back to school from the southern part of the Lower Peninsula. Throughout the drive back to Sault Ste. Marie, I would stare at the repetitive signs proclaiming the "wonder" of the Soo Locks. Over time, without visiting the locks but once or twice, I developed a relationship with the locks. I was interacting with the locks but only through the signs: I knew a version of the place due to my interaction with its highway signs.

The student as traveler is traversing these non-places on a daily basis; even before she becomes a student she has imagined the place of the university. Further, more and more it is words and texts that mediate the interaction between the non-place and student. Like my example of driving back to school, many expressways throughout the state of Indiana contain large billboards advertising Purdue University to drivers. Although this might seem to be deviating from corruption, and from the future of English studies, I see them as intertwined. Again, as we find ourselves working through our days in more non-places, places of excess, of movement and exchange; we find ourselves mediating these surroundings through texts, but our interactions with non-places—especially a place such as the university—is growing corrupt. This movement and exchange and constant flow that is our non-places is one of corruption, of a ceasing to be. This ceasing to be goes hand in hand with economic, social, and technological changes (i.e., "the usual suspects"). These non-places are not just places of generation but of corruption—schools, departments, and majors decompose, move, transform. The constant of movement, of exchange, of mediation is also one of corruption, of de-composition, of interacting through (more than) words and texts. Engaging with these non-places is not done through writing. What might it mean for our field to engage with and explore a rhetoric of corruption for the non-places of our lives? How can the concept of corruption influence and shift our understandings of composition and composition pedagogy? Moreover, how can corruption and non-place provide possibilities for English studies? Very briefly, I would like to consider two aspects of a rhetoric of corruption and point to some (corrupt) work and directions in English studies.

CORRUPT COMPOSITION

Shifting from a more global and abstract consideration of corruption and of the university in a state of change, I want to go back to the role of writing in the future university and the future of English studies. As North, Miller, and Bazerman contest, writing is the tendons connecting the decomposing, the corrupting, body of English. Few writing pedagogies exist that seem to embrace this de-generative process. Just as the university has been remediated for students, so has writing. Students may see "writing," university writing, as far removed from what they do on a daily basis as they compose and communicate. In a computer lab, users may not be writing *per se* but they are busy interacting with various programs, documents, and media. In addition, students are increasingly finding the place of computer labs extinct. From wireless networks to laptops to smaller technologies such as MP3 players, students traverse non-places engaging in (for lack of a better term) non-writing. As writing has tipped, so to speak, both pedagogical and institutional reactions have shown a limited, though growing, reaction to such changes.

A pedagogy beginning to address these issues is witnessed in Jeff Rice's *College Composition and Communication* article "The 1963 Hip-Hop Machine: Hip-Hop Pedagogy as Composition." Within this pedagogy, Rice employs hip-hop as indicative of the ways in which "discourse emerges from the cultural odds and ends we assemble" (455). Rice builds upon Victor Vitanza's whatever-based invention strategy, which Rice argues "allows chance and randomness a prominent role in discursive constructions" (459). Rice's hip-hop writing pedagogy employs the techniques of cuts, pastes, mixes, and playbacks in order for students to see the ceasing to be of corruption in our culture as inventive: "Student writing benefits from choosing contrasting samples and allowing the dissimilarities of the material to function as heuristic" (469). Rice sees this pedagogy as "allow[ing] students to resist the imposed linear methods of critique in favor of practices already working within digital culture" (468–69). Further, I see Rice's pedagogy as a pedagogy recognizing the movement, the excess, of students' lives. It is a cutting and a pasting and a mixing of the mediation of ourselves with non-places; in non-places, we don't necessarily have linearity and we do not necessarily have "writing."

Rice's hip-hop pedagogy calls to mind Gregory Ulmer's claim that a shift from orality to literacy is now rushing towards electracy. Echoing Rice, Ulmer writes, "the change in thinking from linear indexical to network association—a shift often used to summarize the difference between alphabetic and electronic cognitive styles [. . .]—is happening at the level of technology itself" (36). Vitanza, in commenting on Ulmer, writes, "As hardware and software change, so institutions and disciplines [read: places] change. So do the thinking and writing generated by them" (198). Vitanza employs Ulmer in his call for a "writing of the accident," in order to push beyond heuristics, binary thinking and writing. Sounding very corrupt, Vitanza calls for chance, for accidental connections in writing; a procedure already happening in the digital non-place culture noted by Rice.

Institutionally, initial steps are being taken that move beyond traditional writing and writing instruction. For example, Purdue University recently revised its approach to first-year composition. The revised approach combines elements of traditional classroom pedagogy with conferencing pedagogy and computer-mediated pedagogy. This approach pushes at the possibilities for composing without mandating specific multimedia or multi-genre approaches. This move may push in the direction Readings sought for disciplinarity that "holds open the question of whether and how thoughts fit together" (191). And, in turn, this may offer an option for English studies. Corruption points towards the "holding open" as an inventive phase, in which accidental connections are valued.

In addition, corruption allows a different possibility for how we might approach writing and rhetoric that extends Rice's hip-hop pedagogy. Throughout *Generation and Corruption*, Aristotle plays with a notion of prime matter, of a quality that survives generation and corruption. This may point to a consideration of corruption that centers around affect as outlined by Lawrence Grossberg and Brian Massumi among others (see also Edbauer). Although affect is frequently equated with emotion, Massumi, in *Parables for the Virtual,* connects affect with intensity and excess. Similarly, in *We Gotta Get Out of This Place,* Grossberg links affect to "what we often describe as the 'feeling' of life" (80). As he writes, "One can understand another person's life, share the same meanings and pleasures, but still not know how it feels" (80). We have a different affective investment in different objects, and we all find ourselves in varying affective contexts. Affect is preconscious and exists on the surface, relying highly on context. Grossberg contends that "unlike emotions, affective states are neither structured narrative-ly nor organized in response to our interpretations of situations" (81). Further, Massumi writes of a "growing feeling within media, literary, and art theory that affect is central to an understanding of informa-tion- and image-based late capitalist culture, in which so-called master narratives are perceived to have foundered" (27).

Like Massumi and Grossberg, I agree that we live in a culture cen-tered around affect, even more pronounced as I write this chapter only an hour or two after hearing of the *Columbia* shuttle disaster. Images of the shuttle breaking apart in the blue sky are excess—they become emotional later, but center around intensity. It seems that a rhetoric of corruption requires a clearer understanding of the affective contexts students find themselves in and how those affective contexts might influence students' rhetorical lives. A consideration of affect might aid students as they maneuver the situations creating their lived experience in a culture where contexts and situations are linked to intensities, feel-ings that are pre-conscious. However, as Lisa Langstraat has recently written: "compositionists lack a vocabulary to address affect in the classroom" (304). A rhetoric of corruption might see these affective contexts as opportunities for the consideration of seemingly acciden-tal connections. But this means we must also see these affective con-texts as occurring more and more in non-places—in spaces of move-ment and exchange and excess. Again, we perhaps lack a vocabulary to address affect because we must consider it before language: excess is non-linguistic. But herein lies the problem for a pedagogy of affect. Affect, like Ulmer's memory in electracy, lives in connections between loci, not in loci—it lives in the seemingly random connections of non-places and corruption—not solely in the classroom. In a larger sense,

English studies does not exist in any sole discipline or field but rather in the connections between these fields.

How do we get students to consider the accidental connections of corruption and of affect of non-places? Moreover, how do we outline and enact an English studies existing through connections and openness? While I lack pedagogical examples to point to beyond Rice and Langstraat, it seems we must consider the pedagogy of corruption in electracy, in a digital culture of non-places. In addition, we need to extend and disrupt North's writing metaphor institutionally. This will require extending local pedagogical connections and approaches as possibilities for larger situations. Currently, I add some final touches to this paper in a basement computer lab, staring at one of the four, beige, cinderblock walls limiting the space. Fellow computer users come and go, interacting with various aspects of the screen and what it windows to. The texts of the place are signs outlawing smoking, stealing software, using stolen software, and outlining the hours of operation. Soon, I will leave my station and another user will fill my seat. The traditional community of writers does not rule here, nor does generation. Although it has served us well and will continue to do so in the future, the concept of generation provides an equally rich counterpart: corruption. Corruption deserves a more thorough consideration, especially as our field and institutions find themselves in transition to the landscape of non-places. This is no time to lament but rather a prime opportunity to explore counterparts and see fragments as openings and possibilities. What if we let the tipping point tip as opposed to digging in our heels and crying calls of crisis?

WORKS CITED

Aristotle. *Generation and Corruption*. Trans. C. J. F. Williams. New York: Oxford UP, 1982.

Atwan, Robert. *Convergences: Message, Method, Medium*. New York: Bedford/St. Martin's, 2002.

Augé, Marc. *Non-Places: Introduction to an Anthropology of Supermodernity*. Trans. John Howe. New York: Verso, 1995.

Barker, Kathleen, and Kathleen Christensen, eds. *Contingent Work: American Employment Relations in Transition*. Ithaca, NY: Cornell UP, 1998.

Bazerman, Charles. "The Case for Writing Studies as a Major Discipline." *Rhetoric and Composition as Intellectual Work*. Ed. Gary A. Olson. Carbondale: Southern Illinois UP, 2002. 32–38.

Bolter, Jay David, and Richard Grusin. *Remediation: Understanding New Media.* Cambridge: MIT P, 2000.

Bousquet, Marc, Tony Scott, and Leo Parascondola, eds. *Tenured Bosses and Disposable Teachers: Writing Instruction in the Managed University.* Carbondale, IL: Southern Illinois UP, 2003.

Carre, Francoise, Marianne A. Ferber, Lonnie Golden, and Stephen A. Herzenberg, eds. *Nonstandard Work: The Nature and Challenges of Changing Employment Arrangements.* Ithaca, NY: Cornell UP, 2000.

Downing, David B., Claude Mark Hulbert, and Paula Mathieu, eds. *Beyond English, Inc.: Curricular Reform in a Global Economy.* Portsmouth, NH: Boynton/Cook, 2002.

Edbauer, Jenny. "Big Time Sensuality: Affective Literacies and Texts That Matter." *Composition Forum* 13.1–2 (2002).

Gilbert, Sandra M., et .al. "Final Report of the MLA Committee on Professional Employment." 1998. 23 Jan. 2009 <http://www.mla.org>.

Gladwell, Malcolm. *The Tipping Point: How Little Things Can Make a Big Difference.* New York: Little, 2000.

Grossberg, Lawrence. *We Gotta Get Out of This Place: Popular Conservatism and Postmodern Culture.* New York: Routledge, 1992.

Hardt, Michael, and Antonio Negri. *Empire.* Cambridge: Harvard UP, 2000.

Hull, Glynda. "Hearing Other Voices: A Critical Assessment of Popular Views on Literacy and Work." *Changing Work, Changing Workers: Critical Perspectives on Language, Literacy, and Skills.* Ed. Glynda Hull. Albany: SUNY P, 1997. 3–39.

Judd, Dennis R. "The Rise of the New Walled Cities." *Spatial Practices: Critical Explorations in Social/Spatial Theory.* Ed. Helen Liggett and David C. Perry. Thousand Oaks, CA: Sage, 1995. 144–66.

Langstraat, Lisa. "The Point Is There Is No Point: Miasmic Cynicism and Cultural Studies Composition." *JAC* 22.2 (2002): 293–325.

Marshall, Margaret J. *Response to Reform: Composition and the Professionalization of Teaching.* Carbondale, IL: Southern Illinois UP, 2003.

Massumi, Brian. *Parables for the Virtual: Movement, Affect, Sensation.* Durham, NC: Duke UP, 2002.

Miller, Susan. "Writing Studies as a Mode of Inquiry." *Rhetoric and Composition as Intellectual Work.* Ed. Gary A. Olson. Carbondale: Southern Illinois UP, 2002. 41–54.

"A Nation at Risk: The Imperative for Educational Reform." The National Commission on Excellence in Education. United States Department of Education. Apr. 1983. 23 January 2009 <http://www.ed.gov/pubs/NatAtRisk>.

North, Stephen M., with Barbara A. Chepaitis, David Coogan, Lâle Davidson, Ron MacLean, Cindy L. Parrish, Jonathan Post, and Beth Weatherby.

Refiguring the PhD in English Studies: Writing, Doctoral Education, and the Fusion-Based Curriculum. Urbana, IL: NCTE, 2000.

Putnam, Robert D. *Bowling Alone: The Collapse and Revival of American Community.* New York: Simon, 2000.

Readings, Bill. *The University in Ruins.* Cambridge: Harvard UP, 1996.

Rice, Jeff. "The 1963 Hip-Hop Machine: Hip-Hop Pedagogy as Composition." *College Composition and Communication* 54.3 (2003): 453–71.

"The Skills Gap 2001: Manufacturers Confront Persistent Skills Shortages in an Uncertain Economy." National Association of Manufacturers, 2001.

Taylor, Mark C. *The Moment of Complexity: Emerging Network Culture.* Chicago: U of Chicago P, 2001.

Vitanza, Victor. "From Heuristic to Aleatory Procedures; or, Toward 'Writing the Accident.'" *Inventing a Discipline: Rhetoric Scholarship in Honor of Richard E. Young.* Ed. Maureen Daly Goggin. Urbana, IL: NCTE, 2000. 185–206.

Zuboff, Shoshana, and James Maxmin. *The Support Economy: Why Corporations Are Failing Individuals and the Next Episode of Capitalism.* New York: Viking, 2002.

12 English Teachers We Have Known

Christopher Schroeder

Next to garrulous people at PTO meetings or on airplanes, I anxiously await the inevitable conversational turn to careers. As soon as I mention that I am an English teacher, these new acquaintances often say something about not being good with grammar, sometimes even covering their mouths, as if bad grammar is tantamount to bad breath.

While disappointing, these reactions are understandable, at least from my experience. In these, I see the contradictory existence of English studies in the United States, the land, at least in theory, of equal opportunity, where English is simultaneously a protector of cultural heritage and a source of social certification, often in the same classroom.

If this dual function isn't difficult enough, our efforts are further complicated by the increasingly ethnic diversity in our classrooms. Between 1991 and 2001, minority enrollment increased by 52 percent to more than 4.3 million students while white enrollment decreased slightly over the same time from 10.6 million to 10.1 million students (American Council). For many of these students and even more around the world, English is a second or third language.

While many students today exhibit greater control over spoken than written English, they nonetheless bring proficiencies in textual practices, from sending text messages to designing Web content (not to mention expectations for connectivity) that challenge many assumptions we make about meaning-making. Across the U.S., 44 percent of all adult internet users, or 53 million people, contribute materially to the digital world by creating websites, posting to another's site, exchanging pictures or art, using chatrooms, etc. (Lenhart, Fallows, and Horrigan 4). Many, if not most, students today are shaped by electronic texts, from reality shows to online games, in ways that challenge not only the goals of English departments but also the attachment to a print-based society.

Such challenges historically have resulted in cries of literacy crises, but at some point these cries, as the children's story suggests, lose their credibility. After all, such complaints, according to Harvey Daniels, have been a part of the Western world since 2500 BCE (33–34). In the U.S., such declarations have captured the public attention in the 1890s, 1920s, 1940s, and mid-1970s (Hourigan; Ohmann). These complaints, in the U.S., coincide with substantial shifts in college enrollment, leading some to conclude that these ostensible crises are concerted efforts to contain the challenges posed by new and different students (e.g., Trimbur, "Literacy").

While we're complaining about the differences between them and us, I can't help but wonder to what extent we perpetuate, if not create, the conditions that alienate us from the very communities we profess to represent. Sexism aside, although not insignificant, not all of us sport tweed jackets with leather elbow patches and puff on pipes around smoldering fires, but in the minds of students, and the general public, we might as well. Rare is the relevant, interesting, and even hip English teacher, such as Jack MacFarland in Mike Rose's *Lives on the Boundary*, and even he is too immersed in conventional English culture to reach more than Mike, Art, Mark, and a few of their friends.

Despite popular belief, people consume and produce text throughout their everyday lives. In other words, the problem is not *whether* but *what* people consume and produce, and while I don't propose that we merely invert the existing cultural order or exchange the current canon for a more popular one, I suspect that our refusal to recognize these conditions only reinforces our increasing irrelevance. While we can, and do, declare literacy crisis after literacy crisis, we do so, I believe, at our own peril. If we are to regain (or establish) some legitimacy, we must acknowledge the innovative and creative efforts throughout our society even as we must debate, and be able to justify, standards that are relevant.

꙳

After distributing the Warriner's grammar book, he assigned the first chapter and asked for questions. The lanky pitcher across the aisle and I both raised our hands. He pointed, but my classmate didn't answer. He jabbed again, his lazy eye swimming in the space between us.

Me? I mouthed, pointing to myself.

Yes, you, goddamnit, he said, scanning the roster on the podium in front of him. How many Schroeders do I have in here?

Sophomore English hadn't started as I had hoped.

Even before the semester started, I was anxious. According to school legend, he once stuffed a student in a locker for disrespecting his wife, who was substituting for the health teacher.

Some of these stories, I'd later learn, were only partially true. For instance, he had worn a black beret, not a green one, during his two tours in Vietnam, although he refused to answer when I asked if he killed anyone.

Several sessions into the semester, he assigned more grammar exercises and then, on his way to the back of the classroom, stopped at my desk. I hunched over my homework. He said that he heard that I was preparing for a marathon. When I nodded, he motioned for me to follow him.

At the back of the classroom, he dropped into his desk and folded his hands behind his head. With one eye on my classmates' backs, he explained that he had stopped smoking, started running, and hoped to complete a marathon himself.

Also, his father, I learned later, suffered a fatal heart attack in his forties, and he wanted to stay longer with his kids.

Before long, we settled into a routine. He'd slip me a yellow pass during class that would free me from eighth-hour study hall. We'd meet in his classroom and, later, head for the coaches' office. Then as yellow buses began piling up at the curb, we'd slip out the side door, sprint along the sidewalks, and be blocks away from the building by the last bell.

Eventually, we began running together on the weekends. Halfway across the truck road between a field of corn and a field of beans, I'd see him waiting, running in place in order to keep his heart rate high.

As if we owned the roads, we ran, hearts racing and minds beating. We'd talk about books and baseball and bigger things in life, managing our pace in order to maintain our conversation.

༒

Those who want to lament the conditions of literacy in the U.S. can easily find startling statistics. For example, two different national studies report that less than one-half of all U.S. adults read literature, and nearly two-fifths of all high school seniors are hardly ever or never asked to write three or more pages in their English classes (National Endowment; National Commission). Implicit in these and other similar lamentations are beliefs about the inherent benefits of literacy, which include logical, analytic, and rational thinking; general and abstract use of language; skeptical and questioning attitudes; distinctions between myths and histories; a recognition of the impact of time and space; complex modern governments with a separated church and state; democracy, political stability, and greater social equality; a lower crime rate and better citizens; more economic development, as well as wealth and productivity; urbanization; and a lower birth rate (Gee 26). The problem, however, is that these beliefs are based, according to Harvey Graff, on the literacy myth. In fact, historical evidence suggests no causal relationship between reading and writing and social interaction, economic growth, individual wealth, or even democracy (Graff, *Labyrinths*)—although to listen to some of my colleagues, you'd never know it.

Many examples of the complicated connections between literacy and society likely come to mind, so I will limit myself to an obvious one—the literacy tests in the South prior to the 1965 Voting Rights Act. Between August 1964 and July 1965, applicants in Alabama had to choose among 100 different versions of this test, each of which, in general, had three sections: reading excerpts from the Constitution; writing from dictation, or sometimes copying, a portion of the Constitution; and answering questions about both the transcribed excerpt and state and national citizenship, such as naming the two levels of government that can levy taxes (Alabama).

Now, you might be thinking, that's not actually reading or writing, so what, then, is literacy? According to C. H. Knoblauch, arguments about literacy in the U.S. often distinguish among functional, personal growth, cultural, and critical literacies (74). Of these, the one most consistent with the original function of English departments is *cultural literacy.*

As has been extensively documented, the formal study of English in the U.S. emerged in the mid-nineteenth century as a result of the shift from a classical to an elective model of education, which accelerated the development of knowledge by specialists but virtually eliminated the shared cultural experience that was a hallmark of a college education. To remedy this loss, college administrators created the English department, first at Harvard and then at Brown, to certify students as eligible to earn college degrees through both literature classrooms, where students would be exposed to these principles, and composition classrooms, where their mastery could be assessed (S. Miller 51). In other words, the business of English, according to Robert Scholes, is the certification of taste through the business of reading and writing (see also Berlin, *Rhetoric;* Berlin *Rhetorics;* Crowley).

Not surprisingly, the study of English, according to E. D. Hirsch, is a primary source of *cultural literacy,* or to paraphrase his subtitle, what U.S. Americans need to know. According to Hirsch, cultural literacy is the "translinguistic knowledge" necessary for "linguistic literacy," which are interdependent ("Cultural" 165). Moreover, acquiring cultural literacy, Hirsch believes, is being acculturated into literacy culture, which should be the minimal goal of education (166). To this end, Hirsch calls for both extensive and intensive curricula that, he believes, combines both national standards and local choice into the formation of this shared cultural context. At the end of his book-length argument, Hirsch provides a lengthy list—pages and pages and pages—of names, terms, events, and other information that are needed to communicate with each other and participate in society (*Cultural*).

In part, this notion of literacy is so powerful, both inside and outside schools, because it seems so obvious: to understand each other, we must sufficiently share contexts, even if only enough to realize that we misunderstand. This condition is compellingly illustrated throughout Hirsch's book, such as the account of events that seems so incomprehensible, almost random, until a title—washing clothes—provides the context that makes it meaningful (*Cultural* 40). Such experiences occur throughout our lives, whether as section headings in a report or as misunderstood emails among acquaintances.

Nonetheless, this model of literacy has been challenged by critics who have focused on the way Hirsch ignores the politics of canon formation (e.g., Bizzell, "Beyond") or presumes a print-based society (e.g., Tuman). While these critics are correct to challenge Hirsch's universalized context, they must also examine the universalization of textual practices—reading and writing—as shared skills disproportionately distributed across society.

✿

He wasn't the first teacher to befriend me. That was my first grade teacher, a nun who walked me across town, one afternoon, for my first trip to a library. *After she and I selected some books, I watched her haggle with the small town librarian over whether she could check them out without a library card.*

She was one to suggest sending me to the school library during language arts time. While the others completed worksheets and answered comprehension questions, I read alone in the library. Though the selection was limited, the books became familiar—biographies of Abraham Lincoln and Benjamin Franklin, an entire self of the Hardy Boys mysteries, fictionalized accounts of the FBI, and science fiction thrillers sandwiched between The Lives of the Saints *and frayed copies of* The Baltimore Catechism.

For eight years, my teachers assigned the empty school library for my language arts requirement. Occasionally, I was given something specific to read—once 1984 *and another time* A Tale of Two Cities. *Otherwise, I read whatever I wanted.*

In high school, I returned to English classrooms and English teachers. Each fall, honors English used the same grammar handbook, and, in the spring, it focused on a different introduction to canonical literatures.

The first spring focused on Greek mythology. Each class began with a quiz—twenty recall questions from Edith Hamilton's Mythology: Timeless Tales of Gods and Heroes, *each of which had a single short answer that had to be spelled correctly. Fascinated by the stories but unmotivated by the memorization, I barely passed.*

The same teacher was my instructor in the summer gifted program because, when asked, I explained that I wanted to learn to write. Unlike her regular classes, these summer sessions started with debates over movies that the others and she had seen, often the night before at her apartment across town. Then she'd read something or assign an exercise.

One crisp morning, she marched us out the doors and around the football field and the baseball diamond behind the building. We were to observe our environment, she said, and then describe our observations.

Upon our return to the air conditioned relief, all I could recall were a patch of dandelions and our creeping pace, so I tried to recreate the languid distraction in my description of splayed stalks. After listening to me read aloud, she announced that I would never be a writer.

I searched for books to help me. I found a rhetorical handbook, but it was too mechanical. I found a series of new age reflections, but these were too vague. So instead I imitated the things I had read, and I lived by my running-English teacher's advice that writing was not finished until it was read.

ᘒ

To be fair, many within English departments acknowledge differences among practices, including assessment. For example, Stanley Fish suggests that the interpretations of texts suggest more about the disciplines that inform them, and Tom Fox argues that different approaches to student writing lead to different conclusions about their intellectual abilities (Fish; Fox 44). The problem, however, is that these acknowledgments are rarely converted into *praxis*—practices and theories— that challenge conventional approaches to English studies.

To illustrate this problem, I want to turn to the use of Mary Louise Pratt's distinction between the linguistics of community and the linguistics of contact. According to Pratt, a linguistics of community, which presumes a homogeneous and unified world, seeks the general and the universal while a linguistics of contact, which recognizes heterogeneity and inconsistencies, focuses upon the specific and the particular ("Linguistics" 50, 61). A linguistics of community, she argues, dominates the disciplines of linguistics and literary studies, as seen, for example, in the notion of speech communities and interpretive communities, and it reflects larger beliefs about a universal national community and national identity (57–58). At the same time, such an approach misunderstands the ways that cultures compete for power within social spaces, which she designates as contact zones ("Arts" 34). To address these situations, a linguistics of contact is necessary.

These insights have been used to reconfigure English studies. For example, Patricia Bizzell argues that the contact zone, situated in time and space but having fluid boundaries, offers an organizing principle for literary study not as chronological periods or literary genres or even race or gender categories but as historical moments in which competing groups contest culturally specific interpretations of texts and the world ("Contact" 166–67). In a related but more expansive way, James Slevin uses both a linguistics of contact and contact zones both to critique the cultural dominance of English departments, as well as language education more generally, and to argue for new notions of intellectual work (2, 6).

Although potentially powerful, Pratt's insights about the differences between a community and contact linguistics are never fully realized in these reconfigurations of English studies, in part because these largely leave underlying models of literacy relatively intact. In terms of contact linguistics and literacy theories, some have criticized the superficiality of the contact zone, and others have complained about the use of conventional constructs and the denial of socio-economic contexts (e.g., Harris 117; Stuckey 6). In much the same way, I believe that these alternative approaches to English studies nonetheless authorize semi-autonomous models of literacy in which unauthorized differences are framed as educational obstacles to overcome and not potential intellectual resources to use.

Slevin's expansive scope makes his approach more useful for analysis. At its center, he insists, is an effort to reject *absence* or *lack* as organizing principles for the study of English in favor of *difference.* In doing so, he appeals to both sides of traditional disciplinary divides while bringing them together around the notion of literacy. For example, colonial literature, such as the story of Pocahontas or the records of Virginia Tidewater, becomes an account of the ways that assumptions about language and education, in his own words, "were planted, like the colony itself, in the consciousness of invaders and invaded alike" (Slevin 4). At the same time, he both expands and limits the scope of composition (10). For instance, he confronts conventional concerns while challenging conventional thinking, such as distinguishing between *writing across the curriculum,* with its tendency toward academic socialization, and *WID,* with its ability to position intellectual workers, including students, within "an historical and dialogic intellectual project" (190–91). In addition, he addresses larger issues, such as assessment and tenure, arguing in both cases for a more active role of those being evaluated.

Among the strengths of Slevin's approach is the use of particularity, often in the form of experience, as the basis for theorizing, which prevents practices from being limited to, or dismissed as, lore. Together, practice and theory, as *praxis,* becomes the definition of intellectual work, whether depicting his classrooms, explicating *Don Quixote,* or analyzing WPA assessment methods.

At the same time, Slevin relies upon generalizations and reifications—a linguistics of community—that ultimately leave approaches to English and their notions of literacy relatively unchanged. For example, he cites, on several occasions, the symbolic violence of colonizing discourse, the canon, even education itself, as others have done (e.g., Stuckey). While sympathetic, I am nonetheless concerned that such a move conflates symbolic violence, which can be traumatic, with physical violence, which often is, and it dismisses those who believe that symbolic violence is the very experience of these acts (e.g., J. Hillis Miller).

Even worse, it ignores the complexity of enculturation, particularly the differences between pursing it, having it imposed, or some complicated combination. Instead, it frames participants, whether students or immigrants, as (relatively) passive victims of these violations of language and culture. As, however, many, from Keith Gilyard to Mike Rose and Victor Villanueva, suggest, and as others, from Christina Pearson Casanave and Marilyn S. Sternglass, have reported, these experiences are much more contested.

In contrast to what Slevin suggests, most assume any number of selves and perspectives, even before sitting in English classrooms or experiencing formal language education, not to mention informal language education at home or in the neighborhood.

Moreover, their very presence in universities and other social institutions, such as community literacy programs, suggests a desire for such an education, even if only as a means to another end. At the same time, many know that the linguistic shifts they make, or learn to make or even don't or won't make, are temporary, contingent shifts, ones that are often shifted again as soon as they leave a classroom or a workplace, or the home or neighborhood. As their experience suggests, few can survive, let along thrive, in a world without acquiescing to new selves and different values.

In addition to generalizing about people at the expense of actual individuals with differing desires and situations, another example of the power of a linguistics of community is the use of *discourse,* not just as *colonizing discourse* but also *academic discourse* as a relatively uncontested phenomenon. As a part of argument, for example, for critical perspectives on academic genres, Slevin suggests that most will agree upon the importance of joining the academic community and controlling "the genres of academic discourse" (155):

> I think the problem we face rests in the tension between the metaphor of initiation in which we have become ensnared and our desire, finally, to provide for students a critical distance that makes the process of joining the academic discourse community something quite different from an "initiation." (155)

While Slevin recognizes the limits of the language used to talk about literacy, he nonetheless employs the same theoretical concepts, albeit on a somewhat smaller scale.

To be sure, Slevin is merely echoing others in both English studies and other disciplines. For example, according to David Bartholomae's ironic, and often cited, account, students are, and must be, appropriated by specialized discourses. And to cite a second example, literacy theorist James Paul Gee defines literacy as the "mastery of a secondary Discourse," or particular "saying(writing)-doing-being-valuing-believing combination" (143, 127). Such accounts lead to discussions about the discourse of historians or lawyers, as if these are stable and monolithic phenomena into which language users are socialized, through (to use Gee's terms) acquisition, or exposure, and learning, or conscious study (138).

In these and other ways, Slevin's approach authorizes a *semi-autonomous model of literacy*. Autonomous models of literacy, according to Brian Street, are described in "technical terms" and exist separate from contexts (2). In contrast, semi-autonomous models, as I define them, recognize authorized contexts, such as disciplines or professions, while denying unauthorized yet significant ones, from divergent norms to language histories. While language users might now be defined as *different*, this difference is, at best, deficiently different, if not differently deficient. As such, these differences are framed as educational obstacles to overcome and not potential intellectual resources to exploit.

☙

Upon declaring my English major, he gave me an inscribed copy of a rhetorical handbook from one of his classrooms. After I enrolled in graduate school, he loaned me his copy of A Glossary of Literary Terms. *When I thought about dropping out, he urged me to finish.*

After completing my coursework, I returned to St. Louis, the city where I was born, in order to get on with my life, as well as to prepare for comps and write a dissertation. Shortly thereafter, my father called to tell me that my running-English teacher friend had been hospitalized near my new home.

In the hallway on his floor, I heard the machine pumping his blood for him before I saw him in his room. His spirits were as high as ever, but his prognosis was dire.

Over the next few weeks, we talked regularly, and I visited several more times. Late one night, his wife called to tell me that he was being prepped for surgery as we spoke. Before I could arrive, he had departed, on the table, while his surgeons tried to replace his heart.

The next day, I agreed to give the eulogy. When I couldn't compose my thoughts, I went running. As I sprinted down St. Louis streets, I noticed that I was thinking about my missing friend in terms of the stories he had asked me to read, the stories that had shaped so much of our lives.

Like Manolin to his Santiago, I wanted him to get well fast because I had so much to learn, and I too was crying, as I bid farewell with his family and friends, to the old man, dreaming of sunny beaches, I hoped, while others examined the skeleton that had been strapped to his skiff.

❦

In their original configurations, the function of English departments was the certification of a universalized cultural literacy, in which cultural differences were understood in terms of absence or lack. While this understanding has been challenged, more recent approaches acknowledge authorized differences, such as disciplines or professions, while ignoring others. Although improvements, these more recent approaches still certify students in semi-autonomous models of literacy, in which unauthorized differences are understood as educational obstacles to overcome—deficient differences if not different deficiencies—and not potential intellectual resources to use.

As recent research suggests, the practices of reading and writing themselves are contingent upon contexts, not just in terms of content as Hirsch suggests but also in terms of functions and forms, such as the use of reading or standards for acceptable writing. According to James Collins and Richard K. Blot, the earliest efforts to document these differences first appeared almost thirty years ago in Shirley Brice Heath's *Ways With Words,* Ruth Finnegan's *Literacy and Orality,* and Brian Street's *Literacy in Theory and Practice* and *Cross-Cultural Approaches to Literacy* (34). More recent efforts have examined these differences both outside and inside academic institutions, such as John Trimbur's *Popular Literacy* (2001) and A. Suresh Canagarajah's *A Geopolitics of Academic Writing* (2002), as well as work by David Baron, Mary Hamilton, and Roz Ivanič (2000) and Bill Cope and Mary Kalantzis (2000) in situated and multiliteracies.

While most of these critiques have been made by those outside English departments, others, even those within English, have started to examine assumptions within these models, such as those about language policies and language status. For example, Bruce Horner and John Trimbur identify an implicit policy of unidirectional English monolingualism, based upon a series of reifications, in which language use is the source of social identity (596). Expanding this effort, Paul Kei Matsuda, to cite a second example, suggests that at least among those who teach writing, English Only is presumed to be both the current condition and the ultimate goal, in that students are assumed to be native English speakers (637).

While both the proposed solutions involve multilingualism, neither confronts, in any substantial way, the larger questions about standards, which lead to issues of instruction, assessment, and, at least within English departments, literacy. However, such questions, I should confess, are ones that I have too struggled to examine. While the collection I co-edited with Helen Fox and Patricia Bizzell, *ALT DIS: Alternative Discourses and the Academy*, has been praised as an example of the "most progressive" research in composition, it nonetheless has been criticized, fairly I might add, for its failure to address issues of standards, particularly at the level of syntax, grammar, and spelling (Canagarajah, "Place" 595).

These questions about standards are ultimately questions about both models of literacy and institutionalization of instruction. In terms of the former, some have begun to offer the basis for new literacy models. For example, Canagarajah identifies inference models, or those that invoke cultural differences to explain marked language, and the slightly modified correlationist models, which analyze L1 in order to explain marked features in L2, both of which operate on an essentialization of language and culture. In contrast, he advocates negotiation models, in which multilingual writers move back and forth, or shuttle, between languages (589–91). Already, researchers have begun to document the impact of these negotiations on English (e.g., Bhatt), and I have suggested that negotiation is not only a way of thinking about differences of languages, or between other languages and English but also, I suggest, differences of dialects, or between one variety of language and another (e.g., *ReInventing*).

The challenge, however, is not only developing these models but institutionalizing them, which will be more difficult although this difficulty, I predict, will decrease over time in large part because more and more theorists are expanding the scope of their research in ways that will enrich the corpus, or data, for which our models and practices must account. A good example is the relatively recent interest within English departments in community literacies: Linda Flower and her colleagues and the Community Literacy Center; Stephen Parks and Eli Goldblatt and their Writing Beyond the Curriculum program; and Jeffery Grabill and his work with the Western District Adult Basic Education program.

To be sure, such efforts are not immune to the universalization and essentialization of existing literacy models. For example, Flower and her colleagues define community literacy as an alternative discourse that supports social change, intercultural interactions, strategic approaches, and inquiry (Peck, Flower, and Higgins 205). Nonetheless, they expand the evidentiary base on which we build our theories and establish our practices. As long as these efforts insist that experience is theorized, as Slevin suggests, they will challenge institutionalized models of literacy, particularly within English departments, which can only increase the chances that we're doing relevant work with, and not on, those who pass through our hallways and classrooms.

ᕗ

You'd be forgiven for thinking that this is a testimony to the ways that my running teacher changed my life.

Yes, he did change my life. In a rural town where similarity is a virtue, he was the biggest sinner I knew. He was also a father figure, filling in for one too distracted by sick patients and six siblings.

And no, my problems with English were far from finished. As an undergrad, I changed my major to and from English more times than I want to remember.

Once in an American literature survey, a Samuel Clemens lookalike asked for interpretations of Theodore Roethke's "My Papa's Waltz." When he pointed to me, I tried to express an emotional ambiguity of the little boy persona. No, my professor said, stroking his gray goatee, it's actually a celebration of his father.

In my English classes, I learned to do explication de texte and write literary analyses, but when, upon graduating, I still couldn't understand, I thought that maybe graduate school could give me everything that had been missing in my previous classes.

After passing my comps with distinction, I decided to make this search the focus of my dissertation. My committee rejected the project, so I gave them what they wanted. Then during cocktails after graduation, I mentioned that I had obtained a contract for the project they had rejected only months ago.

After moving my pregnant wife and one-year old daughter across the country for a WPA job, my new chair told me that if his department had seen my manuscript, it likely wouldn't have offered me the position.

At another job, a colleague altered and then published my private email, without my consent or even knowledge, in the school paper in order to buttress his argument about declining standards in the English Department.

These stories are not unique, I know. Too many of us, I know, have experienced the ways that reading and writing have been used to exclude and include. Victor tells similar stories in Bootstraps, *for example, of the ways that reading and writing have been used to exclude and include, but in our haste to theorize (and institutionalize), we sometimes lost the particularity of reading and writing in everyday life.*

So what should we say when we're asked what we do?

WORKS CITED

Alabama Department of Archives and History. "Selma-to-Montgomery 1965 Voting Rights March." 2001. 9 Sept. 2008 <http://www.alabama-moments.state.al.us/sec59ps.html>.

American Council on Education. "ACE Releases Its Annual Status Report on Minorities in Higher Education." 14 Feb 2005. 16 June 2005 <http://tinyurl.com/dzjeow>.

Bartholomae, David. "Inventing the University." *When a Writer Can't Write: Studies in Writer's Block and Other Composing-Process Problems.* Ed. Mike Rose. New York: Guilford, 1985. 134–65.

Barton, David, Mary Hamilton, and Roz Ivanič, eds. *Situated Literacies: Reading and Writing in Context.* London: Routledge, 2000.

Berlin, James A. *Rhetoric and Reality: Writing Instruction in American Colleges, 1900–1985.* Urbana, IL: NCTE, 1987.

—. *Rhetorics, Poetics, and Cultures: Refiguring College English Studies.* 1996. West Lafayette, IN: Parlor Press, 2003.

Bizzell, Patricia. "Beyond Anti-Foundationalism to Rhetorical Authority: Problems Defining 'Cultural Literacy.'" *College English* 52.6 (1990): 661–75.

—. "'Contact Zones' and English Studies." *College English* 56.2 (1994): 163–69.

Canagarajah, A. Suresh. *A Geopolitics of Academic Writing*. Pittsburgh: U of Pittsburgh P, 2002.

—. "The Place of World Englishes in Composition: Pluralization Continued." *College Composition and Communication* 57 (2006): 586–619.

—. "Toward a Writing Pedagogy of Shuttling between Languages: Learning from Multilingual Writers." *College English* 68 (2006): 589–604.

Casanave, Christine Pearson. *Writing Games: Multicultural Case Studies of Academic Literacy Practices in Higher Education*. Mahwah, NJ: Erlbaum, 2002.

Collins, James, and Richard K. Blot. *Literacy and Literacies: Texts, Power, and Identity*. Cambridge: Cambridge UP, 2003.

Cope, Bill, and Mary Kalantzis. *Multiliteracies: Literacy Learning and the Design of Social Futures*. London: Routledge, 2000.

Crowley, Sharon. *Composition in the University: Historical and Polemical Essays*. Pittsburgh: U of Pittsburgh P, 1998.

Daniels, Harvey A. *Famous Last Words: The American Language Crisis Reconsidered*. Carbondale, IL: Southern Illinois UP, 1983.

Fish, Stanley. *Professional Correctness: Literary Studies and Political Change*. Cambridge: Harvard UP, 1995.

Fox, Tom. *Defending Access: A Critique of Standards in Higher Education*. Portsmouth, NH: Boynton/Cook Heinemann, 1999.

Gee, James Paul. *Social Linguistics and Literacies: Ideology in Discourses*. 2nd ed. Bristol, PA: Falmer P, 1996.

Gilyard, Keith. *Voices of the Self: A Study of Language Competence*. Detroit: Wayne State UP, 1991.

Grabill, Jeffrey T. *Community Literacy Programs and the Politics of Change*. Albany, NY: SUNY, 2001.

Graff, Harvey J. *The Labyrinths of Literacy: Reflections on Literacy Past and Present*. Pittsburgh: U of Pittsburgh P, 1995.

Harris, Joseph. *A Teaching Subject: Composition Since 1966*. Upper Saddle River, NJ: Prentice-Hall, 1997.

Heath, Shirley Brice. *Ways With Words: Language, Life, and Work in Communities and Classrooms*. Cambridge: Cambridge UP, 1983.

Hirsch, E. D., Jr. "Cultural Literacy." *American Scholar* 52.2 (1983): 159–69.

—. *Cultural Literacy: What Every American Needs to Know*. New York: Vintage, 1987.

Horner, Bruce, and John Trimbur. "English Only and U. S. College Composition." *College Composition and Communication* 53 (2002): 594–630.

Hourigan, Maureen M. *Literacy as Social Exchange: Intersections of Class, Gender, and Culture*. Albany: SUNY P, 1994.

Knoblauch, C. H. "Literacy and the Politics of Education." *The Right to Literacy*. Ed. Andrea Lunsford, Helene Moglen, and James Slevin. New York: MLA, 1990. 74–80.

Lenhart, Amanda, Deborah Fallows, and John Horrigan. "Content Creation Online: 44% of U.S. Internet Users Have Contributed Their Thoughts and Their Files to the Online World." *Pew Internet & American Life Project*. 29 Feb. 2004. 1 July 2004 <http://www.pewtrusts.org/our_work_report_detail.aspx?id=17080>.

Matsuda, Paul Kei. "The Myth of Linguistic Homogeneity in U.S. College Composition." *College English* 68 (2006): 637–51.

Miller, J. Hillis. *On Literature*. London: Routledge, 2002.

Miller, Susan. *Textual Carnivals: The Politics of Composition*. Carbondale, IL: Southern Illinois UP, 1991.

National Commission on Writing in American's Schools and Colleges. "The Neglected 'R': The Need for a Writing Revolution." 2003. 24 January 2009 <http://www.writingcommission.org/prod_downloads/writingcom/neglectedr.pdf>.

National Endowment for the Arts. "Literary Reading in Dramatic Decline, According to National Endowment for the Arts Survey." 8 July 2004. 4 Sept. 2004 <http://www.nea.gov/news/news04/ReadingAtRisk.html>.

Ohmann, Richard. *Politics of Letters*. Middletown, CT: Wesleyan UP, 1987.

Parks, Stephen, and Eli Goldblatt. "Writing Beyond the Curriculum: Fostering New Collaborations in Literacy." *College English* 62 (2000): 584–606.

Peck, Wayne Campbell, Linda Flower, and Lorraine Higgins. "Community Literacy." *College Composition and Communication* 46.2 (1995): 199–222.

Pratt, Mary Louise. "Arts of the Contact Zone." *Profession* (1991): 33–40.

—. "Linguistic Utopias." *The Linguistics of Writing: Arguments between Language and Literature*. Ed. Nigel Fabb, Derek Attridge, Alan Durant, and Colin MacCabe. New York: Methuen, 1987. 44–66.

Rose, Mike. *Lives on the Boundary: A Moving Account of the Struggles and Achievements of America's Educationally Underprepared*. New York: Penguin, 1989.

Scholes, Robert. *The Rise and Fall of English: Reconstructing English as a Discipline*. New Haven, CT: Yale UP, 1998.

Schroeder, Christopher. *ReInventing the University: Literacies and Legitimacy in the Postmodern Academy*. Logan, UT: Utah State UP, 2001.

Schroeder, Christopher, Helen Fox, and Patricia Bizzell, eds. *ALT DIS: Alternative Discourses and the Academy*. Portsmouth, NH: Boynton/Cook Heinemann, 2002.

Slevin, James F. *Introducing English: Essays in the Intellectual Work of Composition*. Pittsburgh: U of Pittsburgh P, 2001.

Sternglass, Marilyn S. *Time to Know Them: A Longitudinal Study of Writing and Learning at the College Level*. Mahwah, NJ: Erlbaum, 1997.

Street, Brian. "The New Literacy Studies." *Cross-Cultural Approaches to Literacy*. Ed. Brian Street. London: Cambridge UP, 1993. 1–21.

Stuckey, J. Elspeth. *The Violence of Literacy*. Portsmouth, NH: Boynton/Cook Heinemann, 1991.

Trimbur, John. "Literacy and the Discourse of Crisis." *The Politics of Writing Instruction: Postsecondary*. Portsmouth, NH: Boynton/Cook Heinemann, 1991. 277–95.

—, ed. *Popular Literacy: Studies in Cultural Practices and Poetics*. Pittsburgh: U of Pittsburgh P, 2001.

Tuman, Myron C. *Word Perfect: Literacy in the Computer Age*. Pittsburgh: U of Pittsburgh P, 1992.

Villanueva, Victor. *Bootstraps: From an American Academic of Color*. Urbana, IL: NCTE, 1993.

13 (Re)defining the Humanistic: Making Space for Technology in Twenty-First Century English Studies

Michael S. Knievel

INTRODUCTION

In the past century, but with particular vigor during the last twenty-five years, English studies has expanded to encompass previously exotic currents like technical communication and computers and writing, both of which hold technology as central to their identities. The expansion has not been seamless, given that many programs in these fields are situated in English departments that are traditionally more interested in literary texts than in the technologies used to create or disseminate those texts, or in the use and development of other texts (MacNealy and Heaton; Selfe, *Technology and Literacy*). In short, while many English departments might recognize, for instance, the personal computer as the writing technology of our time, few would lay any explicit claim to ownership for "matters technological," however technology is understood. Indeed, it would seem that the essence of the "sweetness and light" Matthew Arnold saw emerging from literary study has historically been and remains largely at odds with subdisciplines that take technology as an orienting concern—that take as objects of analysis diverse technologies and technology topics ranging from online help files to hypertext, from military weaponry to wikis.

In light of this history, one ongoing problem for technical communication and computers and writing, which I will collectively refer to here as "technologized rhetorical subdisciplines" of English studies, has been to establish and articulate the nature of each field's respective "humanistic character"—to establish, in essence, what it is about them that warrants association with the humanities and, typically, English studies. Efforts to do so seem to be motivated at once by a desire for self-definition and a need to establish legitimacy within English as a disciplinary context not traditionally disposed toward technology. And while it is clear that technology enjoys a higher profile in English Studies and the humanities than it once did (see, for instance, the National Endowment for the Humanities' Digital Humanities initiative), C. P. Snow's long-recognized binary model separating the "culture" of technology from that of the humanities is more than a mere vestige of the past.

The burden of proof, then, rests with the technologized rhetorical subdisciplines to demonstrate a sense of commonality with what English, predominantly literary studies, *does*. Perhaps not surprisingly, the main thrust of humanistic argument in these fields has often been to emphasize shared terrain or similar points of interest, like the technologized rhetorical subdisciplines' emphasis on rhetoric and interpretation and postmodern concerns like gender, multicultural communication, ethics, ideology, and authorship (Lay; Dombrowski, *Humanistic Aspects;* Markel; Miller; Smith and Selfe; Nold). Patrick Moore notes, for instance, technical communication scholars' particular tendency "to rehabilitate technical communication by redefining it as rhetoric to make it [. . .] fit better within the humanities" (114). While this strategy has proved useful in various ways, I would argue that in their emphasis on rhetoric and overlapping features, these humanistic arguments have frequently relied upon an ironic form of self-effacement that indirectly segregates technology from "authentic" humanistic enterprise, further complicating the position of the technologized rhetorical subdisciplines in the space of the traditional humanities.

In this chapter, I briefly survey humanistic argument in technical communication and computers and writing to sketch a sense of how deep-seated cultural biases and political pressures have overdetermined the nature of humanistic argument in the technologized rhetorical subdisciplines. Then I explore other possibilities for recasting humanistic definition, focusing on pragmatism and the three twentieth-century editions of the *Humanist Manifesto* as alternative, problematizing lenses through which we might gainfully view the remaining effects of the traditional "two culture" bifurcation between literary and technological interests. I argue that by relying on traditional English humanities characteristics and ideals in their humanistic arguments, scholars in the technologized rhetorical subdisciplines have become strangely complicit in reinscribing a bifurcated English Studies that frustrates humanities participation in the technological sphere. These subdisciplines' future and full membership in English Studies—and, I believe, the future of English Studies itself—require a humanistic framework that explicitly claims technology and instrumentality instead of defining itself in opposition to it.

TECHNOLOGIZED RHETORICAL SUBDISCIPLINES: TECHNOLOGY AS DIFFERENCE IN ENGLISH

Before moving forward, it makes sense to pause and consider the label "technologized rhetorical subdisciplines." What makes this characterization appropriate? Working backwards, "rhetorical subdisciplines" may be a somewhat controversial term insofar as it suggests a degree of establishment that some may question. However, both technical communication and computers and writing bear many of the usual marks of such status, each with an emergent critical mass of conferences, scholarly journals, programs, and tenure line faculty. Both derive from writing studies, itself often marginalized in English despite its roots in rhetoric.

More importantly, technical communication and computers and writing are also uniquely joined in English studies by their definitional relationship to different, but similarly visible, technologies: computers and writing and the networked computer, and technical communication and a range of technologies that include the computer but also many others. This definitional reliance on technology not only binds the two but also distinguishes them from other constituent subdisciplines in many English departments, like linguistics, film studies, and creative writing, among others. Technology is not incidental to either technical communication or computers and writing; rather, it is central to their identities.

Indeed, it is important to draw a distinction between the technology of the technologized rhetorical subdisciplines and the types of technology that can be said to already exist in English studies. Liberally speaking, of course, books, pencils—even language—can be called technologies and are the traditional tools of English studies scholars and students (Baron 15). But technology functions differently and features both prominently and definitionally in the technologized rhetorical subdisciplines. Walter Ong describes technologies that have been "interiorized" and thus rendered essentially invisible *as* technologies. Both computers and writing and technical communication take as a large part of their identities technologies (like the personal computer) that have yet to be interiorized, meaning that the technologies each takes as its respective locus of concern command attention and identification *as* a technology or as technologies (145). For instance, computers and writing emphasizes the ways in which the networked computer revolutionizes textual production and distribution, in addition to the ways it changes the nature of that text through the integration of multimedia forms and interactivity. All of these concerns are immediately connected to the computer as a technology and to the nature of mediation made possible by the digital writing environment. The computer as it is situated in computers and writing, then, remains identified as a technology in way that a pencil does not, as "uninteriorized" vis-à-vis traditional English Studies. Similarly, technical communication's technological identity encompasses a wide range of technologies identified, for instance, with high tech industries and the computer itself, technologies and technology sites that are uncommon objects of inquiry in English.

Hence, designating technical communication and computers and writing as subdisciplines of English challenges conventional views of English in an academy and society that has historically positioned literature and the humanities as antidotes or antitheses to technology, as a site "for technologists to come and be instructed by humanists in order to learn why they are hollow, unfulfilled individuals" (Borchert and Stewart 1). In sum, the very nature of the technologized rhetorical subdisciplines signifies a radical shift in scope from an English studies whose primary role vis-à-vis technology has been critique of it to an English studies that should be enable constructive participation in the technological sphere.

Instrumentality, the Humanistic, and Self-Abnegation in the Technologized Rhetorical Subdisciplines

In the technologized rhetorical subdisciplines' respective histories, the question, "what makes our field humanistic?" appears early and lingers as an ongoing concern, flaring up in various ways from time to time in each field's scholarship. While comprehensive examination of these ar-

guments surpasses the scope of this chapter, a brief survey of their nature illustrates ways in which scholars in the technologized rhetorical
subdisciplines have described humanistic character when the terms of
humanistic discourse are largely overdetermined by the broader disciplinary context of English (Knievel, "Technology Artifacts"; Knievel,
"What Is Humanistic?").

In technical communication, arguments for humanistic characterization have ranged from enumerating disciplinary parallels to literary
studies to explicating the field's postmodern and rhetorical notions
of knowledge and truth. For instance, Russell Rutter has linked the
creative and imaginative component of technical writing invention to
that of poetics, while Elizabeth Tebeaux has argued that contemporary literary theory becomes a site of demonstrable overlap between
technical writing and literary study. Others have focused on concerns
that are familiar in the academic humanities, like the role of ethics
in technical communication (Dombrowski, *Ethics;* Dragga; Markel).
Still others (Lay) point to the role of gender in technical writing and
organizational politics, while Dombrowski ("Post-Modernism") and
Wilson have pointed to postmodern epistemology's role in describing
the humanistic character of technical communication. In other words,
these arguments have focused on demonstrating points of overlap with
concepts and concerns traditionally associated with the humanities
and English studies.

In computers and writing, scholars have long been sensitive to the
threat represented by the computer and its applications and have taken
pains to establish connections to recognizable humanist values since
the field's inception (Nold). Some (e.g., Kemp, Schwartz) have offered
ways to fight against the dehumanizing drill-and-practice tendencies
of early computer applications written to support writing instruction,
while others (Schroeder and Boe) have focused on the compatibility
and coexistence of computers and humanist vision in the writing classroom, advocating a "minimalist" approach to computer implementation in an effort to foreground humanistic pedagogical values without
letting technology interfere. Cynthia Selfe ("Preparing English Teachers") and others (Moran, Sommers) have argued for a closer relationship between technology and the humanities, emphasizing the importance of developing and utilizing technologies that reflect humanistic
values. Like in technical communication, other related computers and
writing scholarship has more recently highlighted issues like gender,

sexuality, identity, and postmodern epistemology as they play out in digital environments, which resonates with a broader locus of concerns in literature and contemporary English studies (Handa, Barker and Kemp, Bolter, Faigley, Regan, LeCourt and Barnes, Slatin, Sullivan, Landow).

These arguments contribute meaningfully to each subdiscipline's respective understanding of its range of concern and also construct a sense of common cause with English and literary studies, a view of the technologized rhetorical subdisciplines as closely linked to traditional humanistic interests. Yet, I would argue that by focusing on establishing connections to recognizable humanities concerns and values, these arguments—though legitimate and valid—may indirectly play a role in reproducing a problematic relationship in English where technology exists *alongside and separate from* the humanistic. In such a relationship, technology might be favorably influenced by the humanities, but it is not, in and of itself, humanistic.

Such separation is reflected in the aforementioned moves to reframe both technical communication and computer-based writing as distinctly "rhetorical" and is often, I think, an unintended consequence of arguments that have made significant contributions to our understanding of these fields. For instance, in her landmark essay, "A Humanistic Rationale for Technical Writing," Carolyn Miller, challenges traditionally positivist notions of technical writing, which in their emphasis on clarity reductively hold that technical writing is little more than a "windowpane" overlooking reality or truth (611–12). Miller argues that invention, context, and motive play key roles in technical and scientific discourse, finding in this rhetorical nature a "humanistic rationale" for the field, which she contrasts with the dehumanizing positivism and instrumentality traditionally associated with technical discourse. In addition to gainfully complicating a long-held and problematic perspective on technical writing, "rhetorical," in this view, becomes a way into familiar humanistic terrain, and this premise became a key statement shaping subsequent humanistic argument in the field. Indeed, I discuss Miller here both because of the long-term influence of her essay and because her ongoing scholarly conversation with Patrick Moore (with Moore, in actuality, doing most of the talking) is something of a "ground zero" for these issues in technical communication scholarship.

In "Instrumental Discourse Is as Humanistic as Rhetoric," Patrick Moore offers critique of what he describes as Miller's rhetoric/humanistic conflation and, in doing so, I believe, raises concerns about not only the status of instrumental discourse but also the status of instrumental technology, broadly construed, within humanistic argument in technical communication and the technologized rhetorical subdisciplines. Specifically, Moore challenges Miller's assertion that "instrumental discourse" and its underlying rationality are necessarily not humanistic, decrying, in other words, the exclusion of instrumental discourse from humanistic classification. Of instrumental discourse, he notes, "In many technological situations, a rigid, one-to-one correspondence is required between the signifier and the signified or else someone could die" (110). According to Moore, in such cases (writing cautions or warnings, for instance), technical communicators prioritize efficiency and an instrumental relationship between language and "reality" as it is practically, contextually understood in pursuit of what Moore terms legitimate humanistic goals, like saving lives and keeping technology users safe. In such instances, Moore argues that instrumental discourse can be humanistic, as well.

Most important for the present discussion is Moore's critique of Miller's claim that technical writing is humanistic because it is rhetorical, not instrumental, in nature. While the scope of Moore's critique may be somewhat overextended (in her response to Moore, for instance, Miller argued that instrumental discourse could be considered a part of rhetoric, rather than placed in opposition to it), I would argue that the logic behind Moore's assertion about the humanistic veracity of instrumental discourse sheds light upon another unstated assumption in much humanistic argument in the technologized rhetorical subdisciplines: that technology, as the embodiment of the instrumental *ethos,* does not fall under the rubric of "humanistic." This assumption is evidenced by technology's marginal status—its relative absence—in conversations about what, precisely, qualifies these technologized fields as humanistic.

Put another way, a shared *ethos* links Moore's arguments regarding instrumental discourse and technology more broadly defined, as instrumental technology is often criticized on grounds similar to those that Moore and Miller describe for "windowpane" technical writing— primarily, its fundamental emphasis on linearity and efficiency to the point of overwhelming other values and concerns (Brantlinger, Noble).

Indeed, instrumentality is often characterized as an irresistible, insidious, form of consciousness, the *ethos* enforcing what Neil Postman has called "technopoly," wherein human goals become conditioned solely by efficiency and what technology deems possible to the exclusion of competing ethics and human concerns (Postman 20; Katz; Lyotard). In this view, instrumentality becomes the sworn enemy of a more robust and rhetorical humanistic ethic. Dehumanizing instrumentality, necessarily exclusive of other ethical concerns, the argument goes, yields dehumanizing technology that marches forward unchecked.

It may well be that technology *is* instrumental by definition. But as Moore argues, "instrumental" is not necessarily the opposite of "humanistic." Following Moore's logic, the instrumental *ethos* associated with technology may be intimately linked with humanistic goals, rather than pitted directly against them; indeed, in keeping with Moore's discussion of instrumental discourse, a more liberal reading of "instrumental" suggests that instrumentality is a human construct, a manifestation or efficient synthesis of laudable human goals. Yet, the warrant in humanistic arguments that shift emphasis away from technology and toward other more readily identifiable humanistic characteristics seems to be that technology is, at best, not humanistic and, at worst, the opposite of it. In such arguments, technology is often pushed to the margins, tacitly hailed as something the technologized rhetorical subdisciplines can claim humanistic status in spite of, rather than because of. While historically validated in the humanities, this stance creates a strange continuum that reinscribes marginalization of the technologized rhetorical subdisciplines vis-à-vis humanistic character:

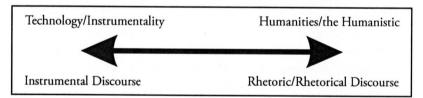

Figure 2: A strange continuum that reinscribes marginalization of the technologized rhetorical subdisciplines vis-à-vis humanistic character.

Again, this is not a general indictment of arguments that foreground traditional, more recognizable humanistic concerns (rhetoric, ethics, style, etc.); such arguments have clarified and expanded our understanding of the technologized rhetorical subdisciplines in meaningful ways. Yet directly or indirectly crowding instrumentality—and thus technology—out of humanistic description in favor of familiar humanities concerns not only threatens the integrity and viability of the technologized rhetorical subdisciplines but also reinscribes the historical division between the cultures of literature and the humanities and science and technology, respectively. Doing so may maintain a false sense of "purity" for the humanities, but it does little to help our students, ensure the long-term viability of our field, or strengthen English studies' contribution to society.

Stated plainly, accounts of what is humanistic about the technologized rhetorical subdisciplines that do not explicitly foreground technology as a humanistic "aspect" are incomplete. We need to consider alternative views of technology and instrumentality that raise the possibility of a dialogic—even synergistic—view of the relationship between technology and the humanistic. When we start to see technology and instrumental epistemology as a manifestation of human values, we must then ponder a view of technology as a legitimate, viable part of the humanities—as "humanistic" by definition and not merely in need of humanistic remediation and rehabilitation, which has historically seemed to be the outer limits set for the relationship between the two. Given their scope, the technologized rhetorical subdisciplines have a foot in both the liberal arts and the sciences (Longo 164)—or, better, stake out a new space entirely. However, when situated in English studies, they are culturally encouraged to differentiate and even quarantine the technological component of this integrated humanistic self-definition, a harmful form of self-abnegation, not only for computers and writing and technical communication but also for English studies.

REASSESSING THE "TWO CULTURES": PRAGMATISM AND THE *HUMANIST MANIFESTOS*

By its nature, pragmatism tests the implications of the traditional division in Snow's "two cultures" metaphor. Louis Menand notes that pragmatists reject the notion (as is common in the analytical philosophy tradition) that there exist abstract explanatory frameworks that might gainfully orient or explain human behavior because "they (pragmatists) believe that these puzzles, when they are not simply wasting the energy of the people who spend their time trying to 'solve' them, actually get in the way of our everyday efforts to cope with the

world" (xi). Acknowledging that there exist variations in how pragmatism is interpreted and practiced, it seems reasonable to claim that
certain fundamental tenets of the philosophy recommend a different
way of thinking about the nature of the technological subordination
that inheres in the "two cultures" as seen from an English humanities
perspective. Pragmatist philosophy does so by reframing traditional
questions of where Truth resides (science vs. humanities)—questions
that have unfortunately focused on which culture is "right"—and instead asks new questions focused on the *consequences* of such a divide.
As William James states, "A pragmatist [. . .] turns away from abstraction and insufficiency [. . .] towards facts, towards action, and
towards power" (28). James describes a philosophical disposition toward contingent decision making that abandons appeals to any sort
of abstract code of beliefs as "truth" bearing. According to James, the
pragmatist asks, instead, what benefits accrue from taking on a given
disposition and whether those benefits, those consequences, are more
desirable than those resulting from another choice in a particular context. Monolithic worldviews become necessarily dispensable in light of
shifting conditions. "Truth" is measured according to whether or not
a belief or course of action yields desirable consequences—what James
calls the relative "cash value" of holding a certain belief (92).

At present, we are faced with re-envisioning and re-assessing the
consequences of the metanarratives represented by the "two cultures"
model. What consequences, for instance, arise when technical communication and computers and writing scholars remain pressured, largely
due to the overdetermined nature of what constitutes "humanistic" in
English circles, to explicitly exclude technology and instrumentalism
from their account of what makes them humanistic when "uninteriorized" technologies are so foundational to their respective identities?
What kind of future in English studies might be possible for these subdisciplines if English remains locked in an unchallenged, two-culture
logic? Conversely, what consequences might emerge when these technologized rhetorical disciplines expand their humanistic definition to
include technology? When humanistic arguments start with the assumption that technology *is* humanistic or is central to the humanistic enterprise? By asking such questions, pragmatism helps to express
differently the relationship between technology and the humanities
by challenging the traditional two-culture binary and questioning the
usefulness of such a model in an increasingly technologized cultural
context.

The *Humanist Manifestos,* three separate documents published during the twentieth century by the American Humanist Association (a fourth was published in 2003), frame one possible competing theory of humanist philosophy that situates technology amidst humanistic endeavors and seems motivated by a pragmatic perspective on technology and the humanities. These documents span over 70 years and are particularly interesting and relevant in that they articulate a leading humanist organization's evolving sense of technology over a significant time span. Some background: the first *Manifesto* was published in 1933 as a brief statement of the Association's values and focused primarily on mapping the legitimacy of a non-theistic worldview. The second was published in 1973 and offered a reflection on the culture of the time, as well as on several issues of contemporary significance, including abortion, nuclear armament, and civil rights. The third was published in 2000 with an eye toward framing a global humanist agenda for the new millennium. The *Manifestos* are fascinating documents to examine alongside the emergence of American Pragmatism (noted pragmatist John Dewey signed the first *Manifesto* in 1933, and pragmatism as variously formulated by Charles Sanders Peirce, William James, and Dewey came to flourish in the first half of the century), given their shared historical overlap and the thoroughly pragmatic disposition they display. Their statements regarding technology are of particular interest here.

The collaboratively authored first *Manifesto* (1933) outlines the Association's fundamental beliefs, rejecting a theocentric perspective and describing humanism as a unifying worldview rooted in mutual respect among people and the belief that the terrestrial world and humanity together contain all the resources necessary for human beings to thrive. The role of technology is for the most part only indirectly hinted at: humanism is to support "the creative in man and to encourage achievements that add to the satisfactions of life" (9). The second *Manifesto* (1973) begins to flesh out a reflective, contingent disposition toward technology and its role in realizing the objectives set forth in a humanistic ideological framework—this in the wake of World War II and the Korean War, and in the late days of the Vietnam War. The authors acknowledge that technological means can realize productive, human ends when appropriated with discretion and disastrous outcomes when misused. They also attack a view often ascribed to the academic humanities: "We deplore any neo-romantic efforts to condemn indiscriminately all technology and science or to counsel retreat from its further extension and use for the good of humankind" (22). Yet they clearly state that technology should not be used without deliberation and scrutiny: "Technology must, however, *be carefully judged by the consequences of its use;* harmful and destructive changes should be avoided [. . .]. Technological feasibility does not imply social or cultural desirability" (22, emphasis added). Technology manifests values, and judicious humanists work to ensure that values yielding desirable consequences guide its development and use.

The third *Manifesto* (2000) is the first to devote an entire section to technological concerns. In its fourth section, "The Benefits of Technology," author Paul Kurtz claims that humans must continue to locate technological solutions to human problems and need to find ways to make these solutions available to all human beings. But while this might seem to suggest a naively optimistic view of technology, Kurtz again demands responsibility and discretion with every advance: "Each technological innovation needs to be evaluated in terms of potential risk and potential benefit to society and the environment" (28). As articulated here, a humanist perspective, as much as it recognizes the value of technology, cannot summarily endorse its use in any and all cases, as the unique contingencies of each case and consequences of use must be considered. Use is pragmatic, contingent. But technology is necessarily—inevitably—a part of this humanistic formulation, a means of effectively instrumentalizing humanistic values, not a pernicious force to oppose.

According to the humanistic framework advanced in the *Humanist Manifestos,* then, the consequences of philosophically opposing or marginalizing technology are undesirable—humans must focus instead on developing technologies that best represent or embody the needs and desires of humanity. In short, the *Humanistic Manifestos* advance an inclusive framework where it is possible and desirable to see technology and the humanities working synergistically toward the same goals, rather than assuming separation and hoping for the humanities to rehabilitate technology. Rather, technology is critically located amidst humanistic interests. While the *Manifestos* are, of course, but one of many formulations of humanism, they raise the possibility that the culture of division that has characterized academe is itself a choice, a possible way, and not a permanent site of tension and distrust.

REORGANIZING HUMANISTIC ARGUMENT IN THE
TECHNOLOGIZED RHETORICAL SUBDISCIPLINES

In light of this brief overview of the *Humanist Manifestos,* it is interesting to look at what we have. English studies and the academic humanities have traditionally taken a very different stance than that of the more integrated, more pragmatic *Manifestos.* Indeed, in his broader discussion of humanism, Corliss Lamont criticizes what he calls "academic humanism" for "setting up a return to the ancient classics as the foundation stone of education and [. . .] opposing the Humanities to science" (23). While Lamont claims that such notions largely disappeared after a brief vogue early in the twentieth century, their roots in English run deeper, and their influence continues to be felt in contemporary English studies.

While the emergence of the digital humanities suggest some progress in moving beyond the traditional humanities/technology impasse, too often, technology—pejoratively cast in terms like "technical," "vocational," and "instrumental"—is seen as a burr beneath the humanities' saddle, rather than a site of humanities' participation. Philosopher Martha C. Nussbaum's humanities-based educational program, which advances multiculturalism and urges the development of students into "world citizens" hints at such a perspective (6–10). Nussbaum argues that liberal education and the "cultivation of the whole person" are too often ignored in favor of technical and vocational education (9). However, Nussbaum seems uninterested in genuinely interrogating and seeking available cultural connections between the liberal arts and "instrumental" interests. Lauding Randolph-Macon College's disposition toward humanities instruction, Nussbaum states: "The institution is committed to giving these students an education that does not focus on these narrow instrumental goals (those purveyed via business and computer science courses), but that gives them something that can impart meaning and discipline to their intellectual lives in a general way" (61). This argument is a familiar one in that it presupposes that technology and the instrumentalism that animates its development and use is divorced from—or, indeed, in competition with—human values. Such a view refuses the possibility that the instrumental might be intimately related to and integrated with the humanistic and reinscribes the familiar, hierarchical "humanities as antidote" view, which in its subjugation of instrumentalism, refuses dialogue between technology and the humanities.

To improve and expand the humanistic scope of technical communication and computers and writing, we must not only focus on rhetoric and more traditionally familiar humanities characteristics but also rehabilitate our views of "instrumentality" and technology. In other words, we need to accept Patrick Moore's argument to the extent that we see instrumental discourse and related instrumental technologies as engaged in manifesting human potential and achieving human goals; consequently, we need to foreground and investigate technology and instrumentalism in humanistic argument. If technology, governed by instrumentality, is consciously or unconsciously deemed to be somehow *inhuman,* damned to the wrong end of some sort of "continuum of humanity," it remains little more than an adversary, an "other," which makes it possible—indeed, necessary and advisable—to stand back from it and thus relinquish responsibility for it. Pragmatism and the philosophical framework of the *Humanist Manifestos* encourage us to make space for instrumentality and technology in humanistic argument in the technologized rhetorical subdisciplines and beyond. Indeed, pragmatism suggests that this traditional cultural disconnect can be reconceived as elective, one worth reconsidering in light of the consequences it yields. The *Manifestos* take an even stronger tack, asserting that technology is vital to a humanistic philosophy and key to realizing humanistic goals. If they do not take on this perspective, the technologized rhetorical subdisciplines remain marginalized—subordinate, probationary members of the *real* humanities given their non-negotiable relationship with technology.

Refusing the provincialism of historically validated visions of the humanities and seeking new, more inclusive models allows for a more holistic approach to technology that might aid those in the technologized rhetorical subdisciplines, as well as English studies broadly defined, in getting into what James calls "satisfactory relation" with technology, which has long been deemed not "other part(s) of our experience" but simply "other" in humanities spaces (30). In this view, the technologized rhetorical subdisciplines become crucial and integral to English studies by usefully extending disciplinary locus in order to gain access to technology conversations and become a site of optimism regarding technology—to become, finally, constructive, rather than simply deconstructive. Such a view challenges radical technology criticism where the oft-vilified "technological imperative" is by definition running roughshod over "real" human concerns and, instead, recognizes such an imperative as a human construct, a pursuit of human concerns, and one competing manifestation of human values. If instrumentality and technology are continually deemed a foil for "what we do" in English, then the contributions of the technologized rhetorical subdisciplines are necessarily invalid in English studies. The result is that English studies lacks a hopeful, optimistic presence in technological dialogue, development, and use, resigning itself to response and critique, rather than a constructive role in the development of technology and its implementation in society.

Some scholars in the technologized rhetorical subdisciplines are already clearly engaged in this more integrated line of thinking, and their work suggests a view of the humanistic that puts other more traditionally recognized human values and interests into contextualized dialogue with supposedly neutral technology and its instrumental rationality. For instance, Robert R. Johnson's user-centered approach to technology development highlights the role of technology users—human beings—who "are allowed to take part in a *negotiated process of technology design development, and use* that has only rarely been practiced" (32). Similarly, Bonni Nardi and Vicki O'Day locate technologies amidst a larger information ecology, not a separate world from which the humanities must hide, and in doing so, I believe, they empower humanists to consider a different relationship between their work and the technological sphere. They rightly note, "As long as we think we do not have enough expertise to engage in substantive discussions about technology, we are effectively prevented from having an impact on the directions it may take" (13). For Nardi and O'Day, new technologies are too often enshrouded in mystery, seen as novelties that people are not to understand but are rather to admire and then watch silently as they shape their lives "as if these technologies were inevitable forces of nature rather than things we design and choose" (14).

By adopting a more integrated view similar to that in the *Humanist Manifestos,* these scholars get us closer to seeing technology as being in constant dialogue with human interests, values, feelings, and hopes, rather than a mere vehicle for an immutable technological *ethos,* something that the humanities can only conscionably define themselves against. They challenge the view that instrumentality is concretely set in opposition to choice and human complexity and an inevitability to be countered, not shaped. Put another way, these scholars suggest a way to extend the reach and influence of the technologized rhetorical subdisciplines and English studies by locating technologies of various types within a cultural and historical context that foregrounds the notion that technology is an iteration of humanistic values, vital to the humanistic enterprise and not some abstraction acting in spite of them or beyond their purview.

CONCLUSION

Affirming technology's centrality to humanistic definition is key to the technologized rhetorical subdisciplines' future in English studies. The *status quo* in many departments—a nominal commitment to the technologized rhetorical subdisciplines out of a sense of obligation to shifting student interests or to access the political capital and resources that follow the large numbers of credit hours often generated by technology-related courses—may well go on indefinitely with both "cultures" being represented, but with only one framing the discourse of legitimacy. Indeed, it is tempting to see the digital humanities as participating in the healing of this fissure. But as Jerome McGann notes, the digital humanities have to date "focused almost exclusively on methods of sorting, accessing, and disseminating large bodies of materials, and on certain specialized problems in computational stylistics and linguistics" (xi–xii), meaning that much of the focus of the digital humanities enterprise remains on manipulating and remediating belletristic texts—on, I would argue, conducting typical English literary endeavors in new ways. Even work of this nature has only recently gained acceptance as legitimate scholarly activity in many English departments around the country.

The technologized rhetorical subdisciplines engage technology in very different and more substantive ways. Hence, seeing the fight to situate technology interests within the English humanities as an unwinnable battle, some would argue for secession, and, indeed, some writing programs with technology-oriented interests have already seceded from English departments. While the stated reasons for such a move are frequently political (e.g., scarce funding, lack of support/respect from colleagues, inability to secure tenure lines), the tie that binds these reasons is technology's poor "fit" within the standard English blueprint. The rich tradition of English studies as the realm of the aesthetic makes union with technology inconceivable to some.

But I am not advocating secession here. A progressive, pragmatic English studies seeks creative responses to this seeming disconnect, and the *Humanist Manifestos* offer one way of rethinking about long-held attitudes and anxieties. As the technologized rhetorical subdisciplines mature, teachers and scholars therein must confidently assert a fundamental, inseparable relationship between technology and the humanities. Working within an evolving English studies that sees and understands this relationship is a best-case scenario for the long-term strength, depth, and influence of these subdisciplines. By positioning technology within our humanistic argument—by insisting on it, rather than only capitulating to traditional humanities characteristics—we help actively recast the larger humanities and better position ourselves to participate in technology development and policymaking.

Such work can reinvigorate English. As university culture becomes more immediately responsive to external influences like legislatures, the corporate sector, and students seeking professional and vocational power, the burden of proof when it comes to demonstrating relevance and long-term viability will only become greater, whether those of us in English studies agree with such assessment or not. Reconstructing the humanistic to centrally accommodate technology, then, becomes a necessary step toward envisioning a new role for the discipline. Doing so is not "selling out" disciplinary turf; rather, it is extending its sphere of influence and agency by thinking pragmatically about what "humanistic" means as a concept-in-time and considering a technologized notion of the humanistic as a logical extension of the work that has long been done in our field. In the twenty-first century, English studies has much to offer, but it must be visible to students and to the public in an increasingly competitive, increasingly technologized society.

By looking to pragmatism and alternative versions of humanist philosophy, the technologized rhetorical subdisciplines can find new ways to envision our orienting sense of the "humanistic," new ways to reframe this complicated term and thus, as pragmatists would offer, "try on" a disposition that relocates technology within the sphere of human activity and value. There is power in doing so—power for the technologized rhetorical disciplines and power for English studies. Denying the humanistic nature of technology might be palliative but of little pragmatic use. Rethinking traditional humanistic notions and core beliefs—moving beyond a cosmetic makeover of our view of technology—offers a real role for English studies in an evolving technology narrative, and a thoroughly humanistic narrative at that.

Works Cited

Barker, Thomas T., and Fred O. Kemp. "Network Theory: A Postmodern Pedagogy for the Writing Classroom." Handa 1–27.

Baron, Dennis. "From Pencils to Pixels: The Stages of Literacy Technologies." *Passions, Pedagogies, and 21st Century Technologies.* Ed. Gail E. Hawisher and Cynthia L. Selfe. Logan: Utah State UP, 1999. 15–33.

Bhatt, Rakesh M. "Expert Discourses, Local Practices, and Hybridity: The Case of Indian Englishes." *Reclaiming the Local in Language Policy and Practice.* Ed. A. Suresh Canagarajah. Mahwah, NJ: Erlbaum, 2005. 25–54.

Borchert, Donald M., and David Stewart. *Being Human in a Technological Age.* Athens, OH: Ohio UP, 1979.

Brantlinger, Patrick. *Who Killed Shakespeare?: What's Happened to English since the Radical Sixties.* New York: Routledge, 2000.

Dombrowski, Paul M. *Ethics in Technical Communication.* Boston: Allyn and Bacon, 2000.

—. *Humanistic Aspects of Technical Communication.* Amityville, NY: Baywood, 1994.

—. "Post-Modernism as the Resurgence of Humanism in Technical Communication Studies." *Technical Communication Quarterly* 4.2 (1995): 165–85.

Dragga, Sam. "'Is This Ethical?': A Survey of Opinion on Principles and Practices of Document Design." *Technical Communication: Journal for the Society of Technical Communication.* 43.3 (1996): 255–65.

Faigley, Lester. *Fragments of Rationality: Postmodernity and the Subject of Composition.* Pittsburgh: U of Pittsburgh P, 1992.

Handa, Carolyn, ed. *Computers and Community: Teaching Composition in the Twenty-First Century.* Ed. Portsmouth, NH: Boynton/Cook, 1990.

—. "Politics, Ideology, and the Strange, Slow Death of the Isolated Composer or Why We Need Community in the Writing Classroom." Handa 160–84.

Hawisher, Gail E., and Paul LeBlanc, eds. *Re-Imagining Computers and Composition: Teaching and Research in the Virtual Age.* Portsmouth, NJ: Boynton/Cook, 1992. 24–42.

Humanist Manifestos I and II. Buffalo: Prometheus Books, 1973.

James, William. *Pragmatism.* 1907. Indianapolis: Hackett, 1981.

Johnson, Robert R. *User-Centered Technology: A Rhetorical Theory for Computers and Other Mundane Artifacts.* Albany, NY: SUNY P, 1998.

Katz, Steven B. "The Ethic of Expediency: Classical Rhetoric, Technology, and the Holocaust." *College English* 54.3 (1992): 255–75.

Kemp, Fred O. "The User-Friendly Fallacy." *College Composition and Communication* 38.1 (1987): 32–39.

Knievel, Michael. "Technology Artifacts, Instrumentalism, and the *Humanist Manifestos.*" *Journal of Business and Technical Communication* 2.1 (2006): 65–86.

—. "What Is Humanistic about Computers and Writing? Historical Patterns and Contemporary Possibilities for the Field." *Computers and Composition.* In press.

Kurtz, Paul. *Humanist Manifesto 2000: A Call for a New Planetary Humanism.* Amherst, NY Prometheus, 2000.

Lamont, Corliss. *The Philosophy of Humanism.* Amherst, NY: Humanist Press, 1996.

Landow, George. *Hypertext: The Convergence of Contemporary Critical Theory and Technology.* Baltimore: John Hopkins UP, 1992.

Lay, Mary M. "The Computer Culture, Gender, and Nonacademic Writing: An Interdisciplinary Critique." *Nonacademic Writing: Social Theory and Technology.* Ed. Ann Hill Duin and Craig J. Hansen. Mahwah, NJ: Erlbaum, 1996. 57–80.

LeCourt, Donna, and Luann Barnes. "Writing Multiplicity: Hypertext and Feminist Theorization of Hypertext." *Computers and Composition* 16.1 (1999): 55–71.

Longo, Bernadette. *Spurious Coin: A History of Science, Management, and Technical Writing.* Albany, NY: SUNY P, 2000.

Lyotard, Jean-François. *The Postmodern Condition: A Report on Knowledge.* Trans. Geoff Bennington and Brian Massumi. Minneapolis: U of Minnesota P, 1984.

MacNealy, Mary S., and Leon B. Heaton. "Can This Marriage Be Saved: Is an English Department a Good Home for Technical Communication?" *Journal of Technical Writing and Communication* 29.1 (1999): 41–64.

Markel, Mike. "A Basic Unit on Ethics for Technical Communicators." *Journal of Technical Writing and Communication* 21.4 (1991): 327–50.

McGann, Jerome. *Radiant Textuality: Literature after the World Wide Web.* New York: Palgrave Macmillan, 2001.

Menand, Louis. "An Introduction to Pragmatism." *Pragmatism: A Reader.* Ed. Louis Menand. New York: Vintage, 1997. xi–xxxiv.

Miller, Carolyn R. "A Humanistic Rationale for Technical Writing." *College English* 40.6 (1979): 610–24.

—. "Comment on 'Instrumental Discourse is as Humanistic as Rhetoric.'" *Journal of Business and Technical Communication* 10.4 (1996): 482–86.

Moore, Patrick. "Instrumental Discourse is as Humanistic as Rhetoric." *Journal of Business and Technical Communication* 10.1 (1996): 100–18.

Moran, Charles. "Computers and the Writing Classroom: A Look to the Future." Hawisher and LeBlanc 7–23.

Nardi, Bonni A., and Vicki L. O'Day. *Information Ecologies: Using Technology with a Heart.* Cambridge: MIT P, 1998.

Noble, David F. *The Religion of Technology: The Divinity of Man and the Spirit of Invention.* New York: Knopf, 1997.

Nold, Ellen W. "Fear and Trembling: The Humanist Approaches the Computer." *College Composition and Communication* 26.3 (1973): 269–73.

Nussbaum, Martha C. *Cultivating Humanity: A Classical Defense of Reform in Liberal Education.* Cambridge: Harvard UP, 1997.

Ong, Walter. "Literacy and Orality in Our Times." *Landmark Essays on Rhetorical Invention.* Ed. Richard E. Young and Yameng Liu. Davis, CA: Hermagoras P, 1994. 135–46.

Postman, Neil. *Technopoly: The Surrender of Culture to Technology.* New York: Knopf, 1992.

Regan, Alison. "'Type Normal Like the Rest of Us': Writing, Power, and Homophobia in the Networked Composition Classroom." *Computers and Composition* 10.4 (1993): 11–23.

Rutter, Russell. "Poetry, Imagination, and Technical Writing." *College English* 47.7 (1985): 698–712.

Schroeder, Eric J., and John Boe. "Minimalism, Populism, and Attitude Transformation: Approaches to Teaching Writing in Computer Classrooms." Handa 28–46.

Schwartz, Helen J. "The Confessions of Professor Strangelove; Or, An Apology for Literacy." *Computers and Composition* 2.4 (1985): 6–16.

Selfe, Cynthia L. "Preparing English Teachers for the Virtual Age: The Case for Technology Critics." Hawisher and LeBlanc 24–42.

—. *Technology and Literacy in the Twenty-First Century: The Importance of Paying Attention.* Carbondale, IL: Southern Illinois UP, 1999.

Slatin, John. "Reading Hypertext: Order and Coherence in a New Medium." *College English* 52.8 (1990): 870–83.

Smith, Elizabeth T., and Cynthia L. Selfe. "Alienation and Adaptation: Integrating Technology and the Humanities." Conference on College Composition and Communication. St. Louis, MO. March, 1988.

Snow, C. P. *The Two Cultures and the Scientific Revolution.* New York: Cambridge UP, 1959.

Sommers, Elizabeth. "Political Impediments to Virtual Reality." Hawisher and LeBlanc 43–57.

Sullivan, Laura. "Wired Women Writing: Towards a Feminist Theorization of Hypertext." *Computers and Composition* 16.1 (1999): 25–54.

Tebeaux, Elizabeth. "Technical Communication, Literary Theory, and English Studies: Stasis, Change, and the Problem of Meaning." *Technical Writing Teacher* 18.1 (1991): 15–27.

Wilson, Greg. "Technical Communication and Late Capitalism: Considering a Postmodern Technical Communication Pedagogy." *Journal of Business and Technical Communication* 15.1 (2001): 72–99.

14 Afterword

From Plainchant to Polyphony

Douglas Hesse

The narrator of Jorge Luis Borges's famous story "The Library of Babel" describes the "Universe (which others call the Library)" as containing every possible text, its endless shelves including, for example, "the Gnostic gospel of Basilides, the commentary on that gospel, the commentary on the commentary on that gospel, the true story of your death" (54). Of course, no one can find anything in that library, which contains myriad false catalogs as well as true. Nonetheless, Borges describes thousands of pilgrims searching for their "Vindications: books of apology and prophecy which vindicated for all time the acts of every man in the universe and retained prodigious arcana for his future" (55).

Lori Ostergaard, Jeff Ludwig, and Jim Nugent re-mark others' remarks on the recent turn within English studies "toward itself as an object of study" (xi), a citational spiral that for me invokes Borgesian commentaries on commentaries. Should I so choose (and perhaps even if I choose not), this afterword will join the meta-reflexive sequence, teaching the conflicts of teaching the conflicts of teaching the conflicts of limning the nature of English studies.

I'd like to ask why we find ourselves so fascinating. There's an unavoidably hostile aspect to that question, but I think its bluntness productive and generative of a few more speculations.

There's clearly the need for reassurance. Institutional, business, and social leaders find whole areas of English studies (chief among them the reading of imaginative literature) far less important than we do ourselves. The importance they do ascribe to literary study comes often in terms many in our field reject (as a repository of cultural values to be passed along), but even this culture war has gone the way of the Crimean. If literature filled religion's departure for Matthew Arnold, we now see religion coming back from its sesquicentennial siesta.

Even more than religion (or perhaps coextant with religion, in such popular books as *The Good of Affluence: Seeking God in a Culture of Wealth*) is economics. How might literary study help people get over in a globalizing economy? Where are English's stem cells, nanotechnologies, financial derivatives? While historically, of course, English studies has scoffed off such pecuniary challenges, our publics think the questions worth asking, and they make us defensive, especially since Michel Foucault and Kenneth Burke don't exactly console them.

In his preface to the 2004 study *Reading at Risk,* Dana Gioia notes that it "is not a report that the National Endowment for the Arts is happy to issue. This comprehensive survey of American literary reading presents a detailed but bleak assessment of the decline of reading's role in the nation's culture. For the first time in modern history, less than half of the adult population now reads literature, and these trends reflect a larger decline in other sorts of reading" (vii). That's not to say we live in a society reading only balance sheets and business plans. American culture remains plenty enthusiastic for imaginative texts, but in the form of movies and television shows and YouTube and James Patterson novels. We seem even happier with nonfiction, in our books, magazines, primetimes, and podcasts. English studies is looking for a stake in this new textual terrain (and one not held by communications or media studies or the social sciences or some of the fine arts), not only for the range of texts it can claim but also what it's supposed to do when it's there. Cultural studies (especially high theory cultural studies) might interest some of us in the profession, but it appeals less to the larger culture.

What makes the depreciation of literary reading and traditional literary study particularly tricky—and what raises anxieties—is that certain historically ramshackle properties within English studies are now getting drive by looks from folks outside the disciplinary neighborhood. Chief among them is writing and composition studies. Reports like the National Commission on Writing's *Writing: A Ticket to Work or a Ticket Out?* offer external validations of writing and its teaching. (Reading matters, too, enough for it to be tested in No Child Left Behind, but almost no one equates teaching reading with anything that happens in a modern college English department—except, of course, in those composition courses that include analyzing nonfiction.) We've now seen a rise not only of writing majors and minors within English departments (a telling but modest enough development; a new subdivision of the same town), but more significantly a rise of freestanding writing programs and, even, writing departments. Composition, rhetoric, and technical writing (as for example, at DePaul University or the University of Rhode Island), sometimes joined by creative writing (as, for example, at places like Loyola College in Maryland or Grand Valley State University), is taking its mule to tend a few acres elsewhere. As emigration sharpens the focus on literary studies in English departments left behind, the change invites even some of those happy with it to wonder, "What's happening in the neighborhood?"

What gives enterprises like rhetoric, composition, writing, or new media studies a certain current advantage is that they can start relatively anew, unbound by calcified curricula (periodicity, for example) or the lineage of faculty lines (the Victorianist is retired; long live the Victorianist). Because they've focused on production and because they've widely and opportunistically selected texts for analysis, these enterprises flexibly accommodate new genres and composing practices, visual and aural as well as verbal.

Realigning resources and redrawing boundaries heightens reflection, even if—and I fully grant this—the number of places making such changes is a small minority and will likely remain so for a few years. The largely philosophical/political questions that have fueled previous introspections—the Dartmouth Conference, *English in America,* and the English Coalition Conference, *The Rise and Fall of English*—have been joined, even occluded, by pragmatic concerns.

Probably none of the latter has been more fretted than the working conditions of English instructors. Various authors in this book have analyzed yet again the historically low status and salaries of writing instructors (certainly since the late-nineteenth century, as Robert Connors has traced), and this ongoing situation further churns questions of the field's identity. Perhaps even at this late date there would be some consolation in the "genteel poverty" of English teaching if folks could be reassured that the work and calling were sufficiently noble, meriting celebration as one of John Ruskin's five great intellectual professions, perhaps. But we scarcely believe those grand narratives ourselves, and we certainly aren't consoled by them. Interestingly, when English departments fracture, writing teachers tend to fare better in new separate programs, adjunct positions and assistantships giving way to better benefited and salaried lectureships/instructorships. That only a fraction of these new positions are tenure track (primarily in an administrative caste that is a synecdoche of the contemporary university professoriate) troubles many of us, but this new "something," if not "all," is materially better than the previous near "nothing." Resources for these new configurations, which reflect how administrators, governing bodies, and something as vague as "the business community" value writing, have to come from somewhere, though. English departments may be the reluctant donor.

᠅

I became an English major my sophomore year at the University of Iowa, in 1975. My first major had been chemistry, but after two semesters of calculus, I didn't understand anything, despite getting B's. A first-generation, working class college student, I hadn't even realized that one could major in something as impractical and pleasant as English. But these were days—they seem now so long ago—when the mere having of a college degree, in anything, had a reasonable reassurance that things would turn out OK in work and life. And I liked to read and write. On the advice of my crusty advisor, Sven Armens, I took at least one literature and one writing course every semester. My formative experience of English studies, then, was not quite plainchant, the single melody of literature, but it was a simple two-part harmony of reading and writing. At that time and that school, reading in literature courses was exclusively of print texts, practiced almost exclusively as close reading in a fairly New Critical vein. Writing courses, whether creative or expository, focused on matters of craft, with a substantial reading component, taught extensively through workshops.

It's dangerous to read one's personal history as representative or idyllic, of course, but I marvel how complicated things have gotten in terms of texts, methods, and pedagogies. The rich new polyphony is largely atonal. We less easily can perceive harmonic relations among the various areas now federated under English studies—or even where English songs begin and those of communications, media studies, history, philosophy, the fine arts end. Atonality is not necessarily bad unless, of course, we worry at the absence of the tonic, the centering pitch. Those worries crop up when administrative structures (like departments, like majors, like general education requirements) depend on coherent, justifiable principles of scope, or when people in a field, like the contributors to this book, wonder whether or how they might understand both themselves and their relationships. That's where we are now. I might, then, start and end with a stark stake in C-major: English studies is centrally concerned with how texts are made, how they mean, and why they matter.

Works Cited

Borges, Jorge Luis. "The Library of Babel." *Labyrinths*. New York: New Directions, 1964.

Connors, Robert. *Composition-Rhetoric: Backgrounds, Theory, and Pedagogy.* Pittsburgh: U Pittsburgh P, 1997.

Gioia, Dana. "Preface." *Reading At Risk: A Survey of Literary Reading in America*. Research Division Report #46. Washington, DC: National Endowment for the Arts, 2004. vii. 27 March 2007. <http://www.nea.gov/pub/ReadingAtRisk.pdf>.

Lloyd-Jones, Richard, and Andrea A. Lunsford. *The English Coalition Conference: Democracy through Language*. New York: MLA; Urbana: NCTE, 1989.

The National Commission on Writing. *Writing: A Ticket to Work . . . Or a Ticket Out?* New York: The College Board. 2004. 2 Feb. 2009 <http://www.writingcommission.org/prod_downloads/writingcom/writing-ticket-to-work.pdf>.

Ohmann, Richard. *English in America: A Radical View of the Profession*. Oxford: Oxford UP, 1976.

Ruskin, John. "The Roots of Honor." (1860). *Unto this Last and Other Writings*. New York: Penguin, 1986.

Schneider, John R. *The Good of Affluence: Seeking God in a Culture of Wealth.* Grand Rapids, MI: Wm. B. Eerdmans, 2002.

Contributors

Matthew Abraham is an assistant professor of Writing, Rhetoric, and Discourse at DePaul University in Chicago. His work has appeared in *Cultural Critique,* the *Journal of the Midwest Modern Language Association, JAC, College Composition and Communication, Logos: A Journal of Modern Society and Culture,* and *Postmodern Culture.* He is author of *Out of Bounds: Academic Freedom and the Question of Palestine* (forthcoming from Pluto Press). He is winner of the 2005 Rachel Corrie Courage in the Teaching of Writing Award.

William P. Banks is an assistant professor of Composition and Rhetoric and director of the First-year Writing Studio at East Carolina University, where he also teaches graduate and undergraduate courses in writing, research, and pedagogy. He recently guest edited, with Jonathan Alexander, a special issue of *Computers and Composition* on "Sexualities, Technologies, and the Teaching of Writing," which won the Ellen Nold Award for Distinguished Contribution to the Field of Computers and Writing. His work has appeared in *College English, Teaching English in the Two-Year College,* and *Dialogue: A Journal for Writing Specialists.* His current book project investigates the rhetorical strategies of queer writers and activists, and explores the implications these strategies may have on writing students in college courses.

David B. Downing is a professor of English at Indiana University of Pennsylvania. An expanded version of his chapter in this collection appears in his most recent book, *The Knowledge Contract: Politics and Paradigms in the Academic Workplace.* His works in English studies reform also include *Beyond English, Inc.: Curricular Reform in a Global Economy* (Heinemann), and *Changing Classroom Practices: Resources for Literary and Cultural Studies* (NCTE).

Lynée Lewis Gaillet is an associate professor of Rhetoric and Composition at Georgia State University. She is a former president of the Coalition of Women Scholars in the History of Rhetoric and Composition and former executive director of the South Atlantic Modern Language Association. Gaillet is the editor of *Scottish Rhetoric and Its Influences* (Lawrence Erlbaum), co-editor of *Stories of Mentoring: Theory and Praxis* (Parlor Press), and author of numerous book chapters and journal articles addressing contemporary writing instruction and the history of rhetoric/writing practices. Her work has appeared in *JAC, The Journal of Basic Writing, Rhetoric Review, Issues in Writing, Rhetoric Society Quarterly, Composition Studies, Technical Communication Quarterly, The Journal of Teaching Writing,* and *English Journal.*

Chris W. Gallagher earned his PhD from SUNY-Albany. He is a professor of English and Coordinator of Composition at the University of Nebraska–Lincoln, where he teaches courses in writing, rhetoric, literacy, and pedagogy. He has published three books: *Radical Departures* (NCTE), *Reclaiming Assessment* (Heinemann), and *Teaching Writing That Matters* (with Amy Lee, Scholastic).

Peter M. Gray earned his PhD from SUNY-Albany. He is an associate professor of English at Queensborough Community College–CUNY and co-director of its writing across the curriculum program. He is currently a Carnegie Foundation Scholarship of Teaching and Learning Faculty Fellow in the CUNY Office of Undergraduate Education.

Douglas Hesse is a professor of English and founding director of the Marsico Writing Program at the University of Denver. He is also the immediate past chair of the Conference on College Composition and Communication and a former president of the Council of Writing Program Administrators. Hesse has taught at Illinois State University, where he directed the honors program, the Center for the Advancement of Teaching, the graduate program in English studies, and the writing program.

Michael S. Knievel is an assistant professor of English at the University of Wyoming, where he teaches courses in composition and technical and professional communication. His research interests include the relationship between technology and the humanities and the position of technology-focused writing programs within the larger curricular geography of English studies. He is currently researching use-of-force policy and the ways in which it mediates relationships between law enforcement agencies and the citizenry.

Jeff Ludwig is a writing instructor at the University of Denver, where he also works to develop WAC/WID initiatives. His specializations include modernist American literature and curricular reform in English Studies. His article "The Rhetorics of Subversion and Silence" appeared in the RSA publication *Rhetorical Democracy: Discursive Practices of Civic Engagement.*

Marcia A. McDonald is an associate provost and professor of English at Belmont University. She received her PhD in English from Vanderbilt University and has been a lecturer at universities in France and China. She has published on Shakespeare and on the humanities curriculum and disciplinary issues. Her teaching areas include composition, Shakespeare, British literature, and interdisciplinary humanities.

Jim Nugent is an assistant professor of Writing and Rhetoric at Oakland University. He holds a PhD in rhetoric and technical communication from Michigan Technological University, a master's degree in technical writing from Illinois State University, and a bachelor's degree in math and computer science from the University of Illinois at Urbana-Champaign. His research interests include neosophistic rhetorical theory, the teaching of technical writing, and certificate programs in technical communication. His latest work on sophistic rhetoric and certificate programs will appear in the collection *Discourse and Design: Composing and Revising the Professional and Technical Writing Program,* edited by David Franke and Alex Reid (forthcoming from The WAC Clearinghouse).

Gary A. Olson is provost and vice president for academic affairs at Idaho State University. Among his works on disciplinary formation is *Rhetoric and Composition as Intellectual Work* (Southern Illinois University Press).

Lori Ostergaard is an assistant professor of Writing and Rhetoric at Oakland University, where she teaches classes in rhetoric, writing with new media, and teaching with technology. She conducts archival research into the teaching of rhetoric and writing at Midwestern normal colleges and high schools in the early twentieth century.

Michael Pennell is an assistant professor of Writing and Rhetoric at the University of Rhode Island. He teaches courses in business communication, writing in digital environments, and research methods.

Matthew T. Pifer earned his PhD from the University of Oklahoma in 2001. He is an associate professor at Husson University where he teaches courses in composition, technical communication, nineteenth- and twentieth-century literatures, and creative writing. His research interests include an analysis of dissent in the underground presses of the 1960s, ethics in technical communication, and the relationship between scholarship and teaching.

Christopher Schroeder is an associate professor of English at Northeastern Illinois University where he teaches undergraduate and graduate courses in composition and literature.

Shari J. Stenberg earned her PhD from SUNY-Albany. She formerly served on the faculty at Creighton University and is now an associate professor at the University of Nebraska–Lincoln. She teaches courses in writing, rhetoric, and pedagogy and coordinates the Faculty Leadership for Writing Initiative. She is the author of *Professing and Pedagogy: Learning the Teaching of English* (NCTE). Her work has also appeared in *College English, Composition Studies,* and *symplokē.*

Caren J. Town is a professor of English at Georgia Southern University in Statesboro, Georgia. She teaches courses in literary theory, American literature, adolescent literature, and English methods for middle grades and secondary education majors. Her scholarship includes articles on Fitzgerald, Wharton, Lewis, and Dreiser; women mystery writers; and a book on female adolescence in Southern fiction, *The New Southern Girl: Female Adolescence in the Works of 12 Women Authors* (McFarland and Company). She is currently working on a book about teaching adolescent novels in high school.

Index

CPSIA information can be obtained at www.ICGtesting.com
Printed in the USA
BVOW080646290513

321879BV00002B/595/P